Greenbank House and the University of Liverpool

Greenbank House and the University of Liverpool

A History

Adrian Allan

UNIVERSITY OF
LIVERPOOL

First published 2022 by
Liverpool University Press
4 Cambridge Street
Liverpool
L69 7ZU

British Library Cataloguing-in-Publication data
A British Library CIP record is available

ISBN 978-1-80085-619-6 paperback

Typeset by Carnegie Book Production, Lancaster
Printed and bound in the Czech Republic by Akcent

Contents

Acknowledgments

When in 1987 the University of Liverpool published a brief history of Greenbank House,[1] the resources available to its author principally comprised the archives of the Rathbone family held by the Special Collections department of the University's Sydney Jones Library, the deeds of the property, and several books about the family, some authored by family members, including Eleanor Rathbone's memoir of her father, William Rathbone the sixth (1905), also Mrs Eustace Greg's edition of *Reynolds-Rathbone Diaries and Letters 1753–1839* (1905), and Mrs Emily Rathbone's *Records of the Rathbone Family* (1913), both of which had been 'printed for private circulation.' Since 1987, the Rathbone family archives have been more fully listed and their exploitation fostered through these lists being made available on the University Library's website (https://sca.archives.liverpool.ac.uk). More particularly, the fruits of research in these and other archives have appeared in a growing number of significant publications about the firm established by the family, Rathbone Brothers, and about individual family members: Lucie Nottingham's *Rathbone Brothers: From Merchant to Banker 1742–1992* (1992), David Lascelles's *The Story of Rathbones since 1742* (2008), Susan Pedersen's *Eleanor Rathbone and the Politics of Conscience* (2004), and Susan Cohen's *Rescue the Perishing: Eleanor Rathbone and the Refugees* (2010); and, drawing on family papers and recollections, Joy Robinson, a great-granddaughter of William Rathbone the fifth, has brought further family members to life in her book, *Relatively Rathbone* (1992). And in the *Oxford Dictionary of National Biography* (published in sixty print volumes in 2004, with further entries, also corrections and additions being made to the online edition) are to be found entries for the fourth, fifth, and sixth William Rathbones, Eleanor Rathbone, Hannah Mary Rathbone (grandmother of Hugh Rathbone), and for a large number of those with whom the family had close connections, as correspondents and as visitors to Greenbank, a veritable dramatis personae. I am much indebted to these publications.

For those wishing to learn more about the context in which Greenbank House grew and developed – the history of Liverpool and of its university – there is also a growing body of literature, also online resources. In advance of Liverpool celebrating the 800th anniversary of the grant by King John of letters patent in 1207, which in effect created Liverpool as a new town on a virtually greenfield site, and the city's celebrations in 2008 as European Capital of Culture, in 2006 Liverpool University Press (LUP) published a substantial new history, *Liverpool 800: Culture, Character and History*, edited by Professor John Belchem. For an account and commentary on how Liverpool's economic collapse of the early 1980s was arrested and its 'economic, physical and social disintegration' was gradually tackled in the 1990s and 2000s, such that it has undergone what has been described as an 'extraordinary, if incomplete renaissance,' see, in particular, Professor Michael Parkinson's *Liverpool Beyond the Brink: The Remaking of a Post-imperial City* (LUP, 2019). The history of the University is covered in Professor Thomas Kelly's centenary history, *For Advancement of Learning: The University of Liverpool 1881–1981* (LUP, 1981), and Dr Sylvia Harrop's study, *A Decade of Change: The University of Liverpool 1981–1991* (LUP, 1994).

I am indebted to David Williams, formerly Senior Project Manager, Facilities, Residential and Commercial Services department, University of Liverpool, for inviting me to produce this history of Greenbank, to celebrate and commemorate the University's major conservation of the house and its grounds. His successor as project manager, Gary Meinert, could not have been more helpful in making the many various records relating to the property's restoration available to me, also arranging meetings with the team of architects and engineers and others on the site. David Harding, Managing Director of the University of Liverpool Construction Company (ULCCO) – Special Projects, has provided much valued additional information. I was pleased to meet Cerys Robinson, Liverpool City Council's Planning Officer (Heritage Specialist) to discuss the Council's role in granting planning and listed building consents. Mark Moppett, Managing Director of Booth King Partnership Ltd, the structural engineers for the project, has been good enough to provide an illustrated account of the structural repair and remodelling of Greenbank House, with which he was heavily involved throughout the project; and Rupert Goddard, a partner in the Manchester Office of Sheppard Robson, the architects for the restoration and refurbishment of Greenbank House, has also kindly provided an account of how the Sheppard Robson team addressed the challenges presented by the design brief for the wider site and for the refurbishment of Greenbank House. Brian McGorry, the site manager, provided details of the conditions in which individual rooms were found and the works carried out to redress the problems encountered.

At the department of Special Collections and Archives, Sydney Jones Library, Robyn Orr and colleagues, library assistants, produced large quantities of archives of the Rathbones and the University and, during the lockdown, kindly checked various texts on my behalf and supplied photographs for reproduction. Ryan Roach, of the University's Corporate Governance department, located and made available minutes of the University Council relating to Greenbank, 1986–2016. Appreciating the changes effected by an increasing reliance on born-digital records, I was sorry to find that certain records were no longer maintained or retained, such that there are a few lacunae in the account.

Principally through the good offices of the University's Alumni Relations Team (in particular, Caroline Mitchell, Head of Alumni Engagement), I was pleased to receive the recollections of Greenbank of a number of former staff and students: Mr Ian Aitken, Mrs Priscilla Bawcutt, Mrs Tina Billinge, Professor Christopher Allmand, Dr Daniel Ching, Mrs Elizabeth Earl, Mr Ron Green, Dr Susan Green, Dr Derek Howard and Mrs Jill Howard, Miss Maureen Jones, Mr Mike Keating, Mr Peter Kenwright, Professor Ann Mackenzie, Mrs Cathy O'Malley, Mr Colin Perchard, Professor Geoffrey Ribbans, Dr Juliette Riddall, Dr Bill Shannon, Mr Ivor Smith, Professor Fredric Taylor, Dr Robert Walker, and Dr Geoffrey Woodcock.

Thanks are also due to the staffs of Lancashire Archives (particularly Mrs Jacquie Crosby, Archives Service Manager) and Liverpool Record Office (Roger Hull) for facilitating access to their holdings, and to Lancashire Archives, Liverpool Record Office and Dr Amanda Draper, Curator of Art and Exhibitions, Victoria Gallery and Museum, University of Liverpool for kindly supplying photographs. I am particularly grateful to the University of Nebraska Press for permission to reproduce extracts from *John James Audubon's Journal of 1826*, edited by Professor Daniel Patterson (© 2011 by the Board of Regents of the University of Nebraska). At Liverpool University Press, I am particularly grateful to Alison Welsby for overseeing the design and production of this book, assisted at all stages by Sian Jenkins of Carnegie Book Production, Lancaster.

As Dr B. L. (Larry) Rathbone observed in his foreword to the brief history of Greenbank, 'the history of Greenbank from 1787 to 1940 cannot be separated from the history of the Rathbone family.' Accordingly, an endeavour has been made to populate Greenbank with family members and some of those many others, visitors and correspondents, who feature in its history and who recorded their recollections of the hospitality and help they enjoyed. Successive generations have cause to thank members of the family for the example they provided of public and private service in support of various causes, to the benefit of mankind.[2] In the succeeding years, as inheritors of Greenbank and its traditions, the University has sought to follow in the family's footsteps in fulfilling the objective of 'the advancement of learning and ennoblement of life' (as inscribed on the iconic redbrick Victoria Building, formally opened by Earl Spencer, Chancellor of the federal Victoria University [of which University College, Liverpool, was a constituent], in December 1892).[3]

It is most fortunate that Greenbank House has now been given a new lease of life through a painstakingly thorough restoration and sensitive adaptation to new uses: a truly remarkable renaissance which is an outstanding testimony to the positive working relationship established between ULCCO–Special Projects (the contractor), the architects, engineers, City of Liverpool Planning Authority, and the many specialist subcontractors. Now providing inspiring seminar and meeting rooms for staff and students in an attractive landscaped setting, those from further afield making a pilgrimage to Greenbank House will be richly rewarded by the experience.

Adrian Allan
July 2021

1   Saint Anslow or Green Bank

'All that messuage and tenement called or known by the name of Saint Anslow or Green Bank and the several closes or parcels of land thereunto belonging or therewith usually occupied and enjoyed called or known by the several names of the Pit Field, the West Field, the Farmost Field, the Middle Field, the Further Croft, the Orchard Croft, and the Garden Croft situate, lying and being in Toxteth Park in the said County [Lancaster] containing in the whole according to a late survey and admeasurement thereof eleven acres one rood and thirty three perches of land, customary measure.' (This acreage, according to the 'customary measure' was based on eight yards to the pole, whereas according to statute measure this acreage totalled 24 acres and 29 perches.)

Such is the description of the modest property given in its lease by Sir Charles William Molyneux, Baronet, Earl of Sefton, and Lord Viscount Molyneux of Maryburgh in the Kingdom of Ireland, to William Rathbone the younger, merchant, of Liverpool, dated 1 May 1788 (just a year before, on the Continent, the storming of the Bastille that set the French Revolution in motion).[1] At the time, the mercantile elite of Liverpool lived close to the town centre, their migration to the planned middle-class areas developed in the former Mosslake Fields (centred on Abercromby Square) only occurring from the early nineteenth century onwards, as the population rapidly expanded, with a still later migration further away from the centre of Liverpool towards the outer suburbs of Wavertree, Mossley Hill, and Aigburth.[2] Already in 1774 William Enfield could write that 'Everton, Wavertree, and Toxteth-Park, are pleasant villages, which have of late years been much improved by country houses, which several of the principal inhabitants of Leverpool have built for their summer-retreat.'[3] That such as William Rathbone was happy to acquire a modest estate, avoiding the burden of a large landed estate, was indicative of his wish to continue in business and not to plough the profits of business into land. Liverpool was not unique among towns in witnessing the gradual desertion by the wealthier townsmen of the centres of towns for residences in the cleaner and healthier suburbs, in many cases signifying a separation of workplace and home. Though the Rathbones were to retain a home in Liverpool, William Rathbone and his wife wished to acquire an additional

'St Anslow' and district, 1754, from R. Lang's map of Toxteth Park.
(Reproduced courtesy of Lancashire Archives, DDM/14/70)

Survey entry for 'St Anslow,' 1754.
(Reproduced courtesy of Lancashire Archives, DDM/14/11)

residence distant from what in 1804 Dr James Currie described as the 'busy, noisy, smoky, money-getting Liverpool,' to provide a home for their delicate first child, William Rathbone the fifth (1787–1868).[4] Initially, Greenbank was generally only to be used as a summer residence, one particularly appreciated by William Rathbone the fourth's wife, Hannah Mary, the Rathbones maintaining their Cornhill home in Liverpool as their principal residence (and also their business address). William Rathbone the sixth was later to recall that he was born at Cornhill (in 1819), the family afterwards moving to a house in Hope Street, facing Falkner Street, and subsequently to a house at the south-west corner of Abercromby Square.[5] Buildings reveal the past and the successive development of Greenbank House was to be moulded by the culture and ideals of its successive owners.

'St Anslow' estate, from a map of Toxteth Park (1769).
(Reproduced courtesy of Lancashire Archives, DDM/14/56)

Toxteth Park, which is shown enclosed by paling on early maps of Lancashire, including that of Christopher Saxton in 1577, was disparked in about 1592 and in 1605 was conveyed to Sir Richard Molyneux of Sefton, remaining in the ownership of the successive earls of Sefton (whose seat was at Croxteth Hall) until the early twentieth century.[6] Whereas parks attached to great estates had originally provided a habitat for hunting, latterly possession of a park was viewed as a form of cultural capital, establishing and displaying one's aristocratic credentials, along, in the sixteenth century, with newly built houses, the original Croxteth Hall being built by Sir Richard Molyneux c. 1575–1600. As expensive luxuries, the years between 1550 and 1660 have been described as a key period in which disparking took place, parks being cleared of woodland and the land divided up into fields. In the early 1770s, Cuthbert Bisbrown, a Liverpool builder, planned to build a 'New Liverpool' in Toxteth Park but was declared bankrupt by February 1776.[7] By a Private Act of Parliament in 1775, several building leases which had been granted of part of Lord Sefton's settled estates in Lancashire were confirmed and he was enabled to grant other building and improving leases. Taking advantage of such powers, the auction of leasehold property in Toxteth Park was advertised. In September 1788, *Williamson's Liverpool Advertiser* advertised the auction of several parcels of land in the park, including one on which a large dwelling house had been erected on High Park Street, 'pleasantly situated on an eminence, commanding a most beautiful and extensive prospect of the town of Liverpool, the river Mersey, county of Chester, part of Wales, and other prospects, equally pleasing' which might accommodate a boarding school or a private family.[8] By the late eighteenth century, the Mount Pleasant and Brownlow Hill areas were also gradually being developed in response to the growth in population and the desire on the part of the wealthier merchants to move their homes out of the centre of the town. In 1800 Liverpool Corporation determined to develop its own estate in the Moss Lake Fields, the carefully controlled grid development, principally of the 1820s and 1830s, having a square, Abercromby Square, for its central focus.

As was the then practice of the earl, the lease to William Rathbone was not for a fixed period of years but for the lives of three persons: William Reid, a merchant formerly of Liverpool but now living in Ireland, aged 60 years or thereabouts, William Rathbone (aged 30 years), and his wife, Hannah Maria Rathbone (aged 27 years), and the life and lives of the survivors and survivor of them.[9] In a separate instrument of 7 June 1788, testimony was given at Dublin by Captain Samuel Lee of Liverpool and Captain William Robinson of Dublin that William Reid, now of Fishmount near Letterkenny, Ireland, was alive and in good health, William Reid himself subscribing his name in a clear hand alongside the signatures of the two captains.[10] William Reid was named in the leases which had been granted of the property by the Honourable T. Molyneux to his father, Samuel Reid, on 25 March and 24 August 1754.

It was presumably shortly before the grant of the lease to William Rathbone that Edward Lerpiniere surveyed the estate, producing its 'plan and admeasurement,' noting that it had late belonged to 'Mr William Reid a Bankrupt.'[11] Edward Lerpiniere may be identified as having matriculated from Lincoln College, Oxford, in 1761, aged 18 years; he later worked for many years as a land surveyor in the Customs and Excise Office, Liverpool.[12] The evidence points to William Reid being the well-known china maker, who, in partnership with others, produced distinctive soft-paste porcelain china at a factory on Brownlow Hill, Liverpool, in November 1756 placing an

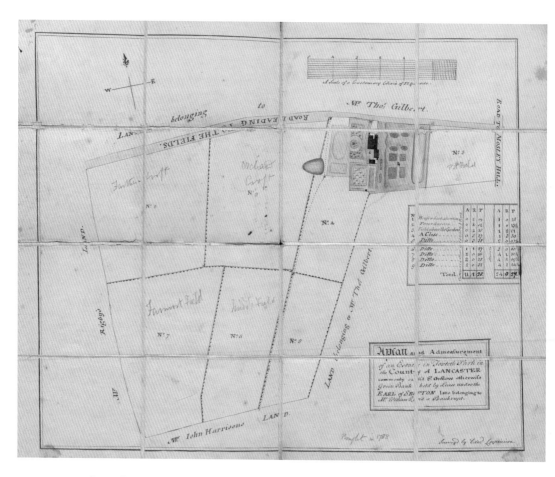

Map of St Anslow/Greenbank (c. 1788).
(Reproduced courtesy of the University of Liverpool Library, RP XX.1.1)

advertisement for the sale of its wares. Though the business was to continue until about 1767 under other management, on 8 June 1761 a Commission of Bankruptcy was issued against William Reid. The Commission was later renewed, *Gore's Liverpool Advertiser* publishing a notice as late as April 1795 calling a meeting of Reid's creditors to take into consideration the state of the proceedings in the suits then carrying on in the Chancery Court of Ireland for the recovery of the money due to his estate from the estate of Daniel MacNeale, his brother-in-law, who, as a Liverpool merchant and partner with Reid, had also been declared bankrupt in 1761.[13] Liverpool was noted in the latter half of the eighteenth century for its pottery and china manufacturers.[14]

The earliest record of a lease of the property, by Caryl, Lord Molyneux, on 25 December 1744 to Samuel Read (sic), was for the term of the lives of Margaret Onslow, aged 61 years, and Sarah Onslow, aged 13, and Thomas Onslow, aged 10, who may be presumed to be her children; the initial lease to Samuel Reid of 25 March 1754 was for the lives of his son, William, and those of Sarah and Thomas Onslow.[15] Though the archives of the earls of Sefton do not reveal when the property was erected, one might suggest that the original lessees, who were perhaps responsible for the original buildings, were members of the Onslow family.

Why the property should have taken 'Saint Anslow or Green Bank' as its name is unknown. There is no known saint of the name of Anslow. Is it conceivable that the name was felt suitable for a small house in the countryside, those responsible perhaps being conscious that the place name of Anslow (in Staffordshire) is derived from an old English word, ansetlleah, one of whose meanings is an open space in a wood with a hermitage, and that the property was leased for the terms of lives of members of the Onslow family (whose surname can be variously spelled as Anslow).

As in the other leases which Lord Sefton granted at this time, he reserved to himself and his successors all trees growing on the property ('excepting so much of the hedging as will be necessary to repair the fences') and all mines and minerals and 'birds and beasts of free warren and chase,' also the right to enter the property to view its condition and enter Garden Croft to repair the tunnel or sough 'in order to turn water out of the ponds or brooks in the tenement adjoining thereto called Green Bank through the said tunnel or sough' for such uses as the earl and his successors thought proper, but not hindering William Rathbone, his heirs and assigns from 'having sufficient water out of the said ponds or brooks to fill the fish ponds in the gardens before the said messuage hereby demised.' Though the 'fish ponds' were evidently later stocked with fish by the Rathbones, they were more in the form of an ornamental lake. 'Canals' and lakes built in the great English gardens of the seventeenth and eighteenth centuries were principally decorative, although they also served as fishponds or reservoirs. On a more modest scale,

Greenbank House's lake was evidently designed to reflect its creator's good taste, in creating and displaying beauty in the house's grounds, no doubt complementing its cultivated creator's presumed taste in the other arts, of literature, etc. Nowadays, the lake forms part of a watercourse which is, in the main, culverted and flows into Sefton Park's lake and hence ultimately to the River Mersey.

To obtain this lease, besides agreement to pay a nominal 10/6d annual rent and a further annual sum of £10 for every acre which William Rathbone, his heirs or assigns should improve through 'push-ploughing, paring or breaking up or burning,' a fine of not less than £450 had to be paid to Lord Sefton. With a view to the value of leased properties being increased at no cost to Lord Sefton, tenants were also obliged to make a commitment to expenditure on various improvements, in the case of William Rathbone a commitment within seven years to expend £300 in buildings 'of housing or outhousing' (providing the earl or his steward in due course with an account establishing that this had been undertaken) and annually to plant ten plants or young trees of oak, ash, or poplar 'for growing up to be timber trees,' using his best endeavours to preserve them 'from the spoil of cattle.' When one of the three persons for whose lives the property was held died, the earl was to be paid £150 for a new lease, naming another person. A more detailed control of the development of housing was to be exercised by Liverpool Corporation in the development of its estate in the late eighteenth and early nineteenth centuries, bequeathing a legacy of long terraces of fine houses and residential squares in what was the Abercromby Ward of Liverpool City Council.[16]

Though the lease to William Rathbone states that at the time he was in occupation of Greenbank, in a letter of 9 August 1788 written from his Liver Street, Liverpool, address, after a visit he had made to Greenbank earlier in the day, he informs his wife that he has 'seen Mrs Hodgson and from her I learn that Mrs White is delivered and Mr White is to be here the latter end of next week. The Appraizer goes to Green Bank on Monday and either then or on Tuesday is to fix on what day the sale is to be advertised and I think it cannot be before the 25th Instant at soonest. Whenever it is Mr White comes again and after it is over we may go into the house as soon as we please.'[17] On 15 September 1788, the local press advertised the forthcoming auction at The Golden Lion, Dale Street, of 'a valuable collection of books of the best French and English authors, Prints, and Books of Prints of the late Thomas Hodgson Esq. (brought from Green Bank) among which is Rollins Ancient History Chambers's Dictionary, Postlethwaite's etc. etc. mostly in fine preservation.'[18] Presumably Thomas Hodgson had obtained a tenancy of the property from William Reid or perhaps, given his bankruptcy, the Earl of Sefton. Already in this letter of 9 August William Rathbone, anxious to involve his wife in planning alterations to the property, asks her to tell him 'what size of a door thou wouldst like between the two Rooms where we intend to sleep, whether, one of the size of all our Room Doors in Liver Street, or smaller say of the size of those two opposite the windows in thy Dressing Room. I have bought some nice seasoned <u>unsmelling</u> stuff for that and other purposes.'

Of the views featuring Greenbank before the Gothic alterations of the early nineteenth century, the last section of the original building, probably dating from the early eighteenth century, to survive nowadays relatively unaltered externally is that nearest Greenbank Lane: the red brick section on the right, facing the pond. One might conclude that the hand-made bricks used to build the house were likely to have come from the brick kilns on whose site is now Greenbank Park: 'Big Brick Kill Field' and 'Little Brick Kill Field' both feature on the map of 1754.

A letter of William Rathbone, written from Liver Street, to his wife, at Ketley, near Shrewsbury, in October 1786 makes reference to building works which, in the absence of any reference to Greenbank, may rather relate to alterations at Liver Street, two months after their marriage:

The Pantry and Scullery are covered in and want only slates to have the roof completed. I wish they may be as high as thou wouldst like, but they are so far finished as not easily to admit of alteration. The fitting up the inside will be wholly left till thou returns. The Kitchen is built up to the first floor and now wants the Store Room raising upon it. The Closets behind the dining Parlor are built up and the Roof finished but all the floors Joiners [and] Plaisterers work within is still wanting. A Terrace Cistern is wanting below the scullery floor. The Back Kitchen floor is unlaid: the Cellar and Back Stairs not yet begun of, nor much done at the intended Closet under the best Stairs and the communication between the best and back Kitchen and between the Nursery and the Store Room is yet to do, all those rooms being now laid open without any door etc. to prevent entrance either by night or day. The intended convenience in the yard is also yet not begun. The communication between our Room and the dressing Room is finished – [?] painting. The fixing of the Water Closet is to begin tomorrow and that nearly finishes up Stairs.

In such circumstances 'we are very rough and I am glad thou art not here.'[19] Writing from Greenbank, enjoying the 'sweet calm of clear night,' on the evening of 26 July 1789, to his wife at Coalbrookdale, having 'just dismissed the servants from reading and they are also retiring to rest,' he observes that 'this is the first time I have ever written to thee from here since we could call the place our own.'[20]

The abstract of a survey of Lord Sefton's Toxteth Park estate in 1754 reveals a total acreage of just over 2,257 (statute) acres.[21] Of the fifty-six individual properties, thirty-three (including Green Bank) were below 30 acres in extent, with the five largest properties being Under Banks (252 acres, George Critchley, tenant), Higher Lodge (243 acres, Mr Edward Trafford), Smoots (109 acres, Dr Ainger), and Danvers's (Mrs Elizabeth Danvers, tenant) and Davises (Roger Brooks, Esq.) each of 107 acres. Already, one notes the names of tenements – including Jericho and Brook House – which are still in use in describing parts of the area, also that some of the properties were taking their names after their then tenants (including Aspinalls, near St Anslow, after Mr Aspinall, and Mathers, after Nathaniel Mather).

2   The second, third, and fourth William Rathbone

William Rathbone the younger (or William Rathbone junior as he occasionally signed his name during the lifetime of his father, William Rathbone the third, 1726–89) was the fourth of the succession of William Rathbones who, originally sawyers from Gawsworth, Cheshire, in the person of William Rathbone the second (1696–1746), had migrated to Liverpool by the mid-1720s. By the 1720s, Liverpool's shipping industry was in the early stages of its rapid development, facilitated by the construction of a wet dock, completed in 1715, the first commercial dock in Britain.

On his third visit in 1721, Daniel Defoe described Liverpool as

> one of the wonders of Britain, and that more, in my opinion, than any of the wonders of the Peak; the town was, at my first visiting it, about the year 1680, a large, handsome, well built and encreasing or thriving town; at my second visit, anno 1690, it was much bigger than at my first seeing it, and, by the report of the inhabitants, more than twice as big as it was twenty years before that; but, I think, I may safely say at this my third seeing it, for I surpriz'd at the view, it was more than double what it was at the second; and I am told, that it still visibly encreases both in wealth, people, business and buildings: What it may grow to in time, I know not … The town has now an opulent, flourishing and encreasing trade, not rivaling Bristol, in the trade to Virginia, and the English island colonies in America only, but is in a fair way to exceed and eclipse it, by encreasing every way in wealth and shipping. They trade round the whole island, send ships to Norway, to Hamburgh, and to the Baltick, as also to Holland and Flanders; so that, in a word, they are almost become, like the Londoners, universal merchants.[1]

By the mid-eighteenth century, Liverpool was becoming one of the leading ports in the British Isles, importing tobacco and sugar from America and the West Indies and exporting coal and salt. The day book for 1742–47, the earliest business archive to survive of what became Rathbone Brothers, provides evidence of the considerable business as timber merchants that the Rathbones had already established by this date. (It is the survival of

William
Rathbone the
third.
(Reproduced
courtesy of
the University
of Liverpool
Library,
RP XXII.A.1.21)

this day book that led Rathbone Brothers officially to date its birth to 1742.)
Demonstrating a readiness to adapt, which has been a marked feature of the
firm throughout its history, the Rathbones were initially timber merchants,
later shipbuilders and shipowners, establishing the firm of William Rathbone
& Son in 1746, trading chiefly to the West Indies, North America, and the
Baltic.

In his will, in January 1789 William Rathbone the third left his 'loving wife
Margaret Rathbone' his interest in a farm in Knowsley, an annuity of £60 (of
which the rents of three houses in Duke Street and Henry Street, Liverpool,
which had been bequeathed to her, were to form part), and all his household
goods, bedding, pewter, brass, linen, plate, china, glass, and books.[2] Though
he refers to the house 'in which we may then dwell in,' he does not identify its
location. In fact, the site of the house and several warehouses and buildings
of 'Mr Wm. Rathbone' are shown on George Perry's plan of Liverpool, 1769,
on a prominent site on the west side of Salthouse Dock, the site nowadays

William Rathbone's premises near the South Dock, from George Perry's plan of Liverpool, 1769. (Reproduced courtesy of Liverpool Record Office)

covered by the Albert Dock; this site was acquired by William Rathbone in 1768 and for the next sixty years the family and business was to be based there. By the time of his death, in August 1789, William Rathbone & Son was one of the largest firms in Liverpool, now a merchant business rather than a timber and shipbuilding business. In his lifetime, Liverpool's population had grown from an estimated 40,000 in 1780, to reach 55,732 in 1790 and 77,653 in 1801, when the first national census was taken.[3] William was buried in the Quakers' Hackins Hey burial ground, where his father had also been buried in 1746.

Both William Rathbone and his father, William Rathbone the second, were Quakers, the father becoming a Quaker in about 1731 and taking as his second wife a fellow Quaker, as was expected of members of the Religious Society of Friends. Particularly noted for their industry and pronounced business sense as also a strong feeling of social duty and commitment towards movements of reform, Quakerism in the instance of the Rathbone family was to be reinforced by a series of marriages between members of the family and other prominent Quaker families, including the Darbys, the Bensons, and the Reynolds, cementing essential social and economic connections, commencing in 1768 when William Rathbone the third's half-brother, Joseph, married Mary Darby, daughter of Abraham Darby of Coalbrookdale.

The eldest son of William Rathbone the third and his first wife, Rachel Rutter, William Rathbone was born at Liverpool in 1757, probably in his father's house. In common with others of the mercantile elite of Liverpool at this time, their home was close to the town's centre, within walking distance of the Town Hall and the Exchange. As the son of Quakers, William Rathbone received a Quaker education, entering his father's office at the age of sixteen or seventeen. Conscious of his lack of formal education at a higher level – and not being a member of the Church of England, he would have been precluded from studying at one of England's universities, Oxford or Cambridge – after long hours spent at his office, he returned home to continue his studies in French, Latin, and Greek, also reading widely in the fields of politics, economics, theology, and philosophy, such that he was in a position to engage in debate and correspondence with learned contemporaries. A friend was later to remark upon his pursuit of knowledge, his 'command of time; by which his understanding, endowed by nature, and in early life unvitiated ... was now extensive in reading and reflection; and between Literature and Science having put the finishing hand to his character, he took that lead in society, which he maintained, thirty years ... a blessing to all connected with him.'[4]

In August 1786, at the Quaker Meeting House at Shrewsbury, William Rathbone married Hannah Mary Reynolds (1761–1839), the young daughter of Richard Reynolds (1735–1816), the Quaker philanthropist and a partner

Hannah Mary
Rathbone.
(Reproduced
courtesy of
the University
of Liverpool
Library,
RP XXV.7.5)

in the ironworks at Coalbrookdale, and of his first wife, Hannah, daughter of Abraham Darby of Coalbrookdale. Richard Reynolds had taken over the ironworks at Coalbrookdale after the death in 1763 of Abraham Darby. Hannah spent most of her youth at the home of her father and his second wife and her siblings at Ketley Bank, Shropshire.

By contrast to his father, who was of a more mild and tranquil spirit, William Rathbone the fourth, though a cautious businessman, was a man of impassioned temperament who took a more prominent part in public affairs. In later life, he was expelled from the Society of Friends following his publication in 1804 of A *Narrative of Events that have recently taken place in Ireland among the Society called Quakers*, expressing sympathy for Irish Quakers who had voiced heretical opinions concerning the authority of the Old Testament and Quaker discipline concerning marriage with non-Quakers.

As Eleanor Rathbone wrote, he was 'too essentially a fighter to be at home in the Society of Friends.' William Roscoe, who was particularly close to William Rathbone, wrote to him on this occasion expressing his concern for his health: 'I know the rectitude of your judgment but I know also the warmth of your temperament and am afraid that your very desire of promoting what is right may lead to injuries and fatal consequences.' He concludes the letter enjoining Rathbone to 'break the chain that binds you to the writing desk and let health and air and exercise be your only study – come and see me at Allerton. I will come and see you at Greenbank – let us apply new fuel to the flame of friendship and those we love shall warm themselves by the blaze.'[5] Henceforth, William Rathbone was to worship occasionally with the Unitarian congregation at Benn's Garden, Liverpool, a church also attended by William Roscoe.

William Rathbone the fourth and 'the Friends of Freedom'

It was as a member of 'the Friends of Freedom,' the party of Reform in Liverpool, that William Rathbone had many friends, proving a staunch supporter of its objectives, a hospitable host, and someone who engaged in a wide correspondence with like-minded persons. The social and professional network enjoyed by this group of public-spirited people allowed them to develop their ideas and to contribute towards an enlightenment movement. The oldest member of the group was William Rathbone's father, William Rathbone the third (1726–89), who joined his son, William Roscoe and Revd John Yates among those few from Liverpool who were prepared openly to oppose the slave trade, in 1788 appearing on the list of subscribers to the Society for the Abolition of the Slave Trade which had been formed in London in 1787. It has to be acknowledged that two decades earlier, in 1768, William Rathbone the third had shipped to Trevor Corry in Danzig 'a young African recommended to me under good character.'[6] The Rathbones refused to have any part in the slave trade, on which many Liverpool fortunes had been founded; besides, they refused to sell timber or ships for use in the trade. The first known ship to depart from Liverpool's docks on a slaving voyage left in 1699 and by the late eighteenth century Liverpool was at its peak as a slave-trading city port, supplanting Bristol as the principal British slaving port in the mid-eighteenth century. Criticism of the trade was fuelled by the ideas of liberty, fraternity, and equality manifest in American Independence and the French Revolution.

The acknowledged leader of the party and by far the best known of the Liverpool reformers was William Roscoe (1753–1831), historian, poet, and politician, whose home, at Allerton Hall, was not far distant from Greenbank. Of a humble background, the son of a Liverpool publican and market gardener, Roscoe left school at the age of twelve, later, in 1774, qualifying as an attorney before turning his attention to property development and then banking. Largely self-taught, in his lifetime Roscoe achieved fame well beyond Liverpool as a scholar, historian, and man of letters, particularly through his biographies of Lorenzo de Medici (1796) and of his son, Pope Leo X (1805). The perceived model of the union between culture and commerce in Lorenzo de Medici's Florence, as pictured in Roscoe's study, clearly had an appeal to his fellow townsmen. Roscoe's first major poem, 'Mount Pleasant,' written at the age of eighteen, contains his first protest against the slave trade; his long abolitionist poem, 'The Wrongs of Africa,' was published in 1787–88. Elected as one of the MPs for Liverpool in 1806, he spoke during the crucial second reading of the Abolition Bill in February 1807, stressing that Liverpool was by no means unanimous in defence of the slave trade and that he wished to represent that 'great and respectable' body which opposed it; he concluded: 'I have long resided in the town of Liverpool; for 30 years I have never ceased to condemn this inhuman traffic; and I consider it the greatest happiness of my existence to lift up my voice on this occasion against it, with the friends of justice and humanity.' Following a decisive vote of 283 in favour and 16 against, the Act received the Royal Assent and came into force on 1 May

William Rathbone the fourth. (Reproduced in Eleanor Rathbone, *William Rathbone, A Memoir*, 1905)

1807, outlawing slave trading. Slavery itself was to be outlawed throughout the British colonies in 1833. In his last speech in parliament, William Roscoe, supported by William Rathbone, also strongly advocated Catholic emancipation, a campaign which was not to be won until 1829. In April 1807 William Rathbone wrote to William Roscoe arguing the case for Catholic emancipation – 'The great points to the British Empire and to mankind is whether an extension of power to the Catholics is not in itself a measure which justice imperiously demands, and which the tranquility of Ireland and the interests of the British empire also requires.'[7] Such outspoken advocacy led William Rathbone to warn Roscoe that knives were being sharpened and that he would not find things easy when he returned to Liverpool; indeed the political climate proved most unfavourable to the Whigs and dissenters, the subsequent election in 1807 returning two candidates who promised that if elected they would restore the slave trade.

Soon after the abolition of the slave trade, the visit to Liverpool of a black man, Captain Paul Cuffee, in command of a small merchant vessel whose cargo was destined for William Rathbone, attracted a good deal of interest. As was customary, he was invited to dinner at Greenbank; among the other guests was William Roscoe, bringing with him Lord John Russell and Professor Playfair. (As a student at Edinburgh University, Lord John Russell [1792–1878], who was later, as a Whig, to serve as prime minister, 1846–52 and 1865–66, lodged with Professor John Playfair [1748–1819], the mathematician and geologist, who latterly held Edinburgh's Chair of Natural Philosophy.) William Rathbone's son later recollected that another of the party, an American or a gentleman who had recently returned from America, told his father that he must on no account ever ask an American to dine with a man who had any black blood in his veins, whatever his culture or position, as the American would probably be deeply affronted and walk out of the room. A portrait of Captain Cuffee hung at Greenbank House for many years.[8]

Another of the members of the Reform party in Liverpool was Dr James Currie (1756–1805). The son of the Presbyterian minister of Kirkpatrick-Fleming, following a short mercantile career in the American colonies, he returned to study medicine at the University of Edinburgh where he also imbibed the work of the philosophers Berkeley, Locke, Hume, and Adam Smith. Settling in Liverpool in 1780, as a physician he had a large practice, second only to that of Dr John Brandreth, his fellow physician at Liverpool Dispensary (which had been established in 1778); in 1785, he was elected a physician to Liverpool Infirmary, his distinction recognised when he was elected a Fellow of The Royal Society in 1792. His biography of his compatriot, Robert Burns, brought him additional renown. Though an early advocate of the abolition of the slave trade, he preferred to work in the background. It

William Roscoe by Sir M. A. Shee, 1815–17.
(© National Museums Liverpool/Bridgeman Images)

took courage in Liverpool to be associated with the campaign. It is said that William Rathbone was so unpopular for denouncing the slave trade and the war with France that a physician attending an illness in his family requested that he be allowed to pay his visits after nightfall, recognising that it would injure his practice for his carriage to be seen standing at William Rathbone's door. In the *Life of Dr Currie*, his son wrote that his father was most strongly attached to William Roscoe and that 'in closest intimacy and friendship with them lived Mr William Rathbone, a man, for whose generous ardour in the cause of civil and religious liberty, native eloquence, fearless vindication of the oppressed, public spirit, and extensive charity, they both felt equal respect and admiration.'[9]

The other members of the party included Edward Rushton, the Revd Dr William Shepherd, and the Revd John Yates. Edward Rushton (1756–1814), formerly a mate of a ship engaged in the slave trade, achieved the widest recognition through his poetry and other writings fiercely attacking the slave trade following his conversion to abolition, being appalled by the inhuman treatment of slaves he had witnessed on an American ship he was working on. In his years of blindness, contracted while treating an outbreak of ophthalmia among the slaves on a ship on passage to Dominica, he was the composer of anti-slavery poetry and one of those who helped establish the Liverpool School for the Blind which opened in 1791.

The son of a Liverpool shoemaker, following training at the Dissenting Academy at Daventry and at New College, Hackney, Revd William Shepherd (1768–1847), a Unitarian, was appointed tutor to the children of Revd John Yates and, in 1791, minister to the English Presbyterian Chapel at Gateacre, where he ran a boys' school which established a fine reputation among the Nonconformist gentry of the north of England. One of the liveliest members of the Roscoe circle, he proved a witty and caustic writer of squibs for the local Whigs to set against the Tories and the unreformed corporation of Liverpool. Reckoned with William Roscoe and James Currie to be part of the 'Liverpool Literary Triumvirate,' his *The Life of Poggio Bracciolini* (1803) earned him an honorary doctorate of laws from the University of Edinburgh; his other publications included a biography of Edward Rushton. The Revd John Yates (1755–1826), a fellow Unitarian, was also an active member of the anti-corporation group in Liverpool; he is reputed to have been in serious trouble with his congregation for his abolitionist sermons in 1788. Revd Yates trained at Warrington Academy, married the heiress daughter of John Ashton of Woolton Hall, and served for many years as minister of Paradise Street Church; living in Toxteth Park, he was a near neighbour of both William Roscoe and William Rathbone.

William Roscoe and his circle of friends, liberal and reformist in politics, Quaker or Unitarian for the most part in religion, took a leading role in every kind of literary, artistic, and scientific activity in Liverpool in the late eighteenth century and early nineteenth century, including in the foundation of the Athenaeum (1797), the Lyceum (1802), Liverpool Botanic Garden (which opened in 1802 on a site near the present Myrtle Street), the Liverpool Academy of Arts (1810), the Literary and Philosophical Society (1812), and the Liverpool Royal Institution (1814), in effect one of the ancestors of the University of Liverpool.[10] Instancing the recent endowment of the Athenaeum and the Botanic Garden, the poet Robert Southey, on a visit to Liverpool in 1802, wrote 'Fortunes are made here with a rapidity unexampled in any other part of England,' but added 'There is too a princely liberality in its merchants, which even in London is not rivaled.'[11] Liverpool's merchants clearly viewed culture as a form of investment worth supporting.

Besides Liverpool, a number of other provincial centres, including Leeds, Manchester, and Newcastle upon Tyne were also witnessing the foundation of their own Literary and Philosophical Societies and Athenaeums in the late eighteenth and early nineteenth centuries. A high value was placed on culture by the merchant elite of this era, in the case of Liverpool their foundations enhancing the town's reputation on the national and international stage. William Roscoe indeed envisaged his native town as a city, as a Florence on the Mersey, a model republic in which the arts and sciences would flourish.[12] As the fifteenth edition of *The Stranger's Complete Guide; or, Liverpool as it is* put it in the early 1850s, William Roscoe 'was himself the Lorenzo de Medicis of Liverpool, and whose genius and talents have essentially contributed to give character and elevation to the town of which he was the distinguished ornament.'[13]

Writing from Manchester to his brother in January 1797, John Dalton, the eminent chemist and natural philosopher, provides an insight into the lives and interests of the cognoscenti of Liverpool following a week's visit:[14]

> went to meeting [presumably of the Society of Friends, of which he was a member] next morning and was introduced to William Rathbone, who invited me to sit by him. At the conclusion he wished me to go home with him into the country to Greenbank (about three miles) ... I agreed, and Wm., his wife, and myself, all rode home in his whiskey. We had a good deal of conversation in the afternoon, and I was highly pleased with his candour, liberality, and good sense, as well as with his amiable wife. Notwithstanding there were seven strangers there besides myself, I was complimented with their most elegant bedroom, a splendid carpet, fire, etc., etc. Next morn we went about a mile across the country to Mr Yates, to breakfast, where I found Wm. Marshall, our classical tutor, James Wild and J.A. Yates, the son, both students. After breakfast, we had some able discussions on points of religion and morality.

Dalton dined at Greenbank the next day,

> where were Yates' family and visitants, Mr and Mrs Roscoe, etc., etc. (The etiquette in Liverpool is to sit down to dinner a little after three; as soon as the cloth is drawn, in winter, candles are brought in; when the bottle has gone round about half-an-hour, the ladies retire, the gentlemen remain till a servant informs them tea is ready, when all meet together again in the tea-room, where they remain till they are informed supper is upon the table.) Mr Roscoe is a gentleman of the law, lately well known in the literary world for his celebrated *Life of Lorenzo de Medicis*; he is also a poet, and man of taste for the fine arts. We dined and drank tea there, a very agreeable company, and went home in the evening.

He concluded that the visit 'was highly pleasant, the respectability of the three principal characters, Yates, Rathbone, and Roscoe, was made more particularly evident to me from the more private interviews I had with them, and it was enhanced to me by their numerous civilities. The stylish manner of living, however, I am not in love with. Breakfasting at nine, getting little till after three, and then eating and drinking almost incessantly to ten, without going out further than to the door, does not suit my constitution.'

Developing Greenbank

In accordance with the conditions specified in the lease of Greenbank, William Rathbone commenced expenditure on improving the property, including the planting of trees. A copious letter-writer, William Rathbone's letters to his wife, Hannah, at Coalbrookdale, visiting her Reynolds family members, provide evidence of these improvements.

Writing from his Cornhill, Liverpool, address in August 1789, he reports that he 'had Matty Wilson and a Labourer in the Hay and since it was finished I keep them till the Garden is got into order.'[15] Of his infant son he reports 'I took Will home last night and much rejoiced he was to find himself there. I left him well this morning and expect he will get plenty of exercise among the Hay-Makers. He bathed yesterday ... Samuel and Peggy continue with us and the latter hath preserved 14 quarts of Gooseberries. She is making more into Vinegar and my Sister Benson hath had a considerable quantity but there will be others left if thou chooses more to be done. The Vinegar Cask, the Jack and the Grate under the Boiler I hope to have attended to.'[16]

In May 1790, he writes,

> Joiners, Painters, Whitewashers and Bricklayers left us yesterday. This week I expect all the rooms to be hung but there is so great a demand for upholsterers that it is a favor to get a.Holland. The Joiners and Painters

A drawing of Greenbank House before 1809.
(Reproduced in Mrs. Eustace Greg., ed., *Reynolds-Rathbone Diaries and Letters 1753–1839*, 1905)

will have something more to do out of Doors about the Gates, etc. I hope
to remember what thou mentions. In the meantime the Dome Bed will be
put up and the Room hung unless the Upholdsterer thinks it will spoil the
paper. The washing Furniture goes to Bootle to be washed and I hope will
be returned by the time we get back ... Our Room is finished and makes
a much better Job than I expected. I hope Joiners, Painters etc. will finish
the inside of the House this week, and next week we are to have the Paper
hanger. Thou art quite right about painting our back Parlor with oil Color
but it would be much more expensive than Paper and the Plaister in one
part is spoiled for paint.[17]

A month later, in June 1790, he almost wishes that his wife was there,

as there is so much that thou wouldest enjoy. The trees shoot with astonishing vigor and the bank is now almost impervious to view as I sit in the
Low Parlor. The double blossomed Cherries trees and thy favorite Lay lock
are in full flower, the Ash trees which we planted at the top of the Bank
field all thrive and so doth the tall Sycamore there about which we were
so hopeless. The Bricklayers are now at the fish pond. It is a troublesome

job but I hope it will at length answer; they have built the Pig Stye; and the Whitewashers have nearly finished their work; the Painters are getting forwards and next week I expect the rooms will be fit to paper. The Joiners begin upon our Room and the Nursery floor tomorrow and I wish that work was well over for I half tremble for the poor old ceiling below it. I hope the new Gates from the Yard into the Garden and the new Gate from the Lane to the front of the House will be finished this week but I remain in doubt about the latter.[18]

The same month he reported that A Holland had been over 'to fix up the White and Down Bed, etc' and 'Thy Cot from Bridgewater is come.'[19] It is presumed that he would also have been responsible for the alterations to the exterior of the house, to transform its appearance from that of a farmhouse to that of a villa: creating a new entrance and frontage. A stuccoed double-bowed façade was added to the existing house, with a central doorway.

Though always under pressure at work, he wrote regularly to his wife, addressing her in affectionate terms, as in July 1792:

I am so much pressed for time that it will be in my power only to inform thee that I am well and that our dear infants are perfectly so. My little Richard chears me with his sweet society and is I think more engaging than ever. Hannah is also as well as she can be and comes on in her walking surprisingly. She will run from the Parlor to the middle of the Kitchen and trot back with ease and pleasure and it would delight thy heart to see her toddling on the Grass plot and playing with her Brother.[20]

In late March 1793, he is glad to receive a good account of the health of his wife and W[ill], though sorry that Hannah has suffered so much in the same way as he has done:

I believe my cough is leaving me tho it is not so much better today as I expected. We were half an hour too late in returning last night and it snowed pretty fast before we reached GBank. I have seen no signs of the Childrens' having caught cold as seemed quite well this morning. Betsy had a very indifferent night, her cough very troublesome and the perspiration profuse, and I left her with a painful headache this morning. She sleeps in the Green Room by her own choice as she thought the fireplace too near the bed in the White Room and I believe her fire is duly attended to and that all in the family will do all they can for her. S.B. is removed into the Dome Room. I don't expect to see Dr Rutter to day but I hope I shall and write thee about Joe Ash tomorrow.[21]

There are few references to his work in this letter besides the report 'We are begun the new Co. house which I hope will not be wanting in a good circulation of air.'

Life at Greenbank

Expressions of his views on life are never far from the thoughts of William Rathbone as he writes to his wife, no doubt conscious that his health was poor for much of his life. Writing from Greenbank in June 1808:

I hear no news about Cotton or Wheat but if we are in health and love one another, I am not anxious about fortune – we may be very happy, tho we spend less money ... a good heart and a humble, not desponding mind, are better than learning or knowledge, tho they are good – but thou knows the distinction I always make between knowledge and wisdom – a good and single hearted man may be useful, happy, and truly wise, tho he be not very learned – be wisely careful of thy health, both of body and mind, – it

A drawing of Greenbank House 'before 1812' by Hannah Mary Rathbone.
(Reproduced courtesy of the late Dr B. L. Rathbone)

is said 'fret not thyself because of evil doers' – thou are already too wise and knoweth too much of thyself, and human nature, to expect perfection in any human being – some failings will not therefore surprise thee, even in the best, but do not dwell upon them – there is some good in every character, and some characters in which it greatly preponderates – when I perceive in myself a quickness to see, and a proneness to dwell upon, the little or great faults of my friends, family, and acquaintances, I am sure that something is wrong in myself, and that I am getting worse, every moment while I indulge it.[22]

The reference to cotton and wheat reminds one that William Rathbone the fourth continued the firm's Irish trade, importing wheat, oats and oatmeal, and linen cloth from Ireland, and that the firm was one of the first Liverpool merchants to import American-grown cotton in the late eighteenth century. In 1801, William Rathbone was among the founding committee of the Liverpool American Chamber of Commerce.

A further insight into life at Greenbank is provided in the diaries which Hannah Rathbone kept up to the premature death of her husband in 1809:[23]

1788: 13 March: 'Went to Greenbank to tea and staid late'; 29 April: 'Went to Greenbank with W.R. and went over the house.'

1790: 3 February: 'Went to Greenbank to breakfast with W.R. and Will [their son, William, born on 17 April 1787] on the cart; left Will there. Drank tea and suped at Dr. [James] Currie's'; 6 February: 'Packed up and sent things to Greenbank'; Sunday 7 February: 'Went to Meeting [of the Society of Friends]. Came to Greenbank. Gave Peggy and Saml. [servants] a month's warning'; 29 June: 'Engaged in the garden dragged the fish pond. Mr Smith at supper'; 3 July: 'In the garden in the morning. Dr Currie and W. Roscoe at dinner and tea Richard Ford Junr. in the evening'; 8 July: 'Some foreigners etc. at dinner 16 in all'; 16 July: 'Molly still confined to her bed. Wrote to my Father, busy morning etc. all the servants at the Hayfield in the afternoon'; 21 July: 'sewing in the afternoon'; 22 July: 'Went to meeting [of the Society of Friends], dined in Castle St., my cousin Harriet with us and went with us to green Bank after drinking tea at Cornhill went round by edge Lane left Betty Strong there. Bessy foald and we found a nice bay Colt in the morning'; 24 July: 'Sent the servants to the Hay'; 4 August: 'Went to the hayfield in the morning with the Children'; 6 August: 'WR kept at home by his complaint, very wet morning passed a quiet day sewing, WR and my Bro[ther, Richard] read in Blair and Price's Sermons' [The sermons of Revd Hugh Blair (1718–1800), a Scottish Presbyterian, were published in five volumes, 1777–1801; the Revd Richard

Price (1723–91), a Nonconformist, published a volume of sermons in 1744.];
25 August: 'Mr Yates at breakfast, WR much the same Drs Currie and
Rutter came';[24] 31 October: 'Went to Liverpool, and to the Catholic chapel
Mr Barrington preached an excellent sermon'; 1 November 'Looking over
fossils etc'; 22 November: 'Coopers in the Cellar etc. hindered me from
writing'; 24 December: 'Went to Greenbank and staid all day with WR, the
partition between the nursery and our room taken down.'

1792: 6 March: 'Went to Greenbank with W.R. and Richard [their younger
son, born on 2 December 1788] in the chair, rode a little way on Black
Bess. Dr Rutter at dinner, drank tea at Mrs. Lightbody's'; 5 April: 'W.R.
returned to tea and told me it was decided in the House [of Commons]
that the slave-trade should be abolished'; 6 April: "Very stormy, wet, cold
day. Dined and drank tea at Mr Roscoe's. Returned behind W.R., and had a
fine moonlight ride'; 7 September: 'Spent the day chiefly with the children
in the cornfields'; 17 November: 'A most delightful day, passed it chiefly in
the garden planting, etc'; Monday 31 November: 'Washing day. The house
very dirty from the workman making the china pantry.'

1793: 28 August: 'W.R. staid at home all day, which we passed sweetly with
our dear children. Dined on the grass plat, and sat by the fish pond most
of the day'; 6 November: 'A very fine day. Planting trees in the lane.'

1795: 8 May: 'went to Liverpool with T.H. [Theophilus Houlbrooke, the
children's tutor],[25] dined at Cornhill & went with my Sister Benson to
W Roscoes and to look at D Dalbys house – returned with T.H. thro
Wavertree to G Bank to tea. Mr Shepperd at supper'; 22 October: 'being
very poorly staid at home & did little but teach my dear girl her lessons
etc. – sent some of the servants to York St. W.R. intending to have
company at supper and to stay all night'; 11 November: 'passed the whole
morning in the garden and by the horse pond planting etc. W.R. staid at
home all day. Dr Rutter at dinner. Wrote to W. Yonge.'

1798: 10 January: 'Returned to Greenbank with T.H. and the children. The
young men from the Counting House, and some others, 13 or 14 in all, at
dinner and tea. Wm. Duncan came in the evening'; 17 [September]: 'Fixed
on a place for the greenhouse, and the foundation began digging for.'

1801: 13 June: 'Too cold to admit of our going out. We sat in the library.
Lord Selkirk came with W.R. to dinner.' [Thomas Douglas, fifth Earl
of Selkirk (1771–1820), studied at the University of Edinburgh where he
joined 'the Club,' an association of students that included Walter Scott and

Adam Ferguson; in 1799 his pamphlet describing the poor relief system of Galloway, as lately reformed under his direction, was published.]

1803: 26 March: 'In the garden with the children, and in the afternoon walked with them to Mrs Baker's field. A very fine day; W.R. too busy writing to enjoy it'; 30 March: 'The workmen began the alteration of the nursery. Dirt, noise, and confusion. W.R. very busy writing; Mr Wilson came to help him'; 16 April: 'Busy upstairs, cleaning pictures, etc., and getting fixed in our new apartments.'

1804: 30 May: 'Our visitors, T.H., Margt. Benson, and I went to Liverpool, rode through the town, saw the Blind School, Botanic Gardens, and returned to a late dinner.' [Founded in 1791, the Blind School transferred in 1800 to premises in London Road.]

1805: 21 September: 'A gloomy day; sat in the library, but was too idle and dispirited to be usefully employed. In the afternoon went into the hothouse with T.H'; 27 September: 'W.R. went with the young men to Liverpool to hear the 'Messiah', and returned to a late dinner'; Saturday 16 November: 'Sat with the children, sewing, etc. In the evening W.R. read in 'Leo the Tenth', Mr Roscoe the author, to Wm. and me.' [Reading as an essential social and domestic activity evolved during the eighteenth century.]

1806: 1 February: 'T.H. and I breakfasted in the nursery with the children. He read to them, and then to me, a history of Botany Bay. W.R. came home very poorly before dinner'; 4 February: 'Read an account of New South Wales, and heard Wm. read in [Samuel] Johnson's 'Lives of the Poets.'

1808: 30 January: 'Hannah read to me in the afternoon in the 'Life of Burns' [by Dr James Currie], and we had a little of Sully [sic] in the evening'; 25 February: 'Mr Roscoe called, and W.R. went to Liverpool with him, and staid all night, and Willm. with him engaged in American business, addressing Parliament, etc. I was buried in the wine cellar with a joiner';[26] 20 May: 'Marking linen for H., knitting, etc. The bees swarmed'; 3 June: 'We went to the Blind school, but were too late to hear them sing'; 2 July: 'Sat on the Sundial while T.H., R. Roscoe, and the little boys were fishing'; 5 July: 'The doctors called and changed W.R.'s medicines; ordered a still stricter regimen. We went to the Blind Asylum and heard the pupils sing'; 11 July: 'Settled accts., etc. W.R. walked with me to the Hayfield, next but one to the garden, but was so weak it was with difficulty he got home'; 21 September: 'W.R. low and poorly, rode out a little way in the morning. The new grate put up. Vidonia wine bottled, etc. Will Smythe called. T.H.

and I weeding in the afternoon. Richd. read [James] Thomson's [poem] 'Castle of Indolence' to us.'

1809: 'Most melancholy is the beginning of this awful year. My dear Husband, after appearing better for several days, again very ill. T.H confined to his bed by the gout. Dr Rutter called, and Hughes, Duncans, Roscoes, and many of our friends – Will Corrie, etc. [...] The journal I keep for the doctors; it best marks my suffering days and nights, which are now all passed in desiring to help and comfort our beloved sufferer.'

There is a gap in the diary between 29 January and 19 February, William Rathbone dying on 11 February, aged 51.

The local press published a generous tribute to William Rathbone:

his loss will be deeply felt and long lamented by those who knew him the best. The poor have lost a warm friend and generous supporter ... As a merchant, he was candid and generous; his knowledge procured him many valuable and respectable connexions in business, which his integrity preserved ... A strenuous defender of civil and religious liberty, he ever stood forward their dauntless champion ... The profession of Christianity he adorned by his example, in the practice of its precepts ... In one word, all his public exertions and his private conversations were directed to one object, – the establishment of peace on earth, and good will towards men.[27]

Quakers believed that by acting as honest and trustworthy businessmen they were fulfilling their commitment towards God. Writing almost a century later, William Rathbone the sixth, ignoring his own major contribution, opined that his grandfather 'was by all accounts the most able and powerful man in will, character and intellect that we have had in our family during the seven generations of which we have traditions.'[28]

The transformation of Greenbank effected by Hannah Rathbone
In his will, dated 3 October 1805,[29] William Rathbone left his 'dear wife,' Hannah Mary Rathbone, his 'messuage and tenement closes and parcels of land called Greenbank within Toxteth park,' which he held by lease from Lord Sefton, also two small freehold houses near Greenbank which he had bought from Mary Mitchell; also left to his wife were all his household goods, his horses, cows and other cattle, carriages, carts, farming stock, hay, corn, and husbandry implements, £500 to be paid to her immediately, and the very large sum of £45,000 for her own sole and absolute use. (Employing the Retail Price Index, the Measuring Worth website calculates that £45,000

in 1805 was worth £3,587,000 in 2018.) Personal bequests were made of one hundred guineas to his 'valued friend' Theophilus Houlbrooke; fifty guineas to his 'excellent friend,' the Revd John Yates, as a last testimony of the value of the friendship which 'throughout the most important period of my life and in some of its most trying conjunctures' he had experienced from him; £100 to his servant, Ann Simkin, in recognition of her long and faithful service; and one year's wages over and above what was due to them to every other of his domestic servants who would have lived in his family for one year at the time of his death. At the time, his children were minors and so besides appointing his wife as their guardian, he left the residue of his property to trustees (Richard Reynolds, his father-in-law, Joseph Reynolds, his brother-in-law, Robert Benson, a nephew, and his friend William Stanley Roscoe) in trust for his children. Evidently he had already acquired other land, authorising his trustees to open 'new roads or streets' through them and in the first of two codicils to his will, dated 10 November 1808, he records that he has since purchased 'sundry lands tenements and hereditaments' in Toxteth Park, Liverpool, Wavertree, and West Derby, which he also left to his trustees, in trust for his children. At this time, he was negotiating with Lord Sefton to acquire the freehold of his Greenbank estate and in his second codicil, dated 29 January 1809, just before his death, he can state that he has contracted with Lord Sefton for the purchase of the estate and also a further small piece of land and a small field called Little Rough in Toxteth Park; this property he leaves to his wife unconditionally.

Dating from July 1800 are two sketches 'of Sundry Lots of Land in Toxteth Park for Sale,' in one case showing two lots close to 'Brook House' (on what is now Smithdown Road) as also lots further afield to the west, closer to the River Mersey and to the north-east of Park Chapel.[30] In the other sketch, the whereabouts of intended streets and individual numbered lots of land are noted within the area bounded by Parliament Street on the north, Northumberland Street and Upper Warwick Street on the south, close to the River Mersey on the west, and what was later developed as Princes Road on the east. The auction advertisement of these 'sundry small farms and valuable parcels of land,' which were among 'the most admired and delightful spots in the kingdom' with their uninterrupted views of Liverpool, etc., noted their 'convenience for business, combining at the same time, a healthy, airy, and picturesque situation.'[31] In his *Topographical and Statistical Description of the County of Lancaster* of c. 1806, George Cooke wrote that 'all the villages in the immediate neighbourhood of Liverpool are filled with the country houses and rural retreats of its merchants and other inhabitants, which give an air of cheerfulness and cultivation to a tract of country, naturally dreary and infertile.'[32] Further sales of parts of the Toxteth Park estate by the Earls of Sefton were to facilitate the creation by Richard Vaughan Yates (a son of

Greenbank House, from Samuel Nicholson's *Lithographic Drawings … in the vicinity of Liverpool*, 1821. (Reproduced courtesy of the University of Liverpool Library)

the Revd John Yates) of Princes Park from 1842 onwards and, through the purchase by Liverpool Corporation of about 370 acres, Sefton Park, laid out between 1867 and 1872.

The conveyance of the Greenbank estate to Hannah Mary Rathbone was effected by deeds dated 4 and 5 October 1809, a total of £3,763/7/6d being paid to the Earl of Sefton. In her diary for 4 October, she noted that her brother, visiting Greenbank, had walked with her in the garden and fields and that 'he talked of making some alterations.' Already on 10 October she was 'looking at plans for altering the house, etc.' On 13 October, Mr Roscoe called and 'talked about the alterations,' bringing 'some plans' when he returned on 16th. Though no later diaries of Hannah are known to exist, in a letter addressed to his mother, 'Mrs Rathbone, Green Bank, near Liverpool,' in November 1810, the twelve-year-old Theodore Woolman Rathbone, during a visit to

Market Drayton with his tutor, the Revd Theophilus Houlbrooke, writes, 'I hope when we get home to see the house covered in and the bow windows finished. Pray are the large arch stones put up? and is our little summer house in the cottage garden pulled down? when do you think of beginning the long covered balcony?'[33]

In his 'Sketch of family history during four generations' (1894), William Rathbone the sixth, who had fond memories of his grandmother, recorded that after her husband's death she altered Greenbank, 'adding the part of the house with the stone front to the old one' and that the iron veranda on the lawn side had been made at the Coalbrookdale works of the Reynolds, being given to her by her father or perhaps her brother, William Reynolds, an engineer and managing partner of the family's iron works in Shropshire.[34] The then fashionable 'Gothic' style, made well known through the fantastical 'Strawberry Hill,' Twickenham, residence of Horace Walpole (d. 1797), who had transformed a modest house into a 'little Gothic castle' between 1748 and 1790, had been adopted. As R. A. Cordingley was later to observe in his article for the *Blue Pigeon*, the magazine of Derby Hall, the design of the arches of the two-storey veranda and that of the arcades of the church of St Michael's-in-the-Hamlet, Aigburth, are the same. The Gothic cast-iron screen of Greenbank, which forms a veranda at ground level and a sheltered balcony at first-floor level, is characteristic of the extensive use of decorative cast-iron work in Liverpool, particularly associated with St George's church, Everton, of 1813–14, and with St Michael's Hamlet, including St Michael's church of 1814–15, the creations of John Cragg, employing cast-iron manufactured at his Mersey Iron Foundry.[35] The general pattern of the tracery and the coupled pilasters of Greenbank's screen are somewhat like those on these two churches, both designed by Thomas Rickman who was based in Liverpool, 1808–21, and who did so much both in his publications and in his buildings to promote an appreciation of Gothic architecture. By the time that the first single-span, cast-iron bridge in the world, spanning the River Severn, had been erected by the Coalbrookdale firm in 1779, Abraham Darby III, Hannah Rathbone's grandfather, was running the company; the town of Ironbridge takes its name from this single-span bridge, whose erection marked a turning point for British engineering.[36] Between 1750 and 1790, Shropshire had become the leading iron producer in Britain and also a leading place of innovation.

In 1811, writing to the Rathbone boys, who were then visiting Market Drayton on their own, Theophilus Houlbrooke reported upon progress on the building works:

> The chimney piece arrived yesterday from Devonshire for the Library room which will be put up on Monday when the room is finished. The dining

A sketch of Hannah Mary Rathbone in the dining room, Greenbank House. (Reproduced in Emily A. Rathbone, ed., *Records of the Rathbone Family*, 1913)

room school room as it is called the little study or William's room and the washhand room are finished. All the bedrooms and vestibule are finished. The drawing room is as you left it. Our bedroom is now ceiled but the last coat is yet to be put on. The ground floor is all levelled before the library windows – and part of it sodded. The hedge is taked away before the little cottage so the field appears from the windows as part of the garden. The barn is covered in and one of the divisions will be flagged on Thursday. The flags for the threshing floor are not yet come. From the same cause the lobby is not yet finished from the kitchen to the [? corner] of the stone staircase. The other part has been done some time ... The fence is finished round Robert's stone jar and a hedge planted on the outside of the paling, and well fenced against the field. It is a mixture of holly privet and whitethorn. The hall is flagged to the arch that separates it from the passage ... The barn will soon be finished, and I hope everything else.[37]

A landscaped garden was being created, and the pastoral scene beyond the house could be enjoyed from its windows. These letters of Theodore Rathbone and his tutor, of 1810 and 1811, suggest that the majority of the internal and external construction works were completed by 1811.

What have been described as the most intact rooms to survive from this period are what was the library and the room immediately above, a bedroom featured in a photograph of c. 1937; the Gothic fireplace in green and white marbles and white marble hearth (with tiles of a later, early twentieth-century, date), the Gothic tracery of the window reveals, and the tracery of the door case and architrave to this bedroom may be dated to the works of 1809–12.[38]

In November 1808, in one of the codicils to his will, William Rathbone had bequeathed his wife an additional £500 'for purposes I have mentioned to her, but which I expressly direct she shall not in any means be called upon to explain.' One might conclude that this bequest was intended to facilitate alterations to Greenbank for, in writing to her children, his widow noted that he intended and desired 'that it should be rebuilt, and made a commodious good house,' that he had added 'Let her have her outward habitation to her mind.' Nevertheless, she 'felt pain and remorse for having, even when it was inadvertently, spent money in ornament, for I know my revered Husband preferred simplicity upon a principle of comprehensive benevolence, not only because his sympathizing heart was more gratified by feeding the hungry and clothing the naked ...than by pleasing his own eye, but also because he thought that each individual had the power of augmenting the general stock of happiness by exciting good, and preventing bad or erroneous feelings in himself, and those around him.'[39]

Hannah Rathbone continued to live at Greenbank until, following the marriage of her daughter 'Annie' to Dr Reynolds in 1831, her younger son Richard had a cottage-house built for her on his own estate nearby, at Woodcroft. In the intervening years we are provided with portraits from the accounts of Henry Chorley and John James Audubon.

Henry Chorley (1808–72), a well-known critic, recollected his stay as a young boy at Greenbank in 1819 when Hannah Mary

> was in the last ripeness of her maturity, looking older than her years, but as beautiful as any picture which can be offered by freshest youth. Though nominally a member of the Society of Friends, she never conformed to its uniform. Her profuse white hair, which had been white from an early age, was cut straight like a man's, to lie simply across her forehead. Above this was her spotless cap of white net ... Her gown was always a dark silk, with a quantity of delicate muslin to swathe the throat, and a shawl which covered the stoop of her short figure ... The welcome of that elderly

woman to the awkward, scared, nervous child, is one of the happiest recollections of my life. She had been throughout her life the admired friend and counsellor of many distinguished men, all belonging to the liberal school of ideas and philosophies. One of so fearless a brain, so tenderly religious a heart, and so pure a moral sense as she, I have never known. Her moral courage was indomitable, her manners shy, gentle, and caressing.[40]

He continues:

Since that time I have been in many luxurious houses, but anything like the delicious and elegant comfort of Greenbank during her reign I have never known. Plenty without coarseness; exquisiteness without that super-delicacy which oppresses by its extravagance. It was a house to which the sick went to be nursed, and the benevolent to have their plans carried out. It was anything but a hide-bound or Puritanical house; the library was copious, novels and poems were read aloud in the parlours, and such men as William Roscoe, Robert Owen, Sylvester of Derby [Charles Sylvester (1774–1825), chemist and inventor], Combe of Edinburgh [Dr Andrew Combe (1797–1847), physician and phrenologist], came and went. There was a capital garden, a double verandah; never shall I see that verandah equalled; there was a piano ... and there was water and a boat.

He might also have made reference to the constant stream of family visitors that the Rathbones entertained.[41] Among those who later visited Greenbank and became lifelong friends was Father (Theobald) Mathew, an Irish Catholic priest, the 'devoted and distinguished apostle of the temperance cause,' who was the guest of William Rathbone the fifth on his visit to Liverpool in 1849. At a meeting attended by William Rathbone at the Hibernian School in Pleasant Street, following an address by Father Mathew, the pledge was administered to about 300 children and the same number of adults; many others later visited Greenbank so that Father Mathew could administer the pledge to them.[42] Another friend and correspondent of William Rathbone the fifth and his wife was Miss Dorothea Dix of Boston, afterwards well known in connection with the reform of mental asylums, who spent a year and a half at Greenbank in the early 1840s before returning to America; she later joined the Rathbones in a visit abroad, to Switzerland.[43] In the obituary of William Rathbone's widow, Elizabeth, who died, aged 92 years, in 1882, the local press paid tribute to her as her husband's 'more than partner in the hereditary hospitality' associated with Greenbank, acknowledging that 'her large-hearted husband always consulted and spoke of her as his better genius.'[44]

A portrait of a visit to Liverpool and Greenbank in 1826–27

In 1826 John James Audubon (1785–1851), the American naturalist and painter, a most extraordinary character who cultivated a rugged backwoodsman image, visited England and Scotland, seeking subscriptions for the publication of his *The Birds of America*, a copy of which he was to present to William Rathbone the fifth. With 435 life-size engravings, the work, in four double elephant folio volumes, was to be offered on subscription from 1827 to 1838. Audubon sold about one hundred sets in England and seventy-five in America, with about one hundred copies surviving nowadays; the copy held by Liverpool Central Libraries remains on public display in the Brown Library.

Setting out for England on 17 May 1826, sailing from New Orleans to Liverpool in a vessel carrying a cargo of cotton, Audubon carried a number of letters of introduction, including one from his German friend, Vincent Nolte, addressed to Richard Rathbone of Liverpool, younger brother of William Rathbone the fifth. Mr Nolte wrote that Audubon has 'spent upwards of twenty years in all parts of [North America] and devoted most of this time to ornithological Pursuits. He carries with him a Collection of upwards of 400 Drawings, which far surpass anything of the kind I have yet seen ... His object is to find a Purchaser, at any rate a Publisher for them; and if you can aid him in this, and Introduce him either in person or by letters to men of Distinction in arts and sciences, you will confer much of a favor on me.'[45]

In Audubon's journals we are provided with a vivid, perhaps somewhat exaggerated picture of Greenbank and of the welcome given him by the Rathbone family and indeed by many others, in effect being treated as a visiting celebrity.[46]

Liverpool, 21 July 1826: 'The next morning when I landed, it was raining; yet the outward Appearance of the City was agreeable, but no sooner had I entered it than the smoak from coal fires was so oppressive on my lungs that I could scarcely breath[e] – I felt the same affecting my eyes also.' Following visits to the Exchange Buildings and the Museum, he took lodgings at the Commercial Inn, the following day visiting the Custom House, paying duty on his drawings, and later receiving 'a Polite Note from Mr Rd Rathbone' inviting him to dine with him and Mr [William] Roscoe. The Rathbones were to prove unsparing in their efforts to help him.

In Liverpool and those other places he visited, Audubon cut an exotic figure, in fringed jacket and his hair slicked down with bear grease, his presence sought at the tables of prominent individuals, besides the great deal of attention the beauty of his collection of drawings of birds attracted. Richard Rathbone's son, then a young child, later recalled the impression Audubon made:

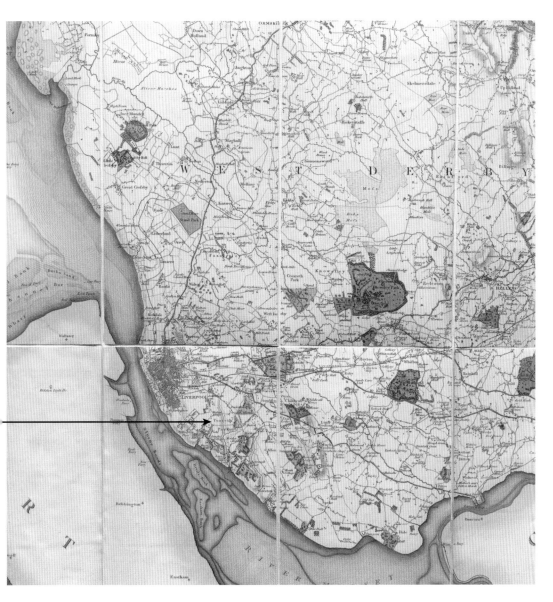

Liverpool and region (including Toxteth Park, arrowed), from C. Greenwood's Map of the County Palatine of Lancaster, 1818.
(Reproduced courtesy of the University of Liverpool Library)

To us there was a halo of romance about Mr Audubon, artist, naturalist, *quondam* backwoodsman, and the author of that splendid work which I used to see on a table constructed to hold the copy belonging to my Uncle William, opening with hinges so as to raise the bird portraits as if on a desk. But still more I remember his amiable character, though tinged with a melancholy by past sufferings; and his beautiful, expressive face, kept alive in my memory by his autograph crayon sketch thereof, in profile, with the words written at foot 'Audubon at Green Bank. <u>Almost</u> happy, 9th September 1826.'[47]

24 July 1826: [In the mid-morning he records that he] 'made as Directly as I could threw the sinuous streets of Liverpool to No. 87 Duke Street, where the Polite English Gentleman Richard Rathbone resides ... the kind Gentleman was not in – I almost ran to his Counting house at Salt Dock down Duke Street &c &c &c – a full dozen of Clerks were at their separate Desks – The Ledgers – Day Books &c &c &c were all under full sails ...

J. J. Audubon, self-portrait, 1826. (Reproduced courtesy of the Victoria Gallery & Museum, University of Liverpool)

An Immense Letter Bag belonging to the Packet that sailed this day for [America] ... stood near the entrance.

Audubon met Richard Rathbone, dining with his family, and then being escorted to the Exchange Buildings to meet the American consul and many others.

> 25 July: [The Rathbones took Audobon to Greenbank:] 'The country opend. To our View gradually, and after having passed under a Cool arbor of English Trees, I entered the Habitation of – Philemon & Baucis [the happy couple referred to in Ovid's moralising fable and later in Jonathan Swift's poem of 1709] !!! – Yes, a Venerable Happy pair received their children with kisses, all kindness, and bid me well come with that natural ease that I thought had deserted this earth with the Golden age ... the good Venerable Couple walked me round a Garden transplanted from abroad, and – my Port Folio was opened in the presence of several females and a younger Rathbone ... I saw as I entered this happy dwelling a Beautiful Collection of the Birds of England well prepared.

In a separate 'true story' that Audubon later wrote for his wife, Lucy, he recorded that

> The Environs of Liverpool are adorned by numerous Seats where in many persons of the Highest Distinction reside ... The Traveller who retires for a few Hours from the Tumult of the City and reaches one of those Seats, laying about 2 and ½ miles South East ... cannot help remarking a Sweet delectable Mansion, in all appearance secluded from the World, and yet filled with a World of Generous Beings = The Building is Gothic. Ever-greens run along its Walls ... A Small piece of Watter slowly moves across the foot of the gentle slope on which it stands – Many Trees embellish the Grounds around, and I recollect myself having seen a Few Sheep grazing peaceably in their shade – There ... the Mistress [Hannah Mary Rathbone, widow of William Rathbone the fourth] lives! And her servant has lived there also 35 Years![48]

On 27 July, Audubon visited William Roscoe's 'place about one and half mile distant' and 'as it was too Early to Dine, a proposition to go to the Botanic Garden was offered and accepted Imediately. Mr Roscoe & I rode there and I was shewn the whole with great attention. This Garden is level, well Drawn and well Kept.' On 28 July, he received a note from William Rathbone at 'Bedford St., Abercromby Square' 'to remind him of his engagement to dine with him to day at six o'clock,' requesting him 'to bring a few of his Drawings with him.'[49]

On 4 August, following a morning spent at Liverpool Royal Institution, where his paintings were being exhibited, and a further visit to William Roscoe's home, Audubon 'passed again under the avenue of Trees leading to Green Banks ... I can easily hear the mirth of many that I suppose on the Green fronting the Building ... the Mother Rathbone meets me with "Oh, I am glad to see You." I was not mistaken: the Green was Covered with beauty – Good sense and pleasure – I was attracted mostly, however, at se[e]ing the Ladies with bows and arrows shooting at a target perhaps 25 paces off.' He records that later that evening he was asked many questions about Indians, and American trees ('things quite unknown here') and that in the parlour 'the table was covered with a profusion of Fruits and refreshments and every one amicably helpd themselves'; with the clock striking 10, 'the Company leave for their own Habitation and I am with the family only,' in a drawing room, being shown 'the New Work [by P. J. Selby] on the Birds of England,' before Richard Rathbone finally showed him up 'the gentle flights of stairs to a chamber where I am again shewn comfort' and he is bid good night. He appreciated sleeping at Greenbank, 'free from the bustling noise of the City.'

On 14 August, he records that 'I have spent a ... Happy half day, at the Green Banks of Mr Rathbone,' seated with [Thomas] Bewick's book on quadrupeds, with Mrs Rathbone with 'a Book of Insects before her,' with one nephew 'examining the Minutious Pistills of a Floweret' and another 'is also engaged on a work beyond my Comprehension'; after they had dined 'I have rambled through the grounds – the Green Houses and Jardin Potagers [vegetable garden].' The following day he 'reached this *enchanted Spot*. Mrs Rathbone, the benevolent Mother, the queen Bee of this honeyed mansion received me alone – and alone I had the pleasure of contemplating her mien and of lessening to the heavenly gifts of her Heart throw her Conversation'; the family later entered, Audubon observing the children 'peaceably engaged in reaping the benefits of a good Education – Seated on their little benches, in different parts of the Room, each held a Book and each held their eyes on the Book before them.' In the afternoon he took a long walk with Miss Hannah Rathbone and her nephew:

> We walked between dreary Walls, contenting ourselves with the distant objects without the sweet privileges of moving freely to & fro ... Thus we reached the Mersey ... It is not very Shocking that whilst in England, all is Hospitality within, all is Aristocratic without their Dwellings – No one dare *trespass*, as it is called, one foot on the Grass – *Signs of Large Dogs* are put up to infer that Further you must not advance ... Beggars in England are like our Ticks of Louisiana – They stick to one and sting our better feelings every moment – England is now Rich with poverty, gaping aghast, which ever way you may look.

Two days later, he walked to Greenbank, lying on the grass a long time listening to the rough voice of a Magpie before at 8 o'clock entering the house where he observes 'the Domestics are Cleaning ... I hear – I see, I kiss the sweet Children – The breakfast Bell is ringing and we are round the table seated – To Town Mrs Rathbone and I are going ... I am now really rolling in the little Carriage with the *Queen Bee* of Green Banks' to Liverpool Royal Institution, 'and this afternoon began a painting of the Trapped Otter with Intention, if well done, to present it to my good Friend's Wife' [Mrs Richard Rathbone].

On 21 August, he recorded that he had 'finished my Otter or Rather Mrs Richard Rathbone's Otter = It was viewed by many and admired' and that 'I was Invited to remove to Green Banks altogether during the Time that I may stay here – but declined going untill I have painted the Wild Turkey Cock for the Royal Institution = say 3 Days.' This painting, presented to the Royal Institution, was in thanks for their hosting an exhibition of his paintings from 31 July until 9 September, he being persuaded by William Roscoe latterly to charge an entrance fee as a form of remuneration; it was through Richard Rathbone and his brother, both active members of the Royal Institution, that Audubon had been put in touch with William Roscoe and other officers of the Royal Institution who had agreed to let him display his work. When, in 1948, the Royal Institution closed and the building was given to the University, forming an extramural teaching centre for a number of years, the gift included a number of works of art, including three oil paintings by Audubon – *American Wild Turkey Cock*, *Hawk Pouncing on Partridges*, and *An Otter Caught in a Trap*. The painting of the trapped otter, presented to Mrs Rathbone, was in 1862 presented to the Royal Institution, her son later recording that it 'hung on our walls for years until my mother could no longer bear the horror of it.' The painting of the otter was Audubon's favourite subject, several versions being in existence.

The 'Painting of the Wild Turkey Cock' was completed – 'Mr Melly, Dr Trail,[50] Mrs William Rathbone and many other Persons were in my Painting Room during the while talking and wondering how I manage to Conceive & finish this fast' – and hung in the Royal Institution's Exhibition room. Then 'At Last I removed to Green Bank, the delightfull Green Bank, and was hailed with the same kind reception ... I had the Study of Mr Theodore Rathbone [the sixth child of the "Queen Bee"] allotted me for my Drawing room = I Cannot tell how much Knowledge the Gentleman took with him to the Continent w[h]ere he is now travelling with his Lucy, but I found an astonishing quantity all around me in his Library – Portfolios, Casts of antiques – &c &c &c.'

Before he departed for Manchester, to seek further subscribers to his work, he returned to Greenbank on 6 September, recording that he was 'told that Lady Isabella Douglass, the sister of Lord Selkirk, former governor of

J. J. Audubon, *An Otter Caught in a Trap*, 1826.
(Reproduced courtesy of the Victoria Gallery & Museum, University of Liverpool)

Canada, was in the house a visitor = I was told that she was now unable to walk and that consequently she moved about in a rolling chair.'[51] At dinner he sat between her and Mrs Rathbone, and much enjoyed the conversation of Lady Douglas, her broad Scotch accent being agreeable to him. It was during this visit that Audubon had drawn what is a rare self-portrait, as a present for Hannah Rathbone, inscribing it 'Audubon at Green Bank. <u>Almost Happy!!</u> – Sept 1826. Drawn by himself.'[52] Through a generous bequest of Dr B. L. ('Larry') Rathbone, this portrait came into the University's possession in 2006.

While visiting Manchester, he reflected on his stay in Liverpool in a letter to his wife, Lucy:

> I have been most kindly received at Liverpool by all those to whom I was introduced either by letters from America or Subsequent means ... There are at Liverpool 3 Families of the names of Rathbones, to all of whom I am particularly indebted ... Thro them I formed the acquaintance of all

J. J. Audubon, *An American Turkey Cock*, 1826.
(Reproduced courtesy of the Victoria Gallery & Museum, University of Liverpool)

the best families, and by their recommendations abroad, I cannot fail
but continue to be received with all the kind Hospitality that renders a
Stranger Happy far from his Friends & relations: To Dr Thomas S Traill,
the President of the Royal Institution of Liverpool, and Mr Roscoe, a most
Eminent person, now known over all the world, I also owe a great portion
of my Success: My Drawings were exibited for 4 weeks without a cent of
Expense to myself and produced me 100 £. My time was spent during the
while at painting & drawing to present pieces of my work as slender marks
of my Gratitude – I gave to the Institution a Large piece of a Wild Turkey
Cock – Mrs Richard Rathbone one of the Otter in a trap, Mr Roscoe, a
Robin, and to Each of my other Friends also a Drawing.[53]

One of the especial friends to receive a watercolour painting was Hannah
Rathbone, who on 10 September received a watercolour of a robin perched on
a mossy stone, the inscription paying tribute to 'her Genial affections – her
most kind attentions and friendly civilities to all who come to repose under
this hospitable roof.' Remaining in the possession of successive generations
of the Rathbone family, with assistance from the Rathbone family trust, this
painting was bought by the University in June 1971 and returned to Greenbank
House. Another of Audubon's watercolours of a robin, also dating from 1826,
inscribed with a poem to Hannah Rathbone, is currently on loan from Mr
R. S. Rathbone and displayed in the Victoria Gallery and Museum, which

J. J. Audubon, *A Robin Perched on a Mossy Stone*, 1826.
(Reproduced courtesy of the Victoria Gallery & Museum, University of Liverpool)

can now lay claim to holding the largest collection of Audubon's paintings outside the USA.

Returning to Liverpool on 28 September, glad to have 'left Manchester and all its smoak' behind him and to be 'warmly welcomed by good Liverpool friends,' he stayed at Greenbank until a return visit to Manchester in early October.

Following visits to Glasgow and Edinburgh, seeking further subscribers to his work, he made his penultimate visit to Greenbank in late November 1827. Rising early, he walked from Liverpool to Greenbank:

> When I reached the house all was yet silent within, and I rambled over the frozen grass, watching the birds that are always about the place, enjoying full peace and security. The same Black Thrush (probably) that I have often heard before was perched on a fir-tree announcing the beauty of this winter morning in his melodious voice; the little Robins flitted about, making towards those windows that they knew would soon be opened to them. ... I entered the hot-house and breathed the fragrance of each flower, yet sighed at the sight of some that I recognized as offsprings of my own beloved country. Henry Chorley, who had been spending the night at Green Bank, now espied me from his window, so I went in and soon was greeted by that best of friends, 'Lady' Rathbone.
>
> After breakfast Miss Hannah opened the window and her favorite little Robin hopped about the carpet, quite at home. I returned to Liverpool with Mr B[Benson] Rathbone, who, much against my wishes, for I can do better work now, bought my picture of the Hawk pouncing on the Partridges.[54]

This oil painting was one of seven paintings which Audubon exhibited at the Liverpool Academy on his return to Liverpool in 1827; presented to the Royal Institution by Benson Rathbone's family in 1840, it thereby also came into the possession of the University.

Just after Christmas 1827, Audubon made a final walk to '"Lady" Rathbone's with my fifth number' (perhaps the drawing of a little wren 'for my good friend Hannah' that he recorded finishing), observing that it was impossible to approach the house in fair weather 'without enjoying the song of some birds ... that sweet place is sacred, and all the feathered tribe in perfect safety. A Redwing particularly delighted me to-day; I found something of the note of our famous Mock-bird in his melody.'[55] After three years in Europe, Audubon finally returned to America in April 1829.

J. J. Audubon, *Hawk Pouncing on Partridges*, 1827.
(Reproduced courtesy of the Victoria Gallery & Museum, University of Liverpool)

3 William Rathbone the fifth

Seven months before his death, in June 1808, writing to his eldest son, William, who was about to reach the age of majority, of twenty-one, William Rathbone the fourth enclosed an 'acknowledgment' for £5,000 (in the name of Rathbone Hughes and Duncan) which he hoped would prove useful as capital 'when there may be a suitable opening for thy entering into business.' Clearly conscious of his mortality, he enumerated the two important duties which he strongly felt the possession of property required: 'the right application of it, while living, as becomes stewards to the great Dispenser of all good' and 'the equitable disposal of it by will,' concluding with a 'fervent wish that the blessing of the Almighty may descend upon thee, and that He may be thy Friend, support and hope this life, in death, and for ever.'[1]

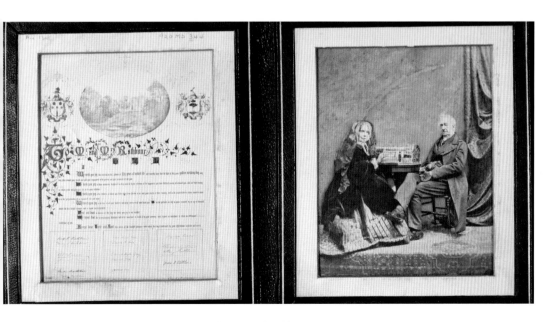

William Rathbone the fifth and his wife Elizabeth, 1862.
(Reproduced courtesy of Liverpool Record Office, 920 MD 344)

In the opinion of his granddaughter, Eleanor Rathbone, William Rathbone the fifth was 'hardly, perhaps, his father's equal in intellectual power nor in his native eloquence; but he had high courage and an ardent, generous nature.'[2] Indeed, his outside interests tended to take precedence over those of the business, which suffered, entering a period of serious decline from the 1820s. It was in the 1820s that he had achieved public recognition as an advocate of Roman Catholic emancipation, finally achieved by the passing of the Roman Catholic Relief Act of 1829 whereby almost all disabilities were removed and Catholics were admitted to most public offices and, after an absence of three centuries, could sit in Parliament. In 1812 William Rathbone had married Elizabeth Greg, elder daughter of Samuel Greg, a prosperous mill-owner, of Quarry Bank, at Styal, near Manchester. (The water-powered cotton mill which Samuel Greg had built on the banks of the river Bollin from 1784 onwards, together with the estate that developed around it, has been a National Trust property since 1939.) As the Gregs were Unitarians, William was expelled from the Society of Friends for marrying out of the Society and though he was later reinstated, he and his family finally severed their connection with the Friends in 1829, joining a congregation of Unitarians, the Revd John Yates, minister of the Unitarian chapel in Paradise Street, Liverpool, becoming a close friend and neighbour.

At the time of his marriage, William Rathbone was already much involved in the politics of Liverpool, actively supporting the movement for reform. In 1831, his action in ensuring the erection of booths at the parliamentary election, so limiting the opportunities for corruption and drunkenness, led to the Reform candidates' success, he being escorted to his house in Abercromby Square by the cheers of the populace.[3] In his address to his 'brother burgesses' in May 1831, written from Bedford Street, he asserted that 'the welfare of my native town has been the object of my increasing anxiety, and, not unfrequently, of my active exertions. The same feelings actuate me on the present occasion, in requesting to be proposed as a candidate to give me the right of demanding a place of voting for each hundred of the burgesses.'[4] Opposing the return of General Gascoyne, the Tory candidate, he urged them 'to return men who will support the rights of the people. Let us gain reform, and you will find in the increasing prosperity of your country, and in the more equal distributions of her burthens, in large profits and better wages, what will amply repay you any loss you may sustain by refusing a paltry and degrading bribe.' The following year, when, in the words of William Rathbone, 'the cholera had awakened the attention of all to the importance of cleanliness,' his wife actively supported the initiative of Kitty Wilkinson, the wife of one of his cotton porters, who 'allowed those of her neighbours who were the most destitute of the means of heating water' to wash their clothes and bedding, an initiative which led, with the support of William Rathbone, to the establishment in Liverpool of the first public wash-house in the country in 1842, Kitty Wilkinson becoming its first superintendent.[5]

His campaigning for municipal reform occupied much of his time, joining fellow townsmen in petitioning Parliament in 1833, exposing the corruption and bribery that had infected the government of Liverpool for many years, justifying Henry, Lord Brougham (one of his acquaintances) in describing Liverpool as 'the greatest of the rotten boroughs.' Following the final passing of the Municipal Reform Act of 1835, public recognition of the major role played by William Rathbone came when he and Robert E. Harvey were presented with services of plate, that to Rathbone being a six-branch acanthus, as a centrepiece, and candelabrum, a chased waiter, two wine coolers, a bread-basket, and a six-quart soup tureen. Engraved on each was the following inscription (or, in several cases, a shortened version): 'Presented to William Rathbone, Esq. by the Reformers of Liverpool assembled at a Public Meeting on the 13th January 1836, as a Testimonial of their Esteem, and as a mark of their Gratitude for his invaluable services in promoting Parliamentary and Municipal Reform as well as for his unflinching Conduct on every trying occasion, whether in defending the rights or extending the Privileges of the People.'

When in May 1978 the University celebrated the centenary of the Town's Meeting held on 24 May 1878 at which it was resolved to establish a University College in Liverpool, Mr William Rathbone the tenth generously presented the silver candelabrum-epergne, a silver basket with hinged handle, and a pair of small oval silver tureens to the University.[6] As Mayor of Liverpool in 1837–38, William Rathbone was to lay the foundation stone for St George's Hall on 28 June 1838, to celebrate Queen Victoria's Coronation, albeit construction of the Hall was not to commence until 1840 when Harvey Lonsdale Elmes's definitive designs for the building, providing both a concert hall and new law courts for the town, were agreed by the corporation.[7] Following municipal reform in 1835, the Corporation of Liverpool had commenced programmes of educational, sanitary, and health reform, the 'new spirit of civic pride' reaching a high point with the construction of St George's Hall.

Overshadowed was the contribution which William Rathbone's wife, Elizabeth, made both to his life in politics and to the cause of education in Liverpool.[8] Her son acknowledged that, inheriting from her family an interest in the provision of schooling and having a great natural aptitude for administration and organisation, she played a major role in the campaign to reform Liverpool Corporation's schools, to introduce 'the Irish National system,' of unsectarian education, the children all receiving secular instruction together before religious instruction was given to the Protestant and Catholic children by their respective clergy.[9] Following the Whigs losing control of the Council

Candelabrum-epergne presented to William Rathbone, 1836. (Reproduced courtesy of the Victoria Gallery & Museum, University of Liverpool)

in 1841, William Rathbone and his wife turned their attention to the Hibernian Schools, making them model elementary schools, following the Irish system. Later on, while the Education Bill of Mr W. E. Forster, in charge of the government's education department, was passing through the House of Commons in 1870, Mrs Rathbone sent her son, then serving as one of the three MPs for Liverpool, a series of memoranda on the practical working of the Bill's various clauses, based on her experience as a school manager, whose value Mr Forster later acknowledged.[10] As provided by what became the Education Act of 1870, locally elected school boards were given powers to levy rates, build schools, provide teachers, and, if they thought fit, insist upon the attendance of all children (under the age of thirteen) who were not being educated in any other way. For the first time, the Act secured local expenditure on elementary education throughout England.

Visitors to Greenbank

William Rathbone the sixth recalled that during the early part of his father's married life, he lived in a house adjoining the business's counting house.

> His home was always open to strangers, of whom he saw a great many. His business connection with America and his friendship with Dr Channing [Dr W. E. Channing, the Boston Unitarian], Robert Owen, etc. brought him numerous introductions from America in favour of those who were foremost in politics, literature, and commerce. His friendship with Dugald Stewart, Lord Murray, Lord Jeffreys [sic] and Lord Brougham[11] procured him many very pleasant acquaintances from Scotland, and these were added to by others formed early in life from the active part he took in politics.[12]

His leadership of the Liberal Party in Liverpool for so many years led him to correspond with Lord Brougham, Lord John Russell, Mr E. J. Stanley, Daniel O'Connell, Henry Labouchere, and many others.[13] Though the published biographies of such persons may not refer to such contacts, one may presume that many of them will have enjoyed the hospitality of the Rathbones at Greenbank. When Lord Ebrington was Lord Lieutenant of Ireland [1839–41], members of the English Ministry of the day stayed at Greenbank; William Rathbone thought that it was at this time that Lord Brougham was at Greenbank, also Lord Russell.[14]

In July 1827, on his return from America to England, Robert Owen – nowadays particularly associated with the mill-town community of New Lanark in Scotland, of which he was the enlightened manager – stayed for a few days at Greenbank, Mrs Elizabeth Rathbone writing shortly afterwards to her mother to provide details of the New Harmony Settlement which he was attempting to establish in Indiana, leaving her with a set of 'New Harmony Papers from the beginning to the present day,' which she reports she had sent to be bound up 'to prevent any being lost.' Robert Owen 'became a legend in his own lifetime as a successful businessman, pioneer social scientist, humanitarian factory reformer, and radical theorist in education, economics and secularism.'[15] On the death of Robert Owen in 1858, his son wrote to Mrs Rathbone acknowledging that 'among the latest friends who visited his sick-bed and ministered to his infirmities – kindness which he himself remembered with gratitude to the last – I shall ever number Mr Rathbone and yourself. With that kindness will ever be associated the pleasant recollection of my renewed acquaintance with you.'[16]

Another of the visitors to Greenbank who became a friend of the Rathbones was the Revd Joseph Blanco White (1775–1841), a former Catholic priest who voluntarily left his native Spain in 1810 and in exile achieved great

Revd Joseph Blanco
White.
(Reproduced courtesy
of the University of
Liverpool Library, Spec
B.W.W5.L72.1845)

distinction as a poet, novelist, literary critic, teacher, and theologian.[17] Following periods spent at Oxford (1826–32) and then in Ireland (1832–35), in the household of Richard Whately, Church of Ireland archbishop of Dublin, Blanco White departed for Liverpool in January 1835, attracted by the reputation of the strong Unitarian community in Liverpool as also by his friendship with a Cadiz merchant engaged in a shipping business in the town. Two weeks after his arrival, in his journal he recorded that he attended Unitarian worship for the first time, noting that 'Sunday after Sunday, going alternately to the two Unitarian chapels in this town, I enjoy the most sublime moral and intellectual treat which the purified religious principle can offer to man.'[18]

Never latterly in the best of health, to a correspondent in September 1836 he refers to his 'regular daily portion of bodily suffering and mental enjoyment,' the latter increased by the frequent opportunity he had of reading German literature with a young man in Liverpool who had studied in Germany.[19] As his health declined, from furnished rooms in Liverpool, Blanco White moved, on his doctor's recommendation, to a cottage in Toxteth Park in the autumn of 1840. By now very weak in body, and though, in a letter to the wife of archbishop Whately, he wrote of Liverpool that the Revd John Thom (minister of the Unitarian Chapel at Renshaw Street) 'alone has obtained my confidence and affection,' in his final weeks he owed much to his Unitarian friends in Liverpool, especially the Rathbones. As the Revd Thom recorded in the three volumes of The Life of the Rev. Joseph Blanco White, written by himself, with portions of his correspondence (1845) which he edited, on 23 February 1841 'he was removed with much difficulty, in a sedan chair, to the house of Mr Rathbone, Greenbank, near Liverpool. This change had frequently, before, been proposed and indeed with earnestness and solicitation pressed upon him; but the pains of removal to a frame distressingly sensible ... made him always shrink from strange places and circumstances ... When he felt his end approaching, this reluctance disappeared: he longed to die among friends.' For a short time his spirits seemed to revive at Greenbank, 'the daily sight of trees and fields, tender nursing, and the face of friends ... soothed and cheered him,' but soon afterwards for nearly three months, in his own words, 'he lingered in the face of Death.' Once in great weakness and pain, on opening his eyes and seeing Mrs Rathbone sitting by him, he said 'Still here: You all are to me the representatives of the merciful compassions of the Almighty.' Though it had been usual to lift him from one large chair to another, wheeling it from room to room, 'to give as much variety and freshness to his life as his condition permitted,' latterly all such change became impossible. Dying, aged 65 years, on 20 May 1841, he was buried, according to the instructions of his will, in the burial ground of Renshaw Street Chapel. Nowadays, the former Central Hall (now the Grand Central Hotel), Renshaw Street, stands on the site of the chapel, its graveyard now forming 'Roscoe Gardens,' fronting Mount Pleasant, the domed memorial structure of 1905 highlighting that in this ground were buried William Roscoe and Joseph Blanco White.

The Greenbank household, 1841 and 1851 – and Christmas Day celebrated at Greenbank, 1851 and 1856

A partial snapshot of the composition of the Greenbank household is provided in the return of those recorded as present on 6 June 1841, when the census was taken. Besides William Rathbone and his wife, George Rathbone, aged fifteen, and a visiting Greg relation of Mrs Rathbone, there were four female and two male servants. Their neighbours were William Ivison, a farmer, and his family at Greenbank Farm, and the Misses Colquitt, of independent means, and their servants. The Tithe Award for Toxteth Park, 1848, records William Rathbone owning 40 acres of land of which just over 35 acres – comprising a cottage and outbuildings, meadow and pastureland, and fields growing potatoes and turnips, mangel wurzel, oats, and wheat – was let to William Ivison.[20] The remaining four-odd acres principally comprised Greenbank with its plantation, garden, and pleasure ground. The 1851 census captures an extended family: besides William (described as a cotton, wool, etc. merchant) and Elizabeth Rathbone were their daughters Elizabeth Paget (with her seven-year-old son, Thomas) and Agnes Rathbone (aged thirty), and their as yet unmarried twenty-eight-year-old son, Samuel Greg Rathbone (also a cotton, corn, and wool etc. merchant); supporting the family were Jane Vaucher, a Swiss-born 'governess' (who was probably responsible for looking after Agnes Rathbone), a cook, a butler, three housemaids, and a stableman, all of whom (with the exception of the butler) were unmarried. Living next door, in three separate dwellings, were other of Greenbank's staff: a gentleman's servant (with his wife), a gardener (also with his wife and their teacher daughter), and the butler's wife with their two young daughters.

Gathering each Christmas at Greenbank, the extended family of William Rathbone paid tribute to him in verse, as in the verses his younger son, Philip H. Rathbone, composed at Christmas 1851:

Though bound on many a varying voyage
With differing freights we roam
Our Barks once more together met
Touch at the Port of Home

Though weather beaten, all as yet
Have braved Life's Tempest rude
So Christmas if it be less gay
Brims still with gratitude

Then once again in the Old House
Raise up the Christmas Tree
If older is the Parent Stem
And older too are we

There are fresh faces and young Hearts
Who yet untouch'd by care
May make it bright with open'ng Flowers
And be what once we were.[21]

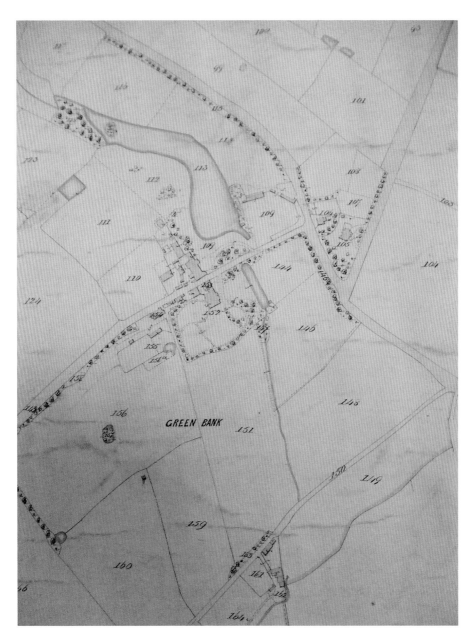

Greenbank House estate, from the Tithe Map of Toxteth Park, 1847.
(Reproduced courtesy of Lancashire Archives, DRL/1/80)

On a more optimistic tone, accompanying a gift from Woodcote (the home at Aigburth of William Rathbone's younger brother, Richard Rathbone, and his son Richard Reynolds Rathbone[22]) are verses celebrating Christmas Day at Greenbank in 1856:

All hail to the Chief of the gallant Clan-Rathbone
The Patriach-Centre of Three Generations.
Who summons this day as he often times <u>hath</u> done,
With generous welcome, his Friends and Relations!
Long, long may he live, and be favoured with health,
Long, long may he live to distribute his wealth
To the aged, the wretched, the destitute poor, –
Who rarely, indeed, are turned back from <u>his</u> door.

All hail! to our Chief! – in green age, may he flourish
With his kindest of wives, as he stiles his 'best-half',
What a blessing it is, these kind feelings to nourish,
And banish all cares, with a good hearty laugh!
Hurra! for our Chieftain! long, long may he live
Our cordial good wishes, from us to receive,
Accept, from our Woodcote, this spiced-wassail Bowl,
And hurra! for our Chieftain! with heart and with soul.
Amen![23]

Recognising the legacy of William Rathbone the fifth

On 1 February 1868 William Rathbone died at Greenbank, aged 80 years. After making the standard testamentary provision for all his debts to be paid, significantly he highlighted the services of plate which had been presented to him for the parts he took 'in promoting municipal reform' and 'in altering the system of voting at Parliamentary elections in Liverpool,' bequeathing them to his wife so long as she resided at Greenbank and after her death or on her ceasing to live there dividing them between his sons, William and Samuel, who were to receive the municipal and the parliamentary plate respectively.[24] Besides a legacy of £2,000, his wife was left an annuity of £1,500, together (with the sole exception of a silver soup tureen) with all Greenbank's furniture and furnishings, including all his 'china, horses, carriages, farming stock and utensils, books, prints, pictures, wines and all consumable stores' absolutely. Greenbank, 'including therein the closes of land I have purchased since my mother's decease adjoining or near thereto,' he left to William and his heirs upon trust to permit his wife to enjoy during her life or so long 'as she should think fit to reside there.' £5,000 was to be paid to Samuel on the death or earlier departure from Greenbank of William Rathbone's wife, perhaps in recognition that he would not inherit the family home. Generous provisions were also made for his other children, Mary, wife of Revd John Thom, Elizabeth, wife of John Paget, and Philip Henry Rathbone. For probate purposes, the effects of his estate were valued at under £160,000, it being noted that there were no leasehold properties.

Though in 1864 the Town Council of Liverpool resolved to erect a memorial in recognition of the respect and esteem in which William Rathbone was held 'by all classes of the community,' it was in deference to his wish that the Council drop the matter, feeling that the erection of a statue would be money misspent, that no action was taken in his lifetime. Following his death, a public meeting at the Town Hall resolved to collect subscriptions towards the erection of a statue. Finally unveiled in January 1877, the statue, featuring William Rathbone, was erected in Sefton Park, close to the Palm House, in response to the Rathbone family's wish that it be sighted in a more public location than in St George's Hall and as close as possible to Greenbank. Set into the statue's pedestal were bronze relief plaques appropriately featuring figures portraying 'Commerce,' 'Education,' and 'Charity.'

In 1865 the portrait of William Rathbone which his friends and admirers had painted of him, to commemorate his mayoralty of Liverpool in 1837–38, was, on the votes of a Tory majority of the Council, finally installed in the Council Chamber, its installation in 1844 being refused by 'the Tory fanatics' who then ruled the Council, the Liberal-supporting organ, *The Porcupine*, observing that William Rathbone, who had begun 'his public life amid stress and storm' now 'closes it in peace and general amity'; 'we think of him as of some of the grand old Florentine citizens who, without title or official position, held a sort of acknowledged and patriarchal rank as leaders and councilors of the people.'[25]

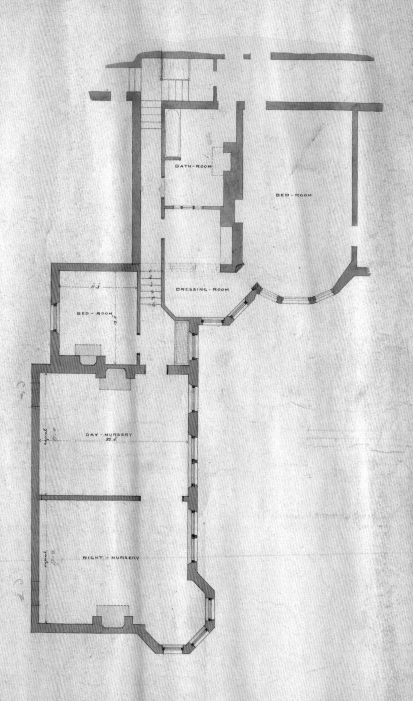

BATH-ROOM

BED-ROOM

BED-ROOM

DRESSING-ROOM

DAY-NURSERY
22.6'

NIGHT-NURSERY

FIRST FLOOR

40   50 FEET

4 William Rathbone the sixth, Eleanor Rathbone, and Hugh Rathbone

Soon after William Rathbone's death, his widow invited her son William and his family (hitherto living at New Brighton) to come and live with her at Greenbank and to regard it as their home. As William later noted, on moving to Greenbank, he altered his father's old study 'into its present form, to make a sitting-room for my wife, adding the conservatory to it, and we afterwards built the large room and nursery over it on to the house.' The plans for this red sandstone western extension to the house were drawn up in March 1868 by Culshaw and Sumners, architects and surveyors, of Liverpool, who were responsible for the design of a large number of buildings in and around Liverpool in the nineteenth century.[1] In 1862 William Rathbone had married Emily Lyle, daughter of Acheson Lyle of Londonderry and a second cousin of his own, through kinship with his mother's family, the Gregs; by 1868, they had a large, growing family – Emily Evelyn born in 1865, Acheson Lyle in 1867, with Eleanor to be born in 1872 and Frank in 1875. The extension provided a large playroom and a storeroom on the ground floor with day and night nurseries and a bedroom above. If, in the words of the architectural historian Professor R. A. Cordingley, these Victorian additions did not improve the appearance of Greenbank, rather adding to its confused skyline, they made Greenbank 'a complete essay in the English art of the Picturesque.'[2] In 1868 Culshaw and Sumners were also responsible for drawing up a plan of the 251 foot by 38 foot 4 inch 'fish pond,' in association with the planned erection of a wall around the pond.[3] Unlike other wealthy individuals, who erected substantial mansions, it is noticeable that William Rathbone did not use architecture to project the influence of his family or assert its status. Successive generations of the family did not want the burden of a large estate; they were happy to retire from the town to their rural residence set in a landscaped park with its ponds, ha-ha, and garden, an Arcadian vision which John James Audubon had enthused about.

Plans of extension to Greenbank House, by Culshaw & Sumners, 1868.
(Lancashire Archives, DDX162/78/09, reproduced with thanks to the partners of Matthews & Goodman LLP, incorporating Edmund Kirby & Sons, and holder of the Edmund Kirby and Culshaw archives)

William Rathbone the sixth was born at the Cornhill, Liverpool, home of his parents and grandparents, in 1819, the family later moving to a house in Hope Street and subsequently to a new-built house at the south-west corner of Abercromby Square; Greenbank at this period principally served as a country retreat for the family in the summer. Attending a variety of schools at Gateacre, Cheam, and Everton, he recalled that he left school, aged sixteen, 'with a distinct desire for knowledge, a fair French and German scholar, but very poor in classics.' Following three years (1835–38) as a junior apprentice in the Liverpool office of Nicol, Duckworth & Co., merchants in the Bombay and Mediterranean trade, and a short time in his father's office, he persuaded his father to allow him a year's leave of absence, joining a school friend in study for a semester at the University of Heidelberg (attending lectures delivered by the professors of history and law), followed by a visit to Italy. Returning for further business training as a junior clerk in the London firm of Messrs Baring Brothers (during which the senior partner took him on a business tour in America), in late 1841 he became a partner in his father's firm, Messrs Rathbone Brothers & Co. In 1838, the firm had left its historic site by the docks for offices at 16 Castle Street, Liverpool.

For about the next twenty-eight years, William Rathbone was an active member of the family's firm, working very hard with his brother, Samuel, to revive and transform the firm's position, establishing a very profitable China business mainly in tea (with houses at Canton and Shanghai), opening an agency in New York (trading largely in cotton), increasing the consignment business in ships from America, and building up a fleet of ships. A study of the firm's accounts led Dr Sheila Marriner to conclude that 1842–72 marked the period of maximum prosperity for the firm.[4] In the 1860s, Rathbones became one of the largest importers of tea, owning a fleet of clippers which ran between China and Liverpool. After ten or twelve years' work, William Rathbone was able to devote a share of his time to public affairs. In September 1847 he had married Lucretia Wainwright Gair, eldest daughter of Samuel Gair, a former partner in Messrs Baring Brothers & Co. in Liverpool, whose family home was close to Greenbank. As B. Guinness Orchard was later to note, William Rathbone came 'of a family which not only prospers itself, but is the cause of prosperity in others.'[5]

Already at this early stage in his life, influenced by the strong moral views of his parents and his religious upbringing, he was determining the proportions of his income that should be spent on public and private uses. 'A man's charity is first to bring up his children well; and secondly, to do thoroughly his daily work, whatever that is.' If a man had secured food and clothing for himself and his family and the means of educating his children and housing them, 'surely all his surplus wealth and leisure are a trust for which he owes an account to himself, to his fellow-men, and to God.' Philanthropy in Britain had, of course, a long-established tradition; for many Christians, there was a belief that salvation was provisional and conditional on 'good works.'[6] One might presume that William Rathbone would have been acquainted with the work of Aristotle, who in his work, *The Politics*, observed that 'every state is an association of persons formed with a view to some good purpose' and 'that man is by nature a political animal; it is nature to live in a state.'[7] In the words of a historian of Western political thought, Aristotle provides 'a clear vision of the moral purpose of society, which is to secure the good life, to produce individuals at once in harmony with the State and fulfilling themselves through it, and yet realizing in themselves those aristocratic moral, physical, and intellectual values to which men, alone of the animals, are able to attain.'[8] It is likely that both William Rathbone and his father would also have been influenced by the arguments advanced by Adam Smith in his *An Inquiry into the Nature and Causes of the Wealth of Nations* (1776) and *The Theory of Moral Sentiments* (1759), that one may pursue one's own interests but not at the expense of others. 'How selfish soever man may be supposed, there are evidently some principles in his nature, which interest him in the fortunes of others, and render their happiness necessary to him, though he desires nothing from it except the pleasure of seeing it' (*The Theory of Moral Sentiments*, Part I, Chapter I, 'Of Sympathy').

In seeking to bring up his children well, William Rathbone wrote to his teenage daughter, Elsie, then absent from home at school, 'As we are so much separated now I think it would be pleasant for you and Willie and I to read every Sunday the same Chapter in the Bible, so that our thoughts may be together though our bodies are absent and if anything occurs to you to remark or ask about it you can do so when writing.'[9] He suggests commencing with chapter 12 of St Matthew's Gospel, teaching them to follow his example – 'to be always willing to help and sympathise with the weak, not to condemn them for their faults or weakness or make harsh ill-natured remarks about others – such remarks generally come from a low mean desire to exalt ourselves by pointing out the faults of others – instead of this we should try to help others to do better.'

As a member of the congregation of Renshaw Street Unitarian Chapel, the influence of its minister, the Revd John Hamilton Thom, on William Rathbone was strong, a relationship strengthened in 1838 on the Revd Thom's marriage to William's sister, Hannah Mary. Eleanor Rathbone believed that her father's doctrinal views were mainly those of the school of Unitarianism represented by the Revd Thom and the Revd William E. Channing, but also contained elements drawn from the Quaker traditions of the Rathbone family.[10] Writing in February 1900 to the Revd Richard A. Armstrong, a Unitarian minister, author of a book on *Back to Jesus*, William Rathbone expresses his support of its object: 'in trying to persuade our orthodox

Lucretia Rathbone
commemorative
bas-relief by
Charles J. Allen,
1894.
(Reproduced
courtesy of the
Victoria Gallery
& Museum,
University of
Liverpool)

fellow-Christians, that even if we have not all that they believe that they have of the truth, they need not shut us out from religious communion, or even co-operation in trying to stem the tide of nihilistic, atheistic, or agnostic unbelief.'[11] As 'an old Quaker,' he believed 'in the Supreme Authority of the divine action of the Spirit of God on the Soul of Man ... in the absolute fatherhood and love of God, and all of His revelation to Man in the life and death of Jesus Christ.'

Commencing in 1849, William Rathbone gained personal experience of the life of the poor in Liverpool through his visiting a district weekly for the District Provident Society. Following his role in unseating the two Conservative MPs for Liverpool, who through corruption had been elected to Parliament in 1852, he commenced a more active part in local politics, becoming chairman of the Liberal Party in Liverpool, also becoming a member of the Dock and Harbour Board.

The pressure of work was such that his health broke down, his doctor finally advising a year's absence. From the spring of 1858 until early 1859, he and his family took a house, with shooting and fishing, at Cumloden in Wigtownshire, Scotland, a break cut short by his wife's failing health. Returning home to New Brighton, and then to Greenbank, it was there on 27 May 1859 that Lucretia died, leaving her husband with five children, of whom the eldest was ten years and the youngest only a few days old. In 1894, William Rathbone was to commission Charles J. Allen, in charge of sculpture and modelling at the School of Architecture and Applied Art at University College, Liverpool, to produce a marble bas-relief, made from a drawing of Lucretia, which was later placed, as he had directed, in the hall of the Liverpool Training School and Home for Nurses.[12]

William Rathbone and the provision of trained nurses

Deeply grateful to Mrs Mary Robinson, who had trained at the Florence Nightingale School of Nursing at St Thomas's Hospital in London and had nursed his wife during her last illness, and conscious of 'what intense misery must be felt in the houses of the poor from the want of such care,' William Rathbone employed Mary Robinson to go into the poorest districts of Liverpool to try 'in nursing the poor, to relieve suffering, and to teach them the rules of health and comfort.'[13] The amount of misery that Mary Robinson demonstrated could be relieved determined him to extend the experiment. Finding that all the nurses trained at King's College and at St Thomas's Hospital, London, and other institutions, including a Nursing Society in Liverpool, were absorbed by work in hospitals and by private nursing, and that there were no nurses regularly devoted to nursing the poor outside hospitals, he consulted Florence Nightingale. Advised by Miss Nightingale that such nurses should be trained in Liverpool's principal hospital, Liverpool Royal Infirmary, he approached the hospital, whose committee, aware of the need to improve the quality of its nurses and of his interest, invited him to join their ranks. Ascertaining that there was a lack of suitable accommodation for either nurses or probationer nurses, he undertook to fund the erection of a Training School and Home for Nurses, and to present it to the Infirmary, without any pledge by the Infirmary to do more than give the system a fair trial; if it failed, the building was to become the absolute property of the hospital. The offer was accepted and, as he noted, 'my savings enabled me to erect the Nurses' Home,' which was opened in 1863.

The work of planning and building the Nurses' Home in Ashton Street was to deepen Rathbone's friendship with Florence Nightingale, upon whose advice he depended for the rest of his life. On 1 July 1862, the nursing of the Infirmary was handed over to the committee of the new 'Liverpool Training School and Home for Nurses,' their new home (on whose site now stands the

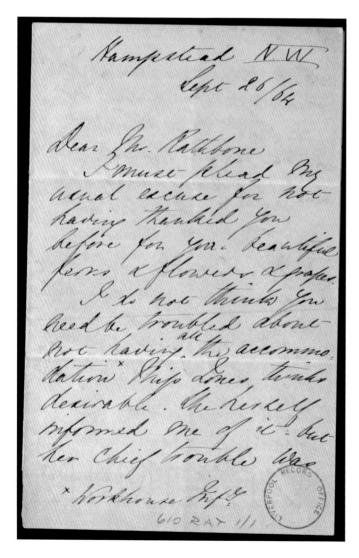

Extract from letter from Florence Nightingale to William Rathbone, 1864. (Reproduced courtesy of Liverpool Record Office, 610 RAT1/1)

University's central boiler house) opening in May 1863.[14] As he later recorded, 'the system has been a complete success.' In two years from the date of his initial conversation with the Infirmary's chairman, seeking to persuade him of the scheme's merits, 'the hospital was nursed by women trained on the Nightingale system, a staff of nurses was gradually thoroughly trained to nurse those who could afford to pay for their services, and in three more years every district in Liverpool was under the charge of a trained nurse and of ladies who provided medical comforts for the poor and supervised the action of the district nurses.' This system of district nursing was later to spread throughout the country. It should be acknowledged that a limited district nursing service had been instituted by the Institution of Nursing Sisters in London by 1854.[15]

Though William Rathbone did not become a member of the Liverpool Select Vestry until 1867, it was through his initiative that in 1865 a parallel reform of nursing in Liverpool's Brownlow Hill Workhouse, for which the Select Vestry was responsible, was effected through the appointment of Agnes Jones (1832–68) to take charge of the introduction of the Nightingale system of nursing, assisted by twelve Nightingale nurses, trained at St Thomas's Hospital, London. For three years he covered the cost of the new system, his identity as benefactor not being revealed to the Select Vestry. Though tragically Agnes Jones fell victim to an attack of typhus, the nurses trained in her school were able to carry on her work, the example of trained nursing spreading to hospitals elsewhere. When in 1874 the National Association for Providing Trained Nurses for the Sick Poor was established, William Rathbone (whose advice on establishing the Association had been sought) was appointed chairman of its subcommittee responsible for district nursing; the report of the subcommittee, issued in June 1875, proved influential in the future development of district nursing. In 1888–89, Rathbone served as honorary secretary of the Provisional Committee responsible for the establishment of Queen Victoria's Jubilee Institute for Nurses, appropriately becoming the Institute's vice-president. In all this work, he remained in close contact with Florence Nightingale and was greatly assisted by his wife, Emily.

In 1867 he had set out his thoughts on the subject of the poor law, charity, and social reform in a book significantly entitled *Social Duties: considered in Reference to the Organisation of Effort in Works of Benevolence and Public Utility; by a Man of Business*. Noting how the growth of large industries and the increasing segregation of different classes in different districts had broken down the old personal relations between employer and employee and between rich and poor, he advocated a system of voluntary charity, to make possible the 'bringing the two classes once more into relations of personal kindness and friendly intercourse, by services rendered without patronage and accepted without degradation.' In the approach of William Rathbone – and indeed the

Emily Rathbone. (Reproduced courtesy of the University of Liverpool Library, RP XXIIA.1.17)

Rathbones over several generations – one witnesses a strong sense of social obligation coupled with a determination to achieve a practical solution; as he expressed it in an address to the Liverpool Institute, 'The faith I believe in is the faith that whatever ought to be done can be done.' As B. Guinness Orchard observed in 1893, 'he is essentially a broad-eyed and sagacious organizer, which leads him to methodize everything,' citing his role in the amalgamation into the Central Relief and Charity Organisation Society of three Liverpool societies, the overlapping of whose work had presented problems to philanthropists and to the detection of 'fraudulent mendacity.'[16]

For advancement of learning: William Rathbone and the establishment of University College Liverpool

Successive William Rathbones supported the desire for a better provision for education at Liverpool. On the initiative of William Rathbone the fifth, the Liverpool Literary and Philosophical Society in 1825 petitioned Parliament for an alteration of the law to facilitate anatomical examinations and thus the training of doctors, an object not achieved until the passing of the Anatomy Act in 1832. As president of the Liverpool Institute – which had originated as the Liverpool Mechanics' Institution – his son in January 1874 addressed a public meeting at the town hall which resolved to establish a Society for the Promotion of Higher Education in Liverpool. Under the leadership of this new body, Liverpool quickly became one of the leading Cambridge University Extension Centres, in Liverpool itself more than forty courses being arranged during the years 1874–80, most of them either in the Liverpool Royal Institution or in the Liverpool Medical Institution.[17] Meanwhile, a younger brother of William Rathbone, Philip Rathbone (1828–95), a Liberal member of Liverpool Town Council, was playing a major role in the establishment of the Walker Art Gallery (whose building, 1874–77, was funded by Andrew Barclay Walker, a brewer), serving as the dominant figure in the chairmanship of the Council's Arts and Exhibitions Sub-Committee, which ran the Gallery.[18]

Although William Rathbone the sixth on several public occasions, including that in January 1874, had spoken strongly of the need in Liverpool for a college like Owens College at Manchester (founded in 1851 under the will of John Owens, a Manchester cotton merchant, who recognised the contribution a university education could make to the community and the business of the surrounding city), the heavy workload he assumed on his active participation in the work of Parliament, following his election in 1868, as a Liberal, as one of Liverpool's three MPs, reduced the occasions on which he could be present in Liverpool. In 1865 he had taken a leading part in the efforts which secured William E. Gladstone's return to the House of Commons representing South-West Lancashire and remained a life-long friend of Gladstone, who, as leader of the Liberal Party from 1867, was to serve as prime minister, 1868–74, 1880–85, 1886, and 1892–94.

For the six months of the parliamentary session, William Rathbone settled with his family in a house in Princes Gardens, close to Hyde Park. Never seeking ministerial office, he represented Liverpool until the election of 1880 when, after declining to support the views of the Home Rule Association on the restoration of an Irish Parliament, he chose to stand aside in Liverpool, instead standing for South-West Lancashire. Though defeated, he was pleased to record that he was now 'left at liberty to devote myself to raising the necessary money for the College proposed in Liverpool.'

Two successive Town's Meetings had been held in 1878, a resolution being passed to establish a college in Liverpool 'to provide such instruction in all the branches of a liberal education as would enable residents in the town and neighbourhood to qualify for degrees in Arts, Science and other subjects at any of the Universities granting degrees to non-resident students, and at the same time to give such technical instruction as would be of immediate service in professional and commercial life.' In writing to the mayor of Liverpool very much regretting that he would be unable to attend the first of these Town's Meetings, William Rathbone observed that 'Liverpool, I believe, at the commencement of this century, was second to no town in the Kingdom, except London and Edinburgh, for its intellectual and literary society; and the formation of such a college [for higher education] would be a natural centre of intellectual life and activity which might aid us to recover that position.' Now that other large towns had stirred or were stirring in this direction, he did not think that Liverpool would be content 'to be left in the rear of intellectual progress.'[19] The civic pride of the Victorians which manifested itself in the erection of buildings, including libraries, schools, and hospitals, in which their people could be proud, often in a spirit of competition with nearby towns, extended to the provision of higher education. It is noticeable that the new higher education institutions were largely the result of the initiatives of local businesspeople. Owens College, Manchester, was by 1873 solidly established, in new premises designed by the Liverpool-born architect, Alfred Waterhouse, on Oxford Road; and at Leeds, the Yorkshire College had been established in 1874.

Having advised the supporters that somewhat more than £15,000 would have to be raised if such an institution was to have a successful launch and to attract support, it was hearing the address of Professor Joseph Barber Lightfoot to the Liverpool Council of Education in January 1879 that inspired William Rathbone to seek out the necessary funds. Professor Lightfoot, a distinguished theologian and biblical scholar, shortly to become bishop of Durham, had returned from Cambridge to his place of birth to 'dream a dream.' As William Rathbone recalled, in his speech Professor Lightfoot dreamed of revisiting Liverpool twenty-five years later, finding 'a magnificent College, of which one wing, or part, had been built by the munificence of one family, another by a firm, a third by individuals; and professorships funded in the same way, in memory of some distinguished Liverpool worthy, or in memory of the success and gratitude of the founder.' With some justifiable pride, in later life he recalled how, through his family, business and political contacts, £80,000 was raised:

> As soon as the election was over in 1880, I went to my brothers [Samuel and Philip] and asked them if they would join me in founding a Professorship.

They agreed to do so, S.G.R. making the condition that it should be called the 'King Alfred Professorship', after England's earliest educationalist. I then went to Alexander Brown, who had promised £5,000, and to William Crosfield, who was the first to promise £1,000, and suggested that if Crosfield would induce each of his partners to do the same, they and Brown could found a 'Gladstone Professorship', which Gladstone being then at the height of his popularity, they cheerfully assented to. I then went to Mr Balfour and Mr Samuel Smith, as Scotchmen, and pointed out that, as the Scotch had been fifty years ahead of us in education, and with the good education they had, many of them came to Liverpool and realized large fortunes – it would be a graceful thing if the Scotch merchants of Liverpool would found a Professorship of Political Economy and Moral Philosophy, two subjects often joined in Scotch Universities. To this they agreed, and raised the necessary funds for it. I then went to my corn-market friends, and Mr Paul and Mr J Bingham taking the matter up and leading off with good donations, this was accomplished. I pointed out to Mr Whitley that the scheme had been started by two Conservative Mayors [A. B. Forwood and his successor T. B. Royden], and it would never do to let us 'Radicals and Infidels', as they chose to call us, have the credit of raising all the money, and suggested that out of the 'Roger Lyon Jones Trust' [of which Mr Whitley was a trustee] he should found a Professorship. He laughed, and was most willing to do it, for he admitted that the Conservatives had not come forward up to that time to do their share. He found that, through the medical school, the Trust allowed him to carry out his good intentions. I then wrote to Lord Derby [the sixteenth earl], pointing out that his father [the fourteenth earl] had handed over to the town a very fine museum of Natural History, and that we hoped he would follow so generous an example, by founding a Professorship of Natural History. This he cordially agreed to do, and so on; and before the year was out, we had raised £80,000 for the College.[20]

Though this account is oversimplified, it was in large measure William Rathbone's energy, initiative and personal influence that translated the academic vision into practical reality.[21] Not an easy man by all accounts, William Rathbone was one who persevered and got things done. It should be noted that it was not until 1889 that the government agreed to make a grant of £15,000 a year for five years for distribution among the university colleges and not until 1919 that the University Grants Committee, the predecessor of the Higher Education Funding Councils, was established to advise the government as to the allocation of grants towards universities and university colleges; even after the increasingly generous grant aid which the state made available, Liverpool and other universities continued to be heavily dependent

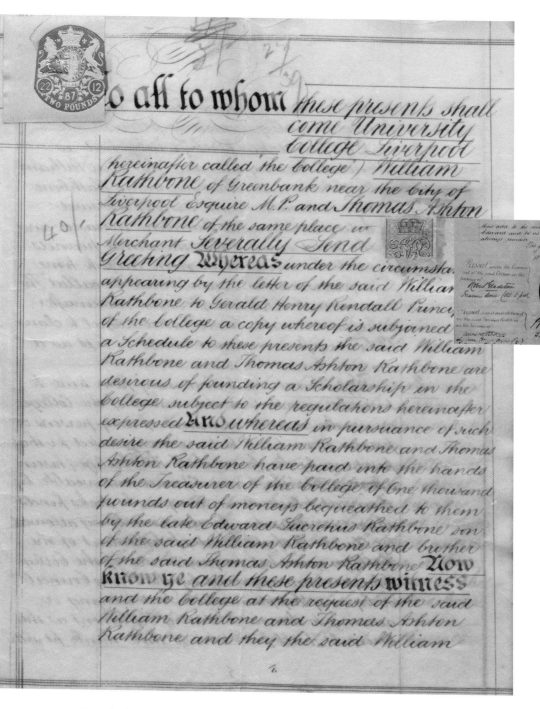

Trust deed establishing Rathbone Scholarship, 1887.
(Reproduced courtesy of the University of Liverpool Library, D.284/2/14)

also on student fees and on philanthropy, on the benefactions of bodies and persons other than central and local government.

Within a year of the inaugural meeting of University College, Liverpool, held at St George's Hall in January 1882, William Rathbone, by now MP for Caernarvonshire, found himself in the thick of the equivalent movement for establishing a University College of North Wales. In the opinion of one of his fellow workers in the movement, he soon became 'the pivot of the whole movement,' finding plenty of scope for what his daughter, Eleanor, later described as his 'undeniable faculty for reconciling divergent views and getting people of conflicting political and religious opinions to work harmoniously together.' In October 1884, the University College of North Wales, based at Bangor, began its first session, William Rathbone inducing some friends to join him in funding a number of valuable entrance scholarships. Appointed vice-president of the College, in 1892 he was made president, remaining in close connection with the College for the rest of his working life, witnessing the creation in 1893 of a federal University of Wales with three constituent colleges, of which Bangor was one.

In the assessment of Professor John MacCunn, University College Liverpool's first holder of the Chair of Philosophy,

> The gain of Wales was never the loss of Liverpool. How else can we read the fact that, as often as our College has made some large stride in its swift progress, this has usually happened, by a coincidence not difficult to explain, when Mr Rathbone was back among us ... Never, since colleges were built, have teachers found a man more ready and eager to give them sympathy without stint, and encouragement that never failed, or to repose in them a more generous and enheartening confidence ... few men have had occasion seriously to converse with him about education, or to mark the passion for the spread of knowledge which possessed him, without taking with them as a result a deepened conviction that Education was one of the great causes worth living for.[22]

Years later, writing in November 1892 to University College Liverpool's first Principal, Professor Gerald Rendall, regretting his absence at the opening of the College's Tate Library and the unveiling of a bust of its donor, Henry Tate, William Rathbone revealed the action he had taken over a period of time to persuade Tate to fund the erection of the wing of the Victoria Building which included the library.[23] When, five years later, responding to a request for a reference for Principal Rendall, a candidate for the headmastership of Charterhouse, Rathbone was pleased to declare that 'heartily backed by his colleagues, the College is saving us from the reproach of being a mere city of money makers.'[24]

Oliver Lodge on a visit to Greenbank House. (Reproduced courtesy of the University of Liverpool Library, P.5506)

William Rathbone, who was appointed as one of the College's two vice-presidents, the Earl of Derby serving as president, enjoyed excellent personal relations with a broad range of the college's staff, taking an informed interest in their work. The surviving letters addressed to him by staff of the college include those of the Shakespearean scholar, A. C. Bradley (the first holder of the King Alfred Chair of Modern Literature and English Language), on the subject of Coleridge and Wordsworth, and John MacCunn, on the course to be pursued by Business Curriculum students during the college's vacations.[25] With Oliver Lodge, Lyon Jones Professor of Physics, the relationship was particularly strong. Writing to Rathbone in November 1891, Lodge discusses the subject of evolution – 'I observe that Mr Balfour argues that the ordinary process of evolution by survival must cease to be effective in proportion as the environment is improved to suit the organism,' concluding that 'the riddle of human life cannot be read by attending to our paltry existence here alone,' confessing a belief in a form of pantheism.[26] At a low point a year later, 'your friend and servant Oliver J Lodge' expressed his appreciation of Rathbone: 'The warmth of your friendship melts opposition I had been getting more and more as I thought strengthened in seeing difficulties ... When low and dispirited I felt doubtful whether it was not now too late to stem the tide and try to achieve real work notwithstanding a large family.'[27]

Writing from his holiday home at Alassio in December 1892,[28] Rathbone expresses to Lodge his concern about Principal Rendall's heavy workload: 'if he is not better we must ship him off to the Riviera,' concluding 'I hope you may bring Ether and a great many other unknowns to book in 1893,'[29] later urging the appointment of a secretary or assistant to whom the principal might delegate his duties. In contributing £500 towards such an appointment, he wrote to Robert Gladstone, the college's treasurer, 'I don't believe that the Liverpool gold-diggings are yet exhausted, but that the good example set by some of our friends will, with usefulness and energy on the part of our financial chief, be followed by others.'[30]

Anxious to retain Oliver Lodge at University College, William Rathbone sought to provide better physical laboratory accommodation than could be provided in the converted former lunatic asylum which formed the College's original home. Writing to Mrs Whitley in July 1899, seeking a contribution towards the cost of a new physical laboratory, Rathbone expressed his admiration for Oliver Lodge: 'one of the most brilliant discoverers and teachers not only in England, but in the world. He was the real discoverer of the means of "Wireless Telegraphy"; but being more interested in his subject than in his own interests, communicated his invention to the scientific world, without taking the precaution of patenting it' and 'another [Marconi] has completed, patented, and is deriving wealth and celebrity from the invention.'[31]

Five months earlier, William Rathbone's eightieth birthday was celebrated at Greenbank by a large family gathering, attended by some hundred of his relations and by a few old friends. In a testimonial, signed by eighty-nine of the staff and students of the Department of Engineering of University College, they expressed their gratitude to him 'as the real founder of the Engineering side of the College,' crediting him with the endowment of a chair for five years, afterwards employing his personal influence 'to induce generous donors to come forward to endow permanently the Chair and build and equip the Engineering laboratories, you yourself having contributed largely to the temporary endowment, also for some years provided the necessary funds for Assistant Lecturers.'[32] His name was to be perpetuated by the William Rathbone Medal and Prizes in Engineering.

William Rathbone aged eighty years. (Reproduced courtesy of the University of Liverpool Library, RP XXV.7.16)

Paying tribute to William Rathbone's life and achievements on this occasion in 1899 were a series of verses by M. F. Rathbone (Mary Frances Rathbone, sister of Hugh Rathbone), each commencing with the initial letters forming the name of Greenbank, including:

E also is found to begin Education,
Where his efforts have proved such a boon to the nation,
Since 'King Alfred's Professorship' started the wheel
Which a Bishop first spoked in his doze after meal.
For it seemed in his dream he was strangely amazed
To find a magnificent College upraised,
As he visited later our seagoing town,
When he told us he thought fifty summers had flown.[33]

G·R·E·E·N·B·A·N·K

 is for Nightingale, nurse of his pen,
Whose handwriting has proved an example to men,
For each new Assistant is led to adopt
Her excellent style, at Greenbank, who had stopped.
But beside the handwriting his model she's been
In his ardour to keep all his countrymen clean.
When providing him first with "luffers" he loves
Preferring to wash with respectable gloves;
And she pointed out once how a mortal could shine
With these "luffers," some soap, and a glass made for wine.
Should he dance in the desert his body to bask
'Neath the scorch of the sun with no aid but a flask.
But when on his birthday a box will arrive,
How his conscience at times with debatings will strive
As the bouquet with "Florence's" label appears,
Till our aunt soon succeeds in dispelling his fears!

---

 is for kindred, for kith and for kin,
For all, yea and more than this room that are in,
Who have leapt from the lengths of our loved British Isles,
Be they Rathbones, or Gregs, Moores, Pagets or Lyles!

Here greet we our chieftain in his 80th year,
Rejoicing in heart his good self to be near;
So we'll join all his hand and our voices the while,
As we raise our Lang Syne, in the old Scottish style.

Walmsley, Printer, Liverpool.

"Della Robbia."

Verses in honour of William Rathbone, 1899.
(Reproduced courtesy of Liverpool Record Office, 920 MD 355)

In a series of tableaux in which members of his family took part, that featuring the University Colleges of Liverpool and North Wales was mounted by, among others, William Rathbone the eighth and Eleanor Rathbone.[34]

Of a popular nature, Doulton Burslem produced a lustreware jug commemorating William Rathbone's eightieth birthday, its portrait of him being accompanied by two verses, the first of which reads:

A man of Deeds not Words; the steadfast Friend
Of all that's weak, or ailing, or distrest;
For others' good his days he loves to spend,
And finds in strenuous Toil, his nobler Rest.[35]

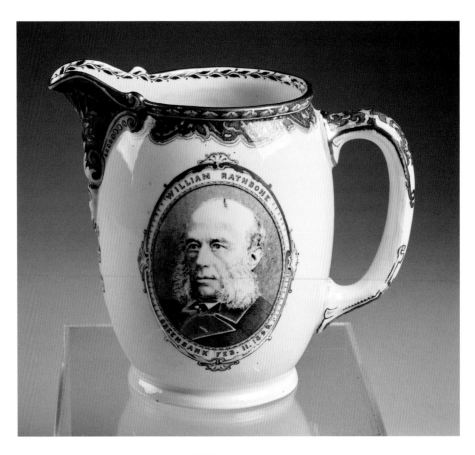

Doulton Burslem jug commemorating William Rathbone, 1899.
(Reproduced courtesy of the Victoria Gallery & Museum, University of Liverpool)

In the same year, William Rathbone expressed the family's sense of obligation and his own hope and endeavour to 'try in some measure to repay that deep debt of gratitude that we as a family owe – under God – to our native City and fellow citizens, for having during eight generations and most of two centuries given us the opportunity of acquiring and enjoying food, raiment, shelter and education and above all a sphere for useful and honourable work in the several vocations to which God has called us.'[36]

Greenbank at the close of the nineteenth century

A snapshot of the occupiers of Greenbank and of the cottages which formed part of its estate is provided by the census taken on 31 March 1901.[37] At Greenbank, eighty-two-year-old William Rathbone and his sixty-eight-year-old (second) wife, Emily, were joined by William's unmarried children, Elizabeth (forty-nine), Eleanor (twenty-eight), and Francis (twenty-six, described as a general merchant); also resident were William's private secretary, Miss Pollard-Kennedy, together with eight unmarried 'servants': a hospital nurse and a nurse (no doubt looking after William), a housemaid, a footman, a cook, an underhousemaid, a lady's maid, and a kitchen maid. As Eleanor recounts, William latterly suffered a series of attacks of a form of eczema which, while not acutely painful, was exhausting and very disabling; 'fortunately he had always been used to dictating his letters to a secretary' and to relying 'a good deal on his wife's help in the composition of speeches and important letters, and thus he was able even when in bed to get through slowly a good deal of correspondence.'[38] Next door lived William Edwards, the thirty-nine-year-old trusted butler of Greenbank (who was to witness the codicils to William's will), his wife, and their six young children. Beyond lived Greenbank's forty-two-year-old coachman, George Grant, his wife, and their four young daughters; and in separate accommodation lived Greenbank's two laundresses.

In a long will, together with no fewer than seven codicils, drawn up over the period 1898–1901, William Rathbone instructed his trustees to permit his wife and her family and servants to occupy, free of rent, a portion of his Greenbank property, namely the house and outbuildings, gardens, and pleasure grounds, also the large field opposite the drawing room window, the field between the pond and the road opposite the dining room window, and the field adjoining the latter field on the south.[39] She was to be permitted to occupy this property for life or until such time as she wished to leave. The Greenbank estate at the time was defined as bounded on the north by Greenbank Lane, on the east by Greenbank Road, on the south by Ibbotson's Lane, and on the west by land used by Greenbank School. The property was to be insured for at least £10,000, his trustees being instructed to put the property (including its 'conservatories, greenhouses, hothouses, gardens')

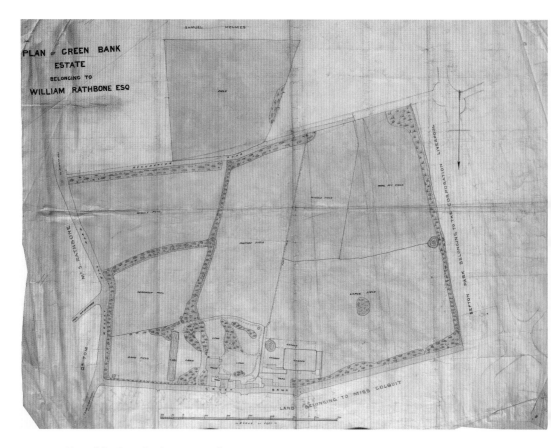

Plan of the Greenbank estate, c. 1892.
(Lancashire Archives, DDX 162/93/78, reproduced with thanks to the partners of Matthews
& Goodman LLP, incorporating Edmund Kirby & Sons, and holder of the Edmund Kirby and
Culshaw archives)

in complete repair and see that his wife had a 'thoroughly satisfactory open
and close carriage (one of each kind) and a pair of really good horses.' Should
Emily leave Greenbank, then she was to be paid an annuity of at least £300
to enable her to acquire and keep up a suitable residence for herself and
those of her children living with her. On the death of Emily or her departure
from Greenbank, Greenbank 'and appropriate land' was to be offered by his
trustees to his son-in-law, Hugh Reynolds Rathbone, and his wife, Emily
Evelyn Rathbone, or to any of his sons or other daughters living in Liverpool
who would wish to purchase the property for £5,000 as were felt able to
'keep up a suitable establishment,' priority being given to Hugh Rathbone
and his wife. Should it become clear that his son, William Gair Rathbone
(William Rathbone the seventh), would never be willing to live permanently

at Greenbank, then he was to receive a legacy of £5,000. Included among the executors was Hugh Rathbone who was joined by his wife among the trustees.

Besides the generous provisions made in the past, in the form of marriage and other settlements, in favour of his children, and now in his will, William Rathbone granted his wife the annual income on an investment of £87,000, and left numerous legacies to family members. Edward Vickers, his late Secretary, was left £300 and each of his domestic servants £50 (if they had served ten years) or £10 (for those whose service extended between two and nine years), besides the wages due them. Of the contents of Greenbank little is revealed. To his wife, he left all his household goods and furniture (without specifying any individual piece), and all china, books, pictures, ornaments, wines and liquors, and other household effects, and his carriage, horses and harness, and garden tools, whether at Greenbank or at his stables or coach houses in Liverpool. The presentation plate which he had inherited from his father was left to his son, William G. Rathbone, with the exception of the large ceiled candelabra which was to remain at Greenbank, in effect as an heirloom, passing to those who purchased the property under the terms of the will; should no such purchase take place, then the candelabra was to go to Hugh Rathbone 'who has since my son Ashton's death inherited his anxieties and work as the Resident Head in his generation of our family and whose wise counsel and aid have greatly lightened the increased labour and thought which my brother's illness and son's death brought upon me and which without such assistance might have proved too much for my age and strength.' The gross value of William Rathbone's estate was declared to be £238,473.

Sadly, William Rathbone, who died at Greenbank on 6 March 1902, his ashes being interred in Toxteth Cemetery, was too ill to attend the unveiling of his statue erected by public subscription in St John's Gardens, behind St George's Hall, on 26 July 1901. Depicted in bronze wearing the gown of a Doctor of Laws of the federal Victoria University (of which University College, Liverpool, was a constituent), which had been conferred upon him, honoris causa, in 1895, the inscription on the pedestal records that William Rathbone was an Honorary Freeman of Liverpool, MP for Liverpool 1868–80 and for Caernarvonshire 1880–95, a guardian of the poor in Liverpool for thirty-five years, a founder of the universities of Liverpool and Wales, and that he instituted the Training School for Nurses 'and brought trained nurses into the homes of the poor and suffering first in Liverpool and later throughout the country.' Below the pedestal's bronze relief panels featuring his advocacy of education, charitable work among the poor, and the nursing of the sick poor in their own homes, are texts encapsulating his beliefs: 'Having faith in God he could never despair of men,' 'He helped the poor by giving his heart with his help,' 'He deemed the fear of obstacles the greatest obstacle,' and 'Seeing the best in others he drew from them their best.'

His ill-health had also prevented him attending the Town's Meeting convened by the Lord Mayor in January 1902, at which the college's University Committee was charged with obtaining a charter for the university and raising the necessary funds, but in one of his last letters to the college's principal he emphasised 'the tremendous and paramount importance for England of straining every muscle to improve the education of her people. The present commercial and industrial state of the country is not so satisfactory that any part of it, and least of all Liverpool, can afford to be weighted in the race with America or with other European countries by defects in her educational machinery.' He was now reassured that 'following on the generous support that the scheme [of a separate University of Liverpool] had already received from a few rich people, the recent resolution of the City Council ensures that the University will be founded and supported in a manner worthy of Liverpool, and of Great Britain.'[40]

William Rathbone's legacy to his daughter, Eleanor, and the forging of her own legacy

The death of William Rathbone was a devastating blow for his twenty-nine-year-old daughter (the tenth of his eleven children), Eleanor, who had worked closely with her father in his last years as both his assistant and collaborator. As a labour of love, she wrote an account of his life, prefacing it with an account of the lives and contributions made by his Liverpool ancestors (William Rathbone: A Memoir, 1905); 'that it might encourage others, especially young men and women in his own city, to trace out for themselves more definitely, and to follow more boldly, a career of public usefulness' was the motive which she felt would, in her father's reluctant view, have reconciled him to the publication of such a memoir. The children of William Rathbone were brought up to regard their wealth and position as a sacred trust, to use to the glory of God and in the service of their fellow men; if Eleanor might later have abandoned her father's certain faith, throughout her life she remained a selfless humanitarian.[41]

Growing up at Greenbank and, while her father was serving in Parliament, at the family's London residence, except for a year at Kensington Girls' School (1889–90), Eleanor's education was conducted at home. Before, with her father's support, she was allowed to go to Somerville Hall, Oxford, to study 'Greats' in 1893, as a day student she attended courses delivered by Professor John MacCunn and his colleagues at University College. There are entries for Eleanor Rathbone in University College's Day Student Address Books for sessions 1891–92 and 1892–93.[42] Also registered as a student at the College in 1892–93 was her younger brother, Francis W. Rathbone, while more

William Rathbone and family on holiday in Scotland, 1892. Back row, left to right: William Rathbone, his wife, Emily, and daughter, Eleanor. Front row, left to right: Emily Evelyn, wife of Hugh Rathbone, Frank Rathbone (with Hannah Mary (Nancy), daughter of Hugh and Emily), Hugh Rathbone (with his son, Richard Reynolds), and Elsie (daughter of William Rathbone and half-sister of Eleanor Rathbone).
(Reproduced courtesy of the University of Liverpool Library, RP XXV.7.90)

distant relations, Miss May Rathbone of Neston, who was later to achieve distinction as a doctor, botanist, and mountaineer, and Miss Freda Rathbone of Greenbank Cottage, later a pioneer worker for the mentally handicapped, were also students at the College in the late 1880s/early 1890s. Awarded second-class honours at Oxford, she returned to Greenbank in 1896, taking over the secretaryship of the Liverpool Women's Suffrage Society and of the local branch of the Women's Industrial Council, also volunteering as a home visitor for the Liverpool Central Relief Society (which had been formed in 1846). Throughout her life, she constantly sought to find ways to make room for voluntary effort in public life; the teachings of her father and the idealist philosophers who had taught her at Oxford led her to see such personal service as an essential duty of a citizen.[43] Already a self-identified feminist by the time she studied at Oxford, Eleanor was a prominent supporter of the moderate, constitutional Women's Suffrage movement, leading the Liverpool Women's Suffrage Society and, from 1896, serving on the executive committee of the National Union of Women's Suffrage Societies (NUWSS), which had been formed in 1877 as a peaceful campaigning organisation determined to achieve votes for women. She helped to shape its policies, participating in its lobbying and writing for its organ, the *Common Cause*; she was to succeed Millicent Fawcett as the NUWSS's president in March 1919.

Over the two decades between her father's death in 1902 and her mother's death in 1918, in the words of her most recent biographer, Professor Susan Pedersen, Eleanor Rathbone 'became the most prominent woman in Liverpool's public life.'[44] In 1903 she began working with the Victoria Settlement for women, which had been established in 1898, in Netherfield Road, Everton, with the active support of staff of University College, with the aim of creating friendship and understanding between rich and poor and promoting a positive response to the problem of poverty. As the Settlement's honorary secretary until 1915, Eleanor worked closely with the Settlement's new warden, Elizabeth Macadam, not only securing the financial basis of the Settlement, recruiting large numbers of supporters and fellow workers, but also promoting 'the more thorough and scientific treatment of the problem of poverty,' establishing a training programme for social workers. Eleanor was to retain a lifelong interest in the Victoria Settlement and what it stood for; one of the last meetings she attended, as a trustee of the Settlement, was in March 1945, when at the launch of an appeal for £20,000 in aid of the Settlement, she said that it was a complete mistake to suppose, as some people did, that such work as the Settlement was doing could be left to the state or municipality, and that the need for voluntary effort was disappearing.[45] This commitment to voluntary service, conducted with 'professional' expertise and training, was one to be strongly advocated by Margaret Simey, who had served an apprenticeship under Eleanor Rathbone and who later also represented the Granby Ward on Liverpool City Council; and this vision of a responsible citizenship has continued to inspire Liverpool's extensive voluntary, community, and social economy sectors.[46]

Initially run from the Victoria Settlement, largely through the efforts of Eleanor Rathbone, Elizabeth Macadam, and others, a Liverpool School of Social Science and Training for Social Work was established at the University in 1905. In 1910 it became an integral part of the University, in 1911 Elizabeth Macadam being appointed as the school's first lecturer in the Methods and Practice of Social Work, the funds to endow the lectureship being raised by

Eleanor and others. Besides Professor MacCunn, among those who lectured on courses offered by the school was Eleanor, on public administration. Meanwhile, in 1909, Eleanor had become the first woman to be elected to Liverpool City Council, representing the Granby Ward as an Independent; she was to hold this seat without a break until 1935, vigorously supporting the Council's house-building policy to address serious house shortages and a needy low-wage population. She also became a member of the University's Council in 1910, serving until 1916.

In completing the schedule of those who were resident at Greenbank on 2 April 1911, when the census was taken, Eleanor's mother, as head of the household, recorded her daughter's occupation as 'Member of City Council (political organizing unremunerated).'[47] Of the six other single women present, there was a companion-secretary (clearly providing support to Eleanor), a cook, a lady's maid, an upper housemaid and an under-housemaid, and a kitchen maid; also a nineteen-year-old footman. Excluding such rooms as a scullery, closet, and bathrooms, there were evidently no fewer than twenty-nine rooms recorded at Greenbank.

Greenbank remained the home and base of Eleanor Rathbone until her mother's death in 1918. Continuing a study into Liverpool's dock labour system which she had commenced with her father, her *Report of an Inquiry into the Conditions of Dock Labour at the Liverpool Docks* (1904) was to be followed by further influential surveys based on research in Liverpool, *How the Casual Labourer Lives* (1909) and *The Condition of Widows under the Poor Law in Liverpool* (1913), in which she advocated the introduction of state pensions for widows raising young children on their own. In 1908 Lloyd George had introduced old-age pensions, initially for those over seventy years of age with an income of less than twelve shillings (60p) per week. And in 1911 the National Insurance Act had provided for a contributory scheme encompassing manual workers aged between sixteen and seventy and non-manual workers earning less than £160 per year; the benefits of the scheme included cash payments during sickness or disablement and provision for the services of a general practitioner.

As Margaret Simey noted, as her father's apprentice, Eleanor had observed 'his invariable habit of applying to social problems the same sturdy common sense as governed his commercial life,' her own succession of publications embodying 'a respect for methodical analysis and fact-finding as a necessary foundation for any programme of social reform.'[48] During the First World War, at the request of the Lord Mayor of Liverpool, Herbert Rathbone (her cousin), assisted by Elizabeth Macadam, as head of a 'Town Hall Soldiers and Sailors' Families Organisation,' Eleanor Rathbone organised assistance for the families of those soldiers and sailors who were serving in the war. Staffed by voluntary workers, the Liverpool organisation that was established, supplementing the state payments of 'separation allowances,' visiting wives and families, became a model for family-based social work, one that led her to develop her later thinking on family allowances.

Towards the end of the war, Eleanor collaborated with Mary Stocks (her future biographer) and other prominent women in publishing *Equal Pay and the Family*, advocating equal pay between men and women; and in 1918 she helped to establish the Liverpool Personal Service Society to carry on the work she had undertaken during the war. As the war was entering its closing stages, the Representation of the People Act, 1918, granted the vote to women over the age of thirty who met a property qualification, and to all men over the age of twenty-one years; and in November 1918 the Parliament (Qualification of Women) Act granted women the right to stand for parliament on equal terms as men.

Following the death of her mother in March 1918, Eleanor Rathbone's principal home became a house in Romney Street, Westminster, which, in 1919, she and Elizabeth Macadam bought, though, with her many continuing Liverpool commitments, from June 1919 she kept a house in Liverpool, White Gables, Mossley Hill Road, which she shared with Elsie, her elder half-sister, until her death in November 1920. In her will, Elsie left Eleanor the bulk of her property including Oakfield, an eighteenth-century villa close to Greenbank, where from 1920 until 1929 she was to live for part of each month. Renting out Oakfield in the early 1930s, thereafter, on her increasingly fewer visits to Liverpool – she ceased to be a member of the City Council in 1935 – she stayed with Hugh Rathbone and his wife, Evie, at Greenbank, albeit her relationship with Evie was probably happier than that with her argumentative husband Hugh, whom relations felt probably bore some degree of resentment at Eleanor's growing fame.[49]

After 1921, Eleanor spent more time working up the campaign for family endowment, the case for 'family allowances' being made in *The Disinherited Family* (1924), her most influential publication.

Eleanor Rathbone as an Independent MP

An avowed feminist who disliked partisanship, Eleanor Rathbone entered Parliament in 1929 on her election as an Independent MP for the Combined English Universities Constituency, a seat she was to hold until her death in 1946. Both Oxford and Cambridge universities had returned Members of Parliament to the House of Commons since 1603, and in 1918, by the Representation of the People Act, the university franchise was extended such that, inter alia, a 'Combined English Universities Constituency,' of the graduates of the universities of Birmingham, Bristol, Durham, Leeds, Liverpool, Manchester, and Sheffield was established, returning two MPs. In her election address, in May 1929, Eleanor referred to her service on the Council and Court of the University of Liverpool and stated that the community should be encouraged to draw freely upon the facilities of the universities for scientific and economic research and should in return be generous towards their finances while respecting their complete intellectual independence. The circular letter of the Joint Committee to promote her as Prospective Independent Candidate (signed by, among others, Professor Patrick Abercrombie, Dr John Hay, and Professor Percy Roxby, from Liverpool) suggested that while casting their residential vote according to their political allegiance, graduates might welcome the idea of having as one of the two MPs 'a woman of Miss Rathbone's qualifications and independent stand-point.' University representation in the House of Commons was criticised and challenged throughout its existence (1603–1950). In rallying the opposition to the Labour government's proposal to abolish the university franchise in 1931, Eleanor made one of many return visits to Liverpool to attend meetings she addressed. Also in 1931, the University conferred an honorary degree of Doctor of Laws upon her, congratulating 'her and ourselves on the working of that special franchise, of which she has proved herself at once a champion and a justification,' acknowledging that in the House of Commons, 'that most hospitable and most critical of assemblies, where almost anyone may enter, but where no one succeeds without character and knowledge,' she was heard with attention.[50]

Already in 1931 Eleanor Rathbone had brought the vice-chancellors and university MPs together to plan the campaign. In her 'The Case for University Representation,' circulated to her constituents, she noted that the great majority of students came from secondary municipal schools or endowed grammar schools; a very large proportion – in the case of Liverpool 66.2 per cent – began their education in the public elementary schools. At Liverpool, 47.9 per cent of the total of full-time students in session 1928–29 were assisted by scholarships, exhibitions, grants, etc. With justification, she could write that 'it is probably safe to say that nowadays a large majority of University graduates have come from homes which cannot be called affluent, and have owed their University education to their own abilities and industry, aided by parental self-sacrifice and – for a great number of them – by scholarships and maintenance grants.'

In the subsequent House of Commons debate, Eleanor Rathbone approvingly quoted John Stuart Mill as having stated that 'It is an essential part of democracy that minorities should be adequately represented' and declared that she regarded university representation as an instalment of proportional representation, because the method of election was by the single transferable vote and 'because it does at least secure the representation in Parliament of those members of the learned professions and of the higher grades of industries and commerce who are too scattered over the ordinary constituencies for their votes to have a controlling influence on elections.' The other (Conservative) MP for the Constituency, Sir Martin Conway – who had held the Roscoe Chair of Art at Liverpool, 1885–88 – reminded the Commons that the granting of the franchise to women in 1918 was part of the bargain by which university representation was maintained and increased.

Eleanor Rathbone addressed the University's convocation on two subsequent occasions, in March 1933 and in March 1934.[51] In 1933 she gave an account of her efforts to secure 'fuller recognition of the claims of graduates' with reference to appointments in the Civil Service and to appointments restricted to graduates of the older universities. This was a long-standing grievance which was not to be rectified for some years. At this meeting the vice-chancellor explained the then policy of the University Council in regard to women lecturers, which dictated that their contract of employment automatically terminated on their marriage. Eleanor Rathbone was one of those who gave her full support to those who opposed this policy; following the receipt of many further protests by the Federation of University Women and others, in March 1934 the Council suspended its rule and agreed that the appointments of women lecturers who married in the course of their service be considered in the ordinary routine at the expiry of their normal tenures.

A fierce critic of the whole policy of appeasement in the 1930s, by 1936 Eleanor Rathbone was spending much time trying to persuade the public of the need to stand up to Hitler and Mussolini. One of the few British politicians to see the refugee issue as a whole, concerning the Jewish population of Eastern Europe as those in the German Reich, in December 1938, with other MPs, she formed a voluntary 'Parliamentary Committee on Refugees,' campaigning tirelessly for their rescue. From 1935 until 1945, she spent almost all of her time on international questions.

In July 1945, Eleanor Rathbone was returned to Parliament for a last time, in a general election which returned Labour, led by Clement Attlee, with a landslide majority, with 394 seats to the Conservatives' 210. With an electorate of 42,312, Eleanor Rathbone (as an Independent) received no fewer than 11,176 of the 20,973 first preference votes cast for the six candidates. Though her election address does not include a specific section on higher education, she refers to the 1944 Education Act as offering bright prospects for the future: of 'higher education to depend on ability rather than on purses.'

Sadly, Eleanor Rathbone died less than six months later, in January 1946; she was cremated and her name added to the family monument in Toxteth Cemetery, Smithfield Road. In a moving letter her elder sister Evie, widow of Hugh Rathbone, wrote to the chairman of convocation, in response to a letter of condolences, 'Many causes will miss her help and still nurse heartfelt sympathy. I think she died of a really broken heart over all the suffering she could not cure.'[52] In the previous June, following years of campaigning,

Eleanor Rathbone: oil portrait by Sir James Gunn, 1933.
(Reproduced courtesy of the National Portrait Gallery)

representations to government ministers and lobbying of fellow MPs of all parties, she was able to witness the final achievement of her lifelong campaign, the passing of the Family Allowances Act. Though she never married and had no children, she had proved the greatest champion of married women and the introduction of family allowances. Throughout her lifetime, Eleanor had wholeheartedly advanced and supported many causes. In the assessment of her most recent biographer, 'she stands as both the most significant feminist thinker and the most effective woman politician of the first half of the twentieth century.'[53]

In declining the offer of a Damehood of the British Empire, which Winston Churchill, the prime minister, had made in December 1943, Eleanor Rathbone had observed that she had 'perhaps as an inheritance from my Quaker ancestors – a dislike of titles, except where they denote in the bearers a long historic tradition.'[54]

Eleanor Rathbone left the bulk of her capital, about £100,000, to aid refugee organisations and to establish an 'Eleanor Rathbone Trust,' which was to support social schemes for the underprivileged. (The Eleanor Rathbone Charitable Trust continues to support charities and charitable projects focused on Merseyside, particularly charities benefitting women and unpopular and neglected causes, but avoiding those with a sectarian interest, as well as international projects.) Winston Churchill joined other prominent politicians in supporting an appeal to endow a memorial lecture at her old college, Somerville College, Oxford, and at the civic universities which she had represented.[55] The University of Liverpool was to commemorate her life and work in the naming of the Eleanor Rathbone Chair of Social Science (now Sociology) in 1964 and of the Eleanor Rathbone Building, opened in 1973. Since the 1970s Eleanor Rathbone's life and her ideas have won renewed attention. In 2008, the Royal Mail issued a special edition of postage stamps featuring six 'Women of Distinction,' including Eleanor Rathbone, 'Campaigner Family Allowance.' And in 2016, the seventieth anniversary of her death, Rathbone Brothers' *Rathbones Review* published an article on 'An unsung heroine,' contributed by Dr Susan Cohen.

Greenbank passes to Hugh Rathbone

Under the terms of William Rathbone's will, Greenbank and its grounds, described as comprising 15 acres and 14 perches, were conveyed to Hugh Rathbone in March 1920.[56] It was the great affection and admiration which Hugh Rathbone had for William Rathbone that made him decide to buy Greenbank and assume its responsibilities. The conveyance was subject to restrictive covenants of September 1912 (to which Hugh Rathbone was a party) which specified that no building should be erected on parts of the property – principally a strip of land running from Greenbank south-west to Ibbotsons Lane – except 'good and substantial private dwelling houses and suitable outbuildings,' which in one case should occupy not less than three quarters of an acre and be of an annual rental value of not less than £100, and in the other case occupying not less than half an acre and of an annual rental

Rear of Greenbank House, 'showing where the corridor was,' 1920. (Reproduced courtesy of the University of Liverpool Library, RP XXV.4.2)

'The corridor in its new position from the road, showing the new front door,' 1920. (Reproduced courtesy of the University of Liverpool Library, RP XXV.4.2)

value of not less than £70. Such restrictive covenants, seeking to maintain the quality of development and ensure it was not put to other than residential use, had long been a feature of conveyances of both freehold and leasehold property in Liverpool.

At the time, Hugh Rathbone was living at Oakwood, Aigburth, a twenty-two-room mansion. In 1911, he and his wife, Emily Evelyn Rathbone, their three student sons and their tutor, Hugh's unmarried sister, Mary Rathbone, and seven female servants, were recorded as resident there. Now the household moved to Greenbank where he was to have his greatest happiness, actively working in his garden or extending delightful hospitality to a wide circle of relatives and friends.

Soon after moving to Greenbank, Hugh Rathbone undertook a number of changes which in a letter of December 1920 Rosalind Paget, granddaughter of William Rathbone the fifth, states were absolutely in keeping with the spirit of the place.[57] With memories going back sixty years, she had seen many changes:

> before the big room was built and the boudoir was two horrid little dark rooms where coats were hung. The Library had a big table in the middle and I picture so vividly Grandma working at one side and myself and any other there one drawing or sewing and grandparents a reading aloud Froude's Queen Elizabeth (about 1864?) [J. A. Froude's *History of England from the Fall of Wolsey to the Death of Elizabeth* was published in twelve volumes, 1856–70.] My grandfather was rather an awe inspiring figure to us children ... After those days I never considered the Library looked homey but in your photo it really does and the mantle piece must be a great addition ... I am interested to see you have kept the old banisters to the moved staircase, how many times have I 'caught it' in progressing upstairs on the banisters instead of the stairs or for leaving my 10 commandments on the wall ... The back is greatly improved and more like the old G.B by the removal of the corridor. It will improve the whole place to change the front door. Some time I hope you will send me a photo. to put with the others of what Evie is doing with the front of the house and the drive. I can foresee great developments.

The removal of the corridor refers to relocation of the corridor from its former position, of running south from the entrance to the extensions of c. 1868, to form a covered loggia, the rear entrance to the house from Greenbank Lane being thereby altered and elongated. Another relative, Elfreda Lilian Rathbone (1871–1940), hoped that the alterations would have made the house drier – and that the cockroaches would have been successfully dealt with.[58] The Virginia creeper to the footman's bedroom in the back yard should not,

The library, with its new mantelpiece and fireplace, 1920.
(Reproduced courtesy of the University of Liverpool Library, RP XXV.4.2)

Hugh was advised, be allowed to reach the window, as it was a familiar ladder for rats (when corn was kept in the yard).

Surviving domestic notebooks[59] reveal that in the 1920s large areas of the house were decorated every year; in 1924 a new ceiling was added to the veranda, the hall distempered in green, the boudoir windows painted white, and the entrance hall and staircase also in green distemper. In 1925 the entrance hall was painted grey, and the meeting room and saddle room also decorated. In 1928 the camellia house and greenhouse were reglazed. In 1933 the servants' hall, maids' bedroom, pantry, cloakroom, lavatory, and bathroom were all decorated.

It is possible that the many modern, mostly Arts and Crafts-style, electric lights featured in the photographs Hugh Rathbone and his wife commissioned also date from their occupation of the house. It has been suggested that the influence of the Arts and Crafts Movement, also to be seen in the furniture and decorative arts pictured, may be associated with Hugh

The lounge hall and adjacent areas, 1920 (opposite top: looking towards the door to the kitchens; opposite bottom: looking towards the dining room door; above: looking towards the garden).
(Reproduced courtesy of the University of Liverpool Library, RP XXV.4.2)

Rathbone's younger brother, Richard Llewellyn Benson Rathbone (1864–1939), an eminent Arts and Crafts metal worker, specialising in brass and copper work from 1900, his three doors of beaten copper with Art Nouveau foliate designs for the Unitarian church in Ullet Road (to which the Renshaw Street congregation moved at this time) being among his most notable work.

Besides changes to the house, there is record of improvements to the grounds. Writing from Greenbank to Mrs Hugh Rathbone, then on holiday in Switzerland, in May 1921, E. M. Midgely reports that

> George is very happy poor lad and thinks he is much better: Brown [the gardener] says he can find him plenty of odd jobs to do. The greenhouse is all but finished and the carpenter will be leaving next week all being well ... The pink pearl rhododendrons and that rich red one are just perfection ... Whit Monday certainly was a great success both as regards

the Workshop-outing and also the crowds at Greenbank. Mr Willink has had the takings of the boat sent to him 13/9. Charles rowed valiantly all afternoon and was very hot! The people stayed until after 8 o/c.[60]

The following day she reported 'Miss Eleanor's visit to lunch today' and that Brown had made a wreath of azaleas and dark plum foliage for the funeral of James Alsop, the university's pro-chancellor, whose death had upset Hugh.[61] There are further references to Greenbank providing a venue for events in aid of local charities as in September 1925, the *Liverpool Echo* reporting on 'Dancing Nymphs,' a group of rhythmic dancers performing at Greenbank in aid of the Liverpool branch of the Women's Citizens' Association.[62]

Details of the buildings which comprised the Greenbank estate are given in a schedule provided by the Royal Insurance Co. in 1932.[63] Besides Greenbank

Corridor, 1920.
(Reproduced courtesy of the University of Liverpool Library, RP XXV.4.2)

House (insured for £6,250), there were the coach house, garage, and boiler house; stables, loose boxes, henhouses, pigsty, and stores; a brick-and-timber-built and slated henhouse; tool and potting shed; stable, barn, and shippon with a timber frontage; a private dwelling house (insured for £500); a greenhouse, conservatory, boiler house, and potting shed; corrugated iron and slated timber stores and laundry; two private cottages (each insured for £300, one occupied by the chauffeur); and a further shed with a corrugated iron roof. The total was insured for £9,050, the value assigned being what it was estimated it would cost to replace the buildings. The boiler house was probably built c. 1919–20 when a central heating system was installed in the house, as seen in the photographs of 1920 and the late 1930s. The coach house was presumably what was the old stable block.

Educated at Eton and at Trinity College, Cambridge, from which he graduated in Modern History in 1884, Hugh Rathbone had taken up a business career, entering the Liverpool office of Messrs Ross T. Smyth & Co., grain merchants and importers, of Liverpool, London, Hull, Manchester, and Glasgow, becoming a partner in 1889 and retiring in 1924.[64] In 1902 William Rathbone the sixth's youngest son, Frank Rathbone, joined Rathbones and, supported by Hugh Rathbone and Henry Gair Rathbone (another of William Rathbone's sons), in 1907 took control of the firm, which in 1912 was restructured to become a wealth manager, a financial services company with new offices in the recently opened Royal Liver Building.[65] In fact, in response to the period of decline the firm endured in the late nineteenth century, William Rathbone the sixth had latterly advocated the firm engaging in 'the management of investments.' By good fortune for the firm, Vere Cotton, who in 1910 had been recruited by Hugh Rathbone to act as tutor for his sons, in 1911 joined the firm as its 'financial analyst,' becoming what has been described as its mainstay for the next fifty years, retiring as senior partner in 1960, to be succeeded by Bertram Lyle ('Larry') Rathbone, one of Frank Rathbone's younger sons who had joined the firm in 1934.

From 1929 to 1937, Hugh Rathbone was chairman of the Maritime Insurance Company and, representing the Liverpool Corn Trade Association, from 1905 until 1933 he was a member of the Mersey Docks and Harbour Board. His extensive knowledge of the grain trade was put at the service of the government during the First World War, when he acted as a member of the Royal Commission on Wheat Supplies; from 1916 to 1920 he played a significant role in the national task of purchasing, transporting, and distributing huge supplies of grain required to meet the needs of Britain and her allies.

Hugh Rathbone's service as a lay officer of the University predated its formal establishment in 1903, succeeding his relative George Rathbone as deputy treasurer of University College Liverpool in 1898, becoming treasurer of the University Committee, charged with obtaining a charter for an independent University of Liverpool, in 1901. Uniquely, in succession he held the offices of University treasurer, 1903–18, president of the Council, 1918–24, before holding the most senior post under the University chancellor (the seventeenth Earl of Derby, 1909–48) of pro-chancellor, 1924–30. Such a long record of service was unequalled in the history of the University, his fellow Unitarian and major University benefactor, Sydney Jones, not quite exceeding the length of his service as an officer. Although, in his oration introducing pro-chancellor Hugh Rathbone for the award of an honorary doctorate of laws in 1925, the University's public orator asserted that he was not excelled in devotion and loyal service by any of his predecessors, he paid due tribute to 'the succession of outstanding leaders of the community who, as office bearers in the Council, have given unstintingly of themselves and of their means, in the promotion of its welfare and of its continued progress.'[66] Hugh Rathbone finally retired as a member of the University Council in 1936. In its farewell resolution, the Senate highlighted 'the admirable skill with which he fostered a spirit of unity, understanding, and good will in the different sections of the University.'

A 'Gifts Book' of the University records over sixty donations Hugh and his wife made over the period of 1904–46.[67] Of their financial contributions, one might single out £10,000 given in response to the University's major appeal in 1920 for £1m to meet the urgent need for new buildings and equipment and additional staff in the immediate aftermath of the First World War, and £5,000 given in 1919 to endow a lectureship in the School of Social Science. Donations towards the erection and equipment of buildings included a contribution towards the provision of triple expansion engines for the Engineering department (1904), £250 towards the Students' Union [building] Fund (1905) and £100 towards the furnishing of its Women's Wing (1911), and £1,000 towards the New Arts Building [now the Ashton Building] Fund (1912), besides their gift in 1929 of 4¼ acres of land on the Greenbank Estate as a site for a residential hall or college for students of either sex. Reflecting their particular interest in students and their accommodation, there was a steady stream of donations towards Rankin Hall (including funding of painting and decorating, donations of furniture and furnishings including candelabra for its dining hall, books for the library, and plants for the garden) and a few towards University Hall (the women students' hall), including a grandfather clock.

Though Hugh Rathbone's main interest, outside the business sector, was in the University of Liverpool, he had a wide range of interests, educational, philanthropic, political, and religious. In a series of account books, he carefully recorded the gifts he made each year to various charities, including Liverpool's voluntary hospitals, district nursing, the Domestic Mission, the Renshaw Street Chapel, the Florence Institute, the University Settlement, and other local charities, larger sums generally being given to the University.

Whereas in 1897–1901 in the region of £300–£400 was annually donated, sums in excess of £1,000 or, on occasion, £2,000, were recorded for later years; in 1915, during the war (in which Hugh's son, Richard Reynolds, served as a captain in the 6th King's Liverpool Rifles, being awarded the MC for conspicuous gallantry and initiative), of £2,673 gifted, the beneficiaries included the Belgian hospital, Prisoners of War, the Quaker Mission, Servian Relief, the Soldiers and Sailors Club, and the University's Officers' Training Corps.[68]

As a politician, Hugh Rathbone was true to the family allegiance. As a staunch Liberal and Free Trader, he fought three parliamentary elections as candidate for the Wavertree Division of Liverpool. At the general election of 1923, he defeated the Conservative and Labour candidates to take the seat, but at the subsequent general elections in 1924 and in 1929 he was unsuccessful. In his message to the electors of Wavertree in May 1929 he declared that 'The first thing to remember is that the main object of all political action is to make people happier; and therefore, its aims should be to remove all those things that tend to create unhappiness,' namely unnecessary unemployment, war, starvation, ill-health, unnecessary loss of life, slums, and bad housing.[69] If the age in which he lived saw the decline of the liberalism of the nineteenth century, 'in his own life [he] prolonged the virtues of its past, surrounding himself by his personal exertions with a kind of Indian summer of Liberalism.'[70] In reflecting on the changes in post-war Liverpool, the historian Philip Waller has noted the decline of the liberal plutocracy, Richard Holt (a partner in Alfred Holt & Co.) recording in 1924 that, at a service in Ullet Road Unitarian Church, he had sat between Sir John Brunner and Hugh Rathbone, 'such of the old fashioned Unitarian gentry as still survive'; in Philip Waller's assessment, 'the public service of the old Liberal Unitarian families was not so much exhausted as superannuated.'[71]

A cultured, well-read gentleman, it is no surprise to find among the surviving papers of Hugh Rathbone a printed programme for a concert at Greenbank marking the centenary of the death of Beethoven on 26 March 1927, those performing works by Beethoven, Brahms, Marcello, Mozart, and Vaughan Williams including Dr James E. Wallace, who was later to serve as lecturer in music in the University's School of Education.[72] An obituarist recalled that, though his interests were mostly of an active kind – sailing, walking, travel, and gardening – his 'sedentary pursuits' included painting in watercolours and, above all, reading the poetry of Wordsworth, himself a Liberal in thought.[73]

In 1936 the University library was the recipient of the first of two substantial donations of books from Greenbank's library which had belonged to several generations of the Rathbone family, reflecting the width of their intellectual and artistic interests; in the opinion of Hugh Rathbone and his wife, 'the most interesting books are those of our great-grandfather William Rathbone IV.' The second of the donations was made in 1940 consequent to the need to find a new home for generations of possessions upon the Admiralty's requisition of Greenbank at short notice. The books include those which reflect the literary, political, and social world of Liverpool in which the Rathbones played such a prominent role in the nineteenth century, works by Joseph Blanco White and William Roscoe (including his two volume *Life of Lorenzo de' Medici*, 1795) and others who visited the Rathbones, Edward Rushton's *Poems and Other Writings* (1824) with an inscription by the author to William Rathbone, and William Scoresby's *Journal of a Voyage to the Northern Whale-Fishery* (1823), also inscribed to William Rathbone the fifth. Also included in the donation were copies of the Revd J. H. Thom's *A Spiritual Faith* (1895) and Oliver Lodge's *Life and Matter* (1905). Descending from Hugh Rathbone's grandmother were a number of books reflecting the wide interests of her father, Joseph Reynolds (1768–1859), in the natural world, epic Scottish poetry, and ancient astronomy, books which later generations clearly felt of continuing interest and so retention. Hugh Rathbone wrote his name in books on a range of subjects, including education, a copy of Joachim Heinrich Campe's *Robinson der Jungere* (1842, originally published in 1779–80) – a pedagogical adaptation of Daniel Defoe's *Robinson's Crusoe*, including a new subplot designed to provide moral and educational instruction to young readers – being inscribed 'H. R. Rathbone, Beechwood, 28 Feb 1885.' Publications by Eleanor Rathbone included *The Ethics and Economics of Family Endowment* (1927) and *The Harvest of the Women's Movement* (1935). Also donated in 1940 were two 'large globes in mahogany frames.'[74]

Several sheets of 'Memorandums as to the history of some articles of interest at Greenbank,' which 'E.A.R.' (Mrs Emily A. Rathbone) compiled from 1896 onwards for the information of younger members of the family, help populate other parts of the house.[75] Of the stuffed birds, there was a puffin on the bookcases in the drawing room which was brought in about 1818 or 1820 by Dr Scoresby from an island which he discovered in the Arctic Ocean, north of Iceland, and called 'Rathbone island'; Professor Alfred Newton had informed her that it was in fact the little Auk in summer plumage. The mocking bird on the right of the bookcase was a pet bird which died of fright in a storm while the family was living in Bedford Street, Liverpool, before the birth of Philip H. Rathbone, William Rathbone the fifth's son, in 1828. In the centre was a hunting falcon which had been shot by Benson Rathbone senior (1800–44), son of William Rathbone the fourth, or had come from a collection of birds that he had made. 'The Rathbone Warbler' was associated with 'Plate 65 Audubon's big book,' a copy of which the family possessed. Of other natural history specimens, 'the whalebones in various places were brought from the Arctic by Dr Scoresby' while E. A. R. recorded the dimensions of a chestnut tree growing near the garden wall in 1896 and noted in September 1899 that she had seen a kingfisher on the railing by the pond, also water hens that year, the pond swarming with very big fish, carp and other species. From their Continental visits came embroidery bought at Alassio; a group of figures, women and children, framed as a picture; also two Russian bronzes of horses from Paris (International) Exhibitions. Presents to family members included an intaglio belonging to a ring inscribed 'Souvenir de Charles Jerome Buonoparte 1827,' presented to William Rathbone the fifth; two watercolours by Thomas Miles Richardson in the boudoir, a wedding present to William Rathbone the sixth from Thomas Ashton; and three Correggio engravings in the library which had been given by a former manager of the Borough Bank.

A Unitarian of national standing, Hugh Rathbone was a leading figure in the Ancient Chapel of Toxteth. During his years as chairman, the Chapel's meeting room was enlarged in 1918. For many years he was chairman of the National Conference of the Unitarian and Free Christian Churches, attending the centenary of the Unitarian Churches in America as a lay representative of the English Unitarian Association (of which he was president in the 1930s). Appropriately, given his interests in higher education, he was for some time president of Manchester College, Oxford, a Unitarian foundation (which more recently, as Harris Manchester College, has become a college of the University of Oxford) and a member of the Hibbert Trust. Mourned, on his death in January 1940, as 'a Christian politician,' his cremated remains were interred in the Ancient Chapel's little burial ground, in the presence of family members (including Eleanor Rathbone and Colonel and Mrs Vere Cotton), representatives of the city (Lord Mayor, Sir Sydney Jones), the University (the vice-chancellor, Dr Arnold McNair, also himself a fellow Unitarian; the deans of the faculties; the warden of Derby Hall; the presidents of the Guild of Undergraduates; and others), and the Anglican bishops of Liverpool and Warrington.

In a moving letter written in January 1939, to Hugh Rathbone, then in failing health, Florence MacCunn (widow of Professor John MacCunn), a family friend, recalled,

> in this University Movement you were so ardent a believer that a rather funny and very touching story was told about you. When you were so ill with typhoid that you were delirious the form it took was the belief that large sums had been left to the University – you were then Treasurer – you were rather disappointed when you realised the actual facts ... the Rathbones of your generation by <u>instinct</u> followed the family habit of finding their main interest in spreading freedom and justice for all men.

Top: Mr and Mrs Hugh Rathbone in the hall (late 1930s).
(Reproduced courtesy of the University of Liverpool Library, D.14)
Above: Mrs Emily Rathbone in the drawing room (late 1930s).
(Reproduced courtesy of the University of Liverpool Library, D.14)

Top: Hugh Rathbone in the library (late 1930s).
(Reproduced courtesy of the University of Liverpool Library, D.14)
Above: A bedroom (c. 1937).
(Reproduced courtesy of the University of Liverpool Library, D.14)

Dining room (late 1930s).
(Reproduced courtesy of the University of Liverpool Library, D.14)

> And in your youth – and in the perpetual youth of dear old Mr Rathbone –
> a new and fascinating element came into Liverpool and into the life of all
> of us – the spreading of a very high standard of learning, scientific and
> humanistic in a large important city.[76]

A friend of Hugh Rathbone wrote that he might not inaptly be described as
the urban counterpart of the ideal country gentleman, in his case finding
in his own city of Liverpool a full and happy outlet for his energies and his
ideals, with little patience with those who thought that life in the provinces
was narrower and less worthwhile than life in the capital; 'possessing great
personal charm, comfortable means, absence of private ambition, a keen
brain and a temperament in which Saxon caution and Celtic impetuosity were
nicely balanced, he was well equipped to play the important part which he did
in the life of Liverpool.'[77] A particularly touching letter was received by Hugh

Rathbone's widow from Vere Cotton, who had been originally recruited as tutor to the Rathbone children and to his surprise had been invited 'to enter RB & Co and make Liverpool my home,' recalling 'the charming courtesy with which he, a much older man, always treated me and his wide tolerance of views which on some points were diametrically opposed to his' (perhaps referring to his support of the Conservative party), and acknowledging that his association with the University was due to him and that 'it was from his example that I first realised I had civic responsibilities.'[78] Colonel Cotton was a member of Liverpool City Council from 1931 until 1955, serving as Lord Mayor of Liverpool in 1951–52; he took a particular interest in the Council's Libraries, Museums and Arts Committee, of which he was chairman, 1939–51. A member of the University Council, over the years from 1932 until 1954 he was successively vice-president of the Council, University treasurer, president of the Council, and pro-chancellor.

The gifts by Hugh Rathbone and his wife of sites for halls of residence of the University

Conscious of the need for more residential accommodation for its students, especially for its male students, who, since 1922, had occupied several houses leased by the University in Ullet Road, as Rankin Hall, and that the University was finding difficulty in finding a suitable site for the erection of a new residential hostel, on behalf of his wife and himself, in July 1929 Hugh Rathbone made a gift to the University of about 4¼ acres of land at the corner of Greenbank Road and Ibbotsons Lane.[79] In November 1925, the University Council had expressed its view 'that a large extension of the Hostel system is most desirable if students, especially those coming from a distance, are to receive all the benefits that they should from their University training,' regretting that the University lacked the resources to adapt and enlarge the buildings in Ullet Road or erect a new hostel. The vice-chancellor, Dr Hector Hetherington, and the then warden of Rankin Hall, Mr W. S. Angus, had made an exhaustive survey of possible sites, reporting that there were few, if any, suitable, near enough to the University. Though the gift was made without any conditions, save the erection of a boundary fence or wall separating the land from the rest of the estate, the Rathbones being anxious not to impose restrictions which in years to come 'might be onerous and unfortunate,' a 'gentleman's agreement' was reached. In a letter to the president of Council, Sydney Jones, Hugh Rathbone envisaged that the site would be primarily used for a residential hall or college for students of either sex, and in a letter to his son-in-law, Godfrey Warr, a London solicitor, he added that 'one would not like a great barracks of laboratories or a veterinary hospital or anything of that kind erected there.'[80] In sending a personal letter to Mrs Rathbone in June 1929, the vice-chancellor expressed the University's gratitude for her special share in the benefaction, her husband having let slip that the idea had originated with her; 'I hope that, before many years have passed, Greenbank will be flanked by a building in which you can have pride, and the amenities of your home safeguarded by a band of stalwarts who let no mischief come near you.'[81]

Appreciating that funds for the erection of the hostel might not be available for some time, the University assured Hugh Rathbone that in the meantime the site would not be ploughed up or cultivated but used as a recreation ground or as grazing land; and that when funds did become available, that it would be the special care of the University to see that the design and position of the buildings would be such that the amenities of Greenbank would not be interfered with in any way, an assurance which would be respected so long as any member of the Rathbone family remained in possession of Greenbank.[82]

'This University lags far behind other universities in its provision of hall accommodation for men,' declared the subcommittee responsible for Rankin Hall, in a report of 1936, adding that 'the educational value of residence in hall for students who come from poor home environments is profound.' In 1938 just 10 per cent of the University's students were resident in halls of residence; 20 per cent of students at Leeds, Manchester, and Sheffield were resident in hostels, and at eight other provincial universities the proportion was even greater.

The Men's Hall Sub-Committee considered a site for a new hall of residence in the light of the information which the vice-chancellor supplied, to the effect that at Newcastle, where the local 'Greenbank site' had been utilised, difficulty had been encountered in filling the new hall because of the distance factor. On behalf of the subcommittee, in 1936, Professor Harold Channon made investigations.[83] The Report of the University Grants Committee 1934–35 had revealed that of the universities of the Northern Group, Liverpool's facilities for halls of residence for men were very poor compared with those of other universities. Of the percentage of students living in halls of residence, Liverpool, with 20.9 per cent provided the least progressive figure save Sheffield's 10 per cent; further afield, Bristol had 61.6 per cent and University College, Exeter, 84.4 per cent. Whereas the majority of students at Rankin Hall walked to the University in thirty minutes, it was recognised that the distance to walk from Greenbank to the University would be too great, though some students might walk across the park to Croxteth Road terminus and take a tram from there, which would take forty minutes. On the subject of domestic staff, the Bursar of Rankin Hall reported that she was encountering considerable problems in maintaining a sufficient supply of maids at Ullet Road and that she believed such difficulties might be accentuated on a more distant site, at Greenbank, a suggestion which, on her copy of Professor Channon's report, Mrs Rathbone described as 'rubbish.' Professor James Chadwick, the Lyon Jones Professor of Physics, wrote to Hugh Rathbone, making a strong case for the Greenbank site, as providing room to develop, whereas a large enough hostel could not be built on the Ullet Road site without destroying some of its amenities such as the tennis courts; one hostel for 100–120 students would be insufficient for Liverpool, meaning that only one man in sixteen would have 'the opportunity of a full life as a student'; 'one must believe that the University will continue to grow and develop. A university which has no faith in its own future has no future.'[84]

It was thanks to the generosity of Hugh Rathbone and his wife, who had presented the site of the hall, and of Sir Robert Rankin and his brother, James Rankin, that it finally proved possible in 1938–39 to realise the long-cherished hope, the erection of the University's first purpose-built hall of residence, Derby Hall, named in honour of the University's greatly admired chancellor, the seventeenth Earl of Derby, who declared the hall open at an informal ceremony on 1 December 1939. Designed by a distinguished graduate of the University's School of Architecture, Harold Dod, of the firm of Willink and Dod, who had already been responsible for the Harold Cohen Library (opened in 1938), the academically respectable neo-Georgian architecture of Derby Hall and its adoption of a quadrangle plan, with porter's lodge built into the entrance archway, perhaps naturally led its early occupants to comment, not unfavourably, on the differences between this hall of residence and the colleges of Oxbridge.[85] In the first number of the *Blue Pigeon*, the magazine of the men's halls of residence, published in 1930, the vice-chancellor, Dr Hector Hetherington, had forecast that Rankin Hall would win for itself a sense of corporate unity and continuance and the move of the men students from Ullet Road to Derby Hall just as war was declared in September 1939 led also to the transfer of the customs and traditions which might be associated with the traditional college, such as the wearing of gowns for dinner, which began and ended with a grace. In the editorial of the June 1940 issue of *Blue Pigeon*, Frank Kermode, who was later to enjoy a very distinguished career as a literary scholar and critic,[86] made clear, however, that the University is an important and integral function of society and that if the hall was to be a worthy nucleus of the University, and not withdrawn from society, it would have to have a larger proportion than in the past of morally and politically mature persons.

Derby Hall proved a most popular hall with students and with conference organisers from an early date. During the war, short courses were held during the vacations by RAMC officers studying at the Tropical School, by the University's Senior Training Corps and Air Squadron, by members of the American and Canadian forces, and by many others. Such was the demand for accommodation in hall by students that, reluctantly, in 1944, it was laid down that the normal period of residence at the hall should be not more than two years, though by 1953 students living in lodgings in the vicinity were permitted to take some meals in the hall.

5   Debating the future of Greenbank

Already by the early 1930s, the future of the Greenbank estate was a matter of interest and concern on the parts of both the University and the Rathbone family. When in 1933 the University had acquired further land in Greenbank Road and Ibbotsons Lane for £5,050 from Hugh Rathbone, Vice-Chancellor Hetherington informed him that there was a very strong desire on the part of every member of the Investments Sub-Committee that if, by any chance, Greenbank should cease to be his family's residence, 'and may the day be long distant,' that the University should have the opportunity of succeeding him in the occupation of 'this fine and historic site.'[1]

In May 1935, Sydney Jones, president of the University's Council, having spoken to the vice-chancellor, wrote to his fellow Liberal and Unitarian, Hugh Rathbone, to welcome his idea that Greenbank, 'which is really the Birthplace of the University,' should be presented and finally belong to the University.[2] While suggesting that Hugh Rathbone might gift the property to the University and continue to remain 'the guardian of its traditions' during his lifetime, regretfully the University was not able to pledge that either the vice-chancellor or his successors would promise to live there; though there was such a desire, the future financial resources of the University were not so clear that it could pledge to keep up the place for the vice-chancellor or be able to continue his present stipend, much less increase it. (In the interwar years, Liverpool was in decline; by the early 1930s, it had become 'a stagnant city, commercially, administratively, and culturally.'[3]) Would Hugh Rathbone consider letting the University have the estate in the hope that financially it would be possible for the vice-chancellor to reside there and that at any rate the University would not use it for other than University purposes, perhaps to use the house as part of a hall of residence? In November 1932, writing from Nice, Henry G. Rathbone (a son of William Rathbone the sixth) had suggested to Hugh Rathbone that Greenbank might possibly become 'a Chequers for the Lord Mayor of Liverpool.'[4] It was in 1917 that Chequers Court, Buckinghamshire, which had been restored by Sir Arthur Lee and his wife, Ruth, was gifted by them to the nation, the house, collections, and estate being placed in trust for the use of future prime ministers. Ruth Lee felt that 'the affairs of the country really go better if the Prime Minister has a place of Peace and rest and beauty in bracing healthful air to go to at weekends where he can be refreshed and reinvigorated.'[5]

In a codicil to his will, in August 1936 Hugh Rathbone left Greenbank, together with the cottage attached to the house (in which his manservant lived), together with Bank Field and that part of the Long Field which had not already been sold to the University, to his three children in equal shares as tenants in common. In doing so, he expressed the hope that it might prove possible for his children to carry out the wishes he expressed in any memorandum signed by him.[6] As he had bought the property at the suggestion of his wife's father, she had felt that he should decide its future. At the time of writing the memorandum, also in August 1936, he observed that as the elder branch of the family (represented by William Rathbone the eighth and his family) had migrated to the south, and had all their friends and interests away from Liverpool, it seemed unlikely that they would wish to 'return to the home of their fathers.'[7] Writing in the *Liverpool Daily Post* in 1928, Hugh Rathbone had lamented the general drift away from Liverpool of the 'old money': without the great merchant families, the great record of voluntary contribution in social welfare and education could not be maintained; the Anglican cathedral and the university would be the last great achievements of 'private initiative and private generosity.'[8]

The whole value of the land on which Greenbank stood and its garden and small field Hugh Rathbone felt would probably be very moderate, probably not more than £3,000; rather the value of the property was one of tradition. 'If, therefore, the future owner is not willing to carry on that great tradition of social and public work for the benefit of the town, accompanied by a Liberal point of view in politics and religion, the tradition is lost, and therefore the value is merely the site value.' If no member of the family wished to live at Greenbank, then if his children decided that the University should inherit, he would be very satisfied, because 'after the interests of my family, the University has been, as you know, my chief interest and occupation outside my business life' as it had been of their grandfather, William Rathbone the sixth. Hugh Rathbone left the contents of Greenbank to his wife, subject to a memorandum listing so-called heirlooms to pass to the William Rathbones. A disincentive was that 'owing to the advance of the town, Greenbank as a private residence becomes yearly perhaps less attractive to anyone unless obliged to live in Liverpool for business, or to be near the University.'

The Second World War and the last days of Greenbank as the family home of the Rathbones

At the outbreak of war in September 1939, in order to know everything it could about the civilian population of England and Wales, the government arranged for registration forms to be issued to households, recording those present on 29 September. The return for Greenbank recorded eleven persons including Hugh and Emily Rathbone, Eleanor Rathbone (visiting Greenbank from her London home), together with Miss Stella Thornton, Hugh Rathbone's personal secretary, Miss Grace Drysdale (the household's sixty-nine-year-old cook), and other servants.[9] In the adjoining cottages, further employees and their families were recorded: Harold Burningham, chauffeur, and his wife and a parlour maid at the Cottage; John Brown, head gardener, and his family at Red Cottage; Isherwood Bentley, gardener, and his wife and a shop assistant at Pavilion Cottage; and William Thornborough, gardener, and his wife and son, at Westfield Cottage. As late as 16 November 1939, Mrs Hugh Rathbone was advertising for a kitchen maid, noting that six staff were employed in the household.

Following the death of Hugh Rathbone in January 1940, at short notice in October the Admiralty took over Greenbank for the duration of the Second World War for use as a hostel for the WRNS, such that his widow continued at Greenbank for only a short time before moving to Bishopton, later to Riverslea, Grassendale Park. Greenbank House was one of the thousands of houses requisitioned by the government during the Second World War. Clearly unaware of the imminence of the requisition of the property, on 20 August 1940, Mrs Rathbone advertised for a head housemaid, offering good wages for an experienced person, with three weeks' holiday, two with board wages.[10] Whereas in the aftermath of the First World War thousands of households had dispensed with the services of a maid living in, because of the cost, the Rathbones were still able to employ a large number of servants. A wages book records a total of five household staff in late 1932 and six in late 1935;[11] in autumn 1932, the wages of the housemaid were £55, the cook £52, the parlour maid £48, and the kitchen maid, afterwards the underhousemaid, £30, the monthly wages bill being £16/18/4d. In a tribute to Hugh Rathbone, Greenbank could be described as 'among the last of those Liverpool patrician houses which are still inhabited by the families who built them in the heyday of Liverpool at the end of the eighteenth century'; its setting in trees and grass was deceptively like the real countryside for 'apart from the grime which darkens its tree-trunks and shortens the freshness of the Spring,' it would be easy to believe the city of Liverpool was many miles away rather than surrounding it.[12]

As the last surviving member of the family of William Rathbone the sixth, Mrs Emily Rathbone died, aged eighty-nine, in July 1954. When in 1945 the University conferred an honorary degree of doctor of laws upon her, tribute was paid to her character: 'at all times and in all things, she has enlivened her industry with a shrewd but unmalicious humour, which has sharpened the flavour of her benevolence and deprived controversy of all bitterness.'[13] What 'the management of a great house and works of charity' had left of her energy had been applied to 'public affairs.' Nourished by her Unitarian faith, Liberal principles and family tradition, she took up and with determination promoted a number of causes.[14] In 1917, she and her husband had bought the Crofton estate, the house being used as a war hospital; in 1922, she gave Crofton and some of the land to the trustees of the Liverpool Hospital Saturday Fund, to be used as a hospital of recovery for women – the first women's hospital as such – for patients too ill for a convalescent home but not ill enough to be kept in hospital. She served as chairman of the hospital's committee from 1930 until 1943. She followed her father in the interest she took in district nursing, serving as a member of the Council of the Liverpool Queen Victoria District Nursing Association and loaning her cottage on the Menai Straits to the nurses for their summer holidays. Her deep compassion for the suffering and her love of children found expression in her support of the Cripples Workshop (which after the Second World War was reorganised, as the Sir Robert Jones Memorial Workshops) and 'The Children's Rest,' a home for crippled and invalid children, which just before the First World War moved to the house which was formerly the Greenbank Boys School, serving as president of both charities. As a member of the congregation of the Ancient Chapel of Toxteth, she helped its Domestic Mission and encouraged the development of its Sunday School.[15]

The last days of Greenbank as a family home are chronicled in the letter which Emily Rathbone wrote to Ruby Rathbone, wife of Hugh Rathbone's cousin, George, on 31 November 1940:

> I am taking a day's rest in bed after three weeks of the most strenuous work I have ever had to do even in my young days. We would never have got through it had it not been for the good nights in 'bed'. Greenbank is absolutely stripped. We arrived at 9.30 a.m. yesterday, after the most hellish night Liverpool has had to endure since the War began, to find the windows to the garden *gone*. All the huge plate glass windows lying in the garden!! All round Edge Hill there are whole streets gone altogether. It is like Coventry, only Liverpool is more scattered and lots of the land mines fell in parks and gardens, like Greenbank, and did not fall on human habitation. Oakfield [Eleanor Rathbone's Liverpool home] is stuffed with our furniture and had all the windows on two sides damaged. Eleanor came to Greenbank last night and I left her to sleep on the couch in Hugh's study which is the last remnant of comfort and is left for the Wrens. She is living in Tufton Court, Westminster, close to her old address which is still standing but not fit for human habitation ... Liverpool is a sorry sight after last Thursday night. Not a window left in all Croxteth Road and the end of Lodge Lane, and about six big houses at the end of Lodge Lane, including the Bank. Mossley Hill looks almost deserted. All the windows out and most of the people gone. In Aigburth, Ashfield Road – six houses gone. The land mines damage one quarter of a mile all around and one fell

there. Only five windows left in Crofton Hospital. We found the parachute of the Greenbank land mine in the trees in Ibbotsons Lane … The marvel is so comparatively few people were killed or injured.[16]

After London, Liverpool was the city worst hit by the intensive bombing campaign against Britain in 1940–41, Merseyside being raided on seven successive nights during the 'blitz' of May 1941.

In response, Ruby Rathbone penned the following memorial[17]:

Greenbank
June 1787–December 1940

Hail and Farewell! –
Thou happy gracious home –
The ever open door, to young and old,
To rich and poor, is closed at last;
Closed to us all, who loved thee –
The long line of gracious womanhood
And noble men, who lived within
Thy walls is cut: No longer
Can they pass the torch of justice
And of Service down the years.
Another generation, other aims, and War
With all its misery and sin, replace
Within thy walls, the happy times of Peace:
Let us Remember we have <u>had</u>
Those years, that kindness, and that
Friendship – and give thanks.

At about the same time, Ethel Whitehead, a granddaughter of William Rathbone the fifth, wrote to Evie (Mrs Hugh Rathbone) commiserating with her 'rescuing so much just in time' and remembering Greenbank as 'a paradise of happy memories,' later as 'treasure house of family traditions,' recollecting it 'beautiful and unscathed with you and Hugh giving us tea in the hall below the Polar Bears.'[18]

Mrs Rathbone endeavoured to give what help and support she could to the Wrens stationed at Greenbank. In a letter of September 1942, Margaret Cooke (responsible for both Greenbank as well as Oakfield) wrote to thank her for the dance tickets she had sent them, also the first instalment of stair rods: 'it will make such a difference if we can get a carpet down on the stone stairs in the winter.'[19] She also reported that she had been trying very hard to get the big lawn looking like a lawn and would be recruiting a man to scythe the rest of the grass so that it might be mown properly the next year. A further insight into Greenbank during its occupation by the WRNS is provided in the letter of January 1943 that Sybil Rathbone wrote to her mother-in-law on her journey home:

> with two SRNS – one from 'Ackerly' ... which is what they call the Children's Rest. They are at great rivalry with Greenbank she tells me and consider themselves superior in every way! I heard all about Mrs Roosevelt and how she did her broadcast from the ante-room there ... Mrs Roosevelt said the Children's Rest was the warmest home she'd been in in England and she was much interested in the inscriptions over the cots. I hear the Greenbank WRNS keep Basil Rathbone's photograph displayed and declare it was his house or at any rate that he lived there – so I undeceived the lady and she said she would tell the girls. She was rather a nice girl (not particularly high class!) who keeps a red Setter dog at the Children's Rest.[20]

(A Shakespearean stage actor, Basil Rathbone, MC [1892–1967] achieved worldwide fame for his portrayal of Sherlock Holmes in fourteen Hollywood films made between 1939 and 1946; he was a great-grandson of William Rathbone the fifth.)

The gift by the children of Hugh Rathbone of Greenbank to the University

Given the wartime situation, it was impossible to predict what conditions would be like at the end of the war – 'Greenbank itself may not be standing' observed Colonel Vere Cotton, one of Hugh Rathbone's executors, in December 1941, in advising one of Hugh's children that it would be wise not to delay a decision as to the future of Greenbank, it being unlikely that their mother would wish to return.[21] After a long discussion, all three children wrote to their mother in spring 1943 to report that they had come to the unanimous conclusion that they should like Greenbank to be given to the University, as a free gift.[22] They had previously declared that none of them wanted to 'sell at a fancy price nor to sell to a speculative builder nor do any other iniquity of that sort!,' suggesting that the University might perhaps make an offer for the property.

The deed of gift and trust deed conveying Greenbank, with its garage, yard, and gardens, a total of slightly over 5 acres in all, by way of gift, in memory of Hugh Rathbone, to the University, was dated 17 May 1944.[23] Hugh Rathbone's three children, Dame Hannah Mary Reynolds Warr of Kensington, London, Richard Reynolds Rathbone, of Pulborough, Sussex, and Hugo Ponsonby Reynolds Rathbone, of Royston, Hertfordshire, conveyed the property to the University 'to be retained and used by the University as a residence for the Vice-Chancellor of the University or other member of the staff or Graduate Students of the University or for such other purposes in connection with the educational work of the University as the Council of the University shall from time to time determine.' On its behalf, the University covenanted 'that no buildings shall at any time be erected on the said land except buildings to be used for the purposes of the University and that no building now erected or which may hereafter be erected thereon shall be used for any other purpose,' and that 'so far as may be reasonably practicable nothing shall at any time be done which would cause "Greenbank" to lose its 18th Century character.' Concerned to safeguard Greenbank 'from damage by trespassers or neglect or any other cause,' in letting land abutting on Greenbank Lane with 'Red Cottage' and including the Greenbank kitchen garden, greenhouses, potting sheds, barn, and loft over the stable to John Brown in March 1945, the University required him to maintain the kitchen garden, including the pruning of the fruit trees, and to keep all walks and pathways in good order.[24]

For many years, the University's Department of Botany had felt the need for a small garden for systematic beds for teaching, for the growing of plant stocks, and for the housing of fairly large experimental shrubs. Unlike botany departments in many other universities, Liverpool had never had such a garden. Before the war, Professor John McLean Thompson (Holbrook Gaskell Professor Botany, 1921–52) had made investigations of other universities' garden provisions and in October 1938 he suggested to the vice-chancellor that the walled garden at Wyncote, at Allerton, where the University's Geoffrey Hughes Athletic Grounds were situated, might prove suitable.[25] The intervention of the war delayed consideration of this suggestion but shortly after the end of the war in Europe, in June 1945 the University's Departmental Grants Committee viewed with sympathy the recommendation of the Faculty of Science that a departmental garden be provided for the Department of Botany. Professor McLean Thompson was able to report that Greenbank House's walled kitchen garden of about three-quarters of an acre had a range of three glass-houses, together with potting sheds and other structures which were hidden within the kitchen garden or stood behind it, also a pool 'of some usefulness.' Within the garden yard, there was an additional small greenhouse. Close by was the 'original Rathbone Garden,' of about 3¾ acres, which Professor Thompson had known at one time 'as a thing of beauty and of some richness in trees and shrubs'; following a long period of inattention, he was surprised to find that 'many interesting trees and shrubs have suffered little' and that it still held 'noteworthy herbaceous plants in various positions,' in a 'well-planned and tranquil garden,' whose restoration he strongly advocated. He was satisfied that the kitchen garden was of a sufficient area for the department's immediate purposes for teaching and research and that its natural extension was the Rathbone garden. Mr Brown had informed him that five gardeners had generally been available for the maintenance of the gardens as a whole.

The officers of the University Council approved in principle the proposal that the kitchen garden be used as a departmental garden 'provided that the scheme is a simple one,' and Council in April 1946 approved the appointment of two gardeners in the department 'subject to the formal approval by Council of a Scheme for the development of a Departmental garden.' Though Professor Thompson supplied a provisional plan and sketch map for the grounds, estimating an annual expenditure of £2,500 (including the employment of a head gardener and four journeymen gardeners), besides capital expenditure (including a new heating system for the greenhouses), and the Fabric Department commenced some enquiries, in February 1947 Charles Stewart, the assistant registrar, wrote to Professor Thompson regretting to inform him that 'the matter' must be regarded as 'indefinitely deferred since the Council's recent decision on the necessity of building additional Student Hostels makes it necessary to consider whether the garden at Greenbank may not have to be included in the site of one of the new buildings.' Though a great disappointment to Professor Thompson, in 1948 Ness Gardens, in the Wirral, were generously presented to the University by Miss A. L. Bulley, together with a house and a handsome endowment, part of the grounds and most of the greenhouses being reserved by the University for experimental work, of considerable value to the work of the Botany department in the years ahead.

Greenbank House as an annex of Derby Hall of Residence

In November 1946, the University's newly established Development Committee discussed the future use of Greenbank, inviting Mr Harold Dod, a graduate of the University who had already been responsible for the design of the Harold Cohen Library (opened in 1938), to submit alternative plans and estimates of cost for adapting Greenbank as a temporary hostel for students and for converting it into a permanent residence for the vice-chancellor.[26] The president of the Council, Colonel Vere Cotton, and the University treasurer, Sir John Hobhouse, were of the view that it would be wasteful to spend money on the adaptation of Greenbank to provide temporary hostel accommodation, preferring to press on with all speed with the erection of a new wing at Derby Hall, and indeed at subsequent meetings Harold Dod submitted plans for such a wing, to accommodate approximately forty students, and a treasury grant in aid of the erection of such a building was sought in 1948. The policy of the Development Committee in the immediate post-war period was to develop residential areas outside the University precinct; in the City's Development Plan, an area around Derby Hall of about 38 acres was scheduled for the University, for hostels.[27] The Committee was informed that the estimated cost of converting Greenbank as 'a temporary auxiliary hostel' for a maximum of twenty-one students was £2,000 and for use as residence for the vice-chancellor, £6,000. Within two months of the Committee deciding that it would be better to adapt the house for use as a vice-chancellor's residence rather than incur the cost of a temporary conversion for a period which might be as short as one session, Sir Sydney Jones died in February 1947, leaving his home (and its contents), Eastbourne, Princes Park, to the University, 'for such purposes as the Council of the University shall think fit,' the University determining that it should become the vice-chancellor's official residence, the Vice-Chancellor's Lodge (with a postal address of 12 Sefton Park Road). Accordingly, on the assumption that an annex to Derby Hall would be in use for not less than five years, Harold Dod was instructed to submit plans and obtain estimates.

In June 1947, the Halls of Residences Joint Committee approved the plans for the conversion of Greenbank.[28] Donald A. Coult, a lecturer in botany, was appointed senior tutor, to be responsible for discipline in the Greenbank Annex, besides giving general assistance in the administration of Derby Hall, whose new warden, Professor David Seaborne Davies (Professor of Common Law, 1946–71) was shortly to take up his post. The senior tutor was to be given a remuneration of £75 (per session), together with free board and lodgings at Greenbank, £10 of his remuneration being regarded as an entertainment allowance. Over the course of the next year various alterations were made to the property and its furnishing to supply the needs of its planned twenty-nine residents.

As a member of the Halls Joint Committee, Mrs Rathbone took a particular interest in the conversion of Greenbank, expressing her regret that objects of such artistic value as the Adam fireplace had to be encased to preserve it from all possible damage. She was assured that a temporary wall would not be in contact with the mahogany bookcase and that there would be a wooden partition edged with felt between the temporary wall and the bookcase, so that the mahogany would not be damaged. (The former library has been described as the most complete room within the house, the inlaid and veneered Regency-style floor-to-ceiling bookshelf with cupboards below being the only piece of original fitted furniture to survive in the house; the fine classical marble chimney piece was added by Hugh Rathbone c. 1920.[29]) The task set the architect was that of accommodating the maximum number of students in Greenbank without involving the University in difficult and costly structural alterations. The use of light partitions which could be removed without damage to the original moulding and walls would allow the house to be restored to its previous condition. In the course of conversion, besides the subdivision of several rooms, the main entrance on the east side was blocked up. To provide extra accommodation, the room formerly used as a pantry was converted into living accommodation for two students, and an attic room let to a student. Such was the pressure on student accommodation that, in October 1949, of the 135 students at Derby Hall, two were temporarily housed in the warden's house and thirty-one students and the senior tutor at Greenbank. The house was rewired, electric fires and meters installed, and fire-doors fitted. In 1951 'experimental decorations of six rooms' were authorised.

The estimate for furnishing Greenbank, at a cost of £6,350, was based on supplying the residents with the same type and amount of furniture as provided at Derby Hall, where all main meals, including breakfast, would be served; a piano and a radiogram were to be purchased for the public rooms. Individual members of the Halls Committee generously made gifts in kind – Mrs C. O. Stallybrass, a table-tennis table for the Games Room, and Mrs Rathbone, further gifts to the halls: framed prints, three old German decorative panes for a window at Greenbank, also shrubs.

To look after the garden at Greenbank, George Timms was employed as a gardener at a wage of £4/10/- per week, his work overseen by Derby Hall's head gardener, Mr Ricketts, a night watchman being additionally employed as an extra gardener during the vacation. In 1957, on the appointment of a new head gardener, he was also assigned the role of caretaker and boilerman at Greenbank; as part of his duties, he was required to occupy the caretaker's cottage at Greenbank. It was suggested that the vegetable garden might supply Derby Hall with fresh vegetables.

Of the closing years of Greenbank as an annex of Derby Hall, Ron Green (BEng Hons Electrical Engineering, 1963) recollects that

> the interior of the house had seen better days but was still quite grand, the lovely curved staircase having a good banister rail for sliding down. The lounge was large and Reg [Davies, the resident warden] had to be very stern about not playing football in it because the ball tended to knock the pictures off the wall and make a din when it hit the piano. The cellar was strictly out of bounds but I did once get to sneak down there to look at all the wine storage racks ... There was a small galley kitchen with a cooker which we used to make toast in the evening ... Next to the kitchen there was a small cubicle (or cell) with a pay-phone; that was our communal 'cell-phone' ... The bathroom was towards the Greenbank Lane side of the house, its brick floor at a lower level than the entrance hall. The baths were all in cubicles as were the toilets. It was great sport to fill the baths to the point of overflow and then jump in and cause a tidal wave to spread throughout the whole area. There was a caretaker who fed the hot water furnace with coke. His objective always seemed to be to break his previous

best hot water temperature record. On one occasion, he had the pipes loudly knocking as the water was nearly at boiling point. He gleefully explained that it was due to a dead cat which he had tossed in along with coke. He apparently believed that cats had a higher calorific value than coke. In any case, it was often like a steam room down there.[30]

To better inform the students at Derby Hall, in 1949 R. A. Cordingley, the distinguished architectural historian, who at the time held the Chair of Architecture at Manchester University, contributed an article to the hall's Magazine, *Blue Pigeon*.[31] In a short account of three of Liverpool's small country houses and estates which had been absorbed into the outer suburbs and which now formed 'oases amidst a barren suburbia' – Childwall Hall, Hale Hall, and Greenbank – he suggests that, though there is no known architect of Greenbank, it was probably influenced by John Nash, architect of country houses in the Gothic manner, including Childwall and Hale halls. In contrast to Childwall Hall, 'the mock Gothic flavour' at Greenbank is gayer than at Childwall, 'the battlements frown genteelly on to the sloping lawn, the sundial, and the ornamental lake. But the casements and the dim religious air of the lakeside front is not retained on the south front, where, on the double verandah, with its full length casements, all is sweetness and light.' Even 'with its portioned library, its zealously pruned garden and its cinder tracked lawns,' Greenbank, as a University hostel, had, in its new lease of life, received 'a more civilized treatment than has either Childwall or Hale, with their wanton destruction or desolate decay.'

Professor Seaborne Davies established a unique relationship with his students, both those in the Faculty of Law and those (male) students resident at Derby Hall. On his retirement in 1971, one of his fellow professors wrote of him that 'in a university ..., where, however competent we may be, some as academics, some as administrators, a few even as both, there are too few that can impress themselves on staff and students alike as teachers, friends and personalities into the bargain.' He received many letters from his former students, reporting on their careers, inviting 'Prof.' to their marriages (and he was well known for his matchmaking), and reporting on their athletic achievements (particularly in rugby football in which he took a particular interest). At Derby Hall he exercised what a senior student described as a 'benevolent dictatorship.' In his homily to freshmen he was accustomed to stating that 'there are no wules and wegulations in this place. I am a Libewal,' though he expected his men to behave themselves and respect one another's freedoms. (He had served for a brief spell, in 1945, as Liberal MP for the Caernarvon Boroughs in succession to Lloyd George.) When in 1955 the principal of I. M. Marsh College of Physical Education at Barkhill Road, Liverpool, complained to him about hall students having removed the key from one of the College's outside doors at a dance they had attended, Seaborne Davies annotated the letter 'Where will the baby's dimple be? That is not the question! Where is the Barkhill key? If it is in Derby Hall or Greenbank, please return it <u>at once</u> to the Senior Student, Mr Jackson – who will be <u>delighted</u> to take it back. D.S.D.'[32]

The *Blue Pigeon* reported on the multifarious activities of the hall's residents, which included not only fielding rugby, soccer, cricket, tennis, table tennis, and billiards teams but also productions mounted by a dramatic society (founded in 1947), films projected by the Cine Society, the reading of plays by members of the Reading Society, and discussions organised by both the Discussion Group and the Evangelical Christian Union, besides the entertainments organised each Session – Fresher's Smoker, Formal and other dances, hops, and a Christmas dinner in hall. Though meals for those living at Greenbank were taken in Derby Hall, with gowns being worn for dinner, and students socialised there, a close bond was established among those forming the small community at Greenbank; as Ian Aitken (BA Hons English Language and Literature, 1963), resident at Greenbank from 1960 until 1963, recalls, 'we felt we were a breed apart; somehow we were privileged, special even.'[33] The 'togetherness' those who lived in Greenbank came to feel was illustrated by their participation in the Guild of Undergraduates' 'Rag Weeks'; the Greenbank 'float' 'wasn't part of the general mayhem and wouldn't have won first prize. In truth, it was a less than impressive contraption: Ron Green's Austin 7 dressed up for the occasion with one or two students sitting precariously on its roof. But it was ours!'

In the summer of 1952, Mr Reg Davies, a lecturer in the Department of English Language and Literature, and a tutor at Derby Hall, transferred to Greenbank as tutor-in-charge. In 1960, belatedly, he was given the title of senior (resident) tutor. An affectionate portrait of Reg Davies is provided by Ron Green who recollects, on arriving at Greenbank in autumn 1960, being greeted warmly by Mr Davies,

> who introduced himself and showed me round. He was always quite formal and used our full names. He took me to the room which I had been allocated and then said 'Now Ronald, we lock the outside doors at *** (I'm not sure of the actual time but it was quite late) but for when you come back later at night I'll show you where they climb over the wall and in through the window.' The preferred window was one below Reg's study so we had to be quite stealthy so as not to disturb him. Disturbing the occupant of the room was not a consideration. Reg was a cultured, kind and tolerant man who we all greatly respected. After a night out, having drunk too much ale, one could wake up with a hangover and find a glass of water and some Alka Seltzer tablets which Reg had placed at the bedside ... It was a custom for Reg to ask us in turn to join him in his study

for an evening coffee and biscuits. We would return his hospitality by asking him for afternoon tea in our rooms, with cakes or some crumpets which we toasted in the kitchen. Rhubarb and ginger jam was a favourite accompaniment for these teas.

Ian Aitken adds that

it seemed to us at the time that Reg was ill-equipped to offer advice or administer discipline to his hot-blooded charges who, not infrequently on a Saturday evening, returned from the Brookhouse on Smithdown Road rather the worse for wear, chanting in unison 'Here we are again, Reg, pissed as f...ing newts'. He reacted, as best he could, believing himself to be a good sport, with a peculiarly nervous and exaggerated laugh. Though we discovered, later, that Reg was only in his thirties, and still relatively young, he seemed to us of a different era and that he was out of his time, as we were beginning to be in ours. But we were fond of him notwithstanding, and he contributed to our Greenbank experience and our lasting memories.

A devoted member of the Church of England, following service as first warden of Gladstone Hall (1965–72) and of Roscoe and Gladstone halls (1972–86), Reg Davies was to retire, as reader in English literature, in 1983 to a home in Cathedral Close, in the shadow of the Anglican Cathedral; his services to the University (not least as founder-chairman of The Friends of the University of Liverpool, 1984–2000), to the world of scholarship, and to the wider community were recognised when the degree of Doctor of Letters, honoris causa, was conferred upon him in 2000. Reg Davies died in 2002, remembered with gratitude for all the pastoral work he unobtrusively undertook for the diocese of Liverpool; through his involvement with the University's Anglican Chaplaincy and the Diocesan Higher and Further Education Committee, he had acted as a sort of bridge between the diocese and the University.

The constant need for repairs to an old building is reflected in the minutes which dwell on the subject – in 1951, guttering repairs and the cleaning out of the Greenbank pond by Liverpool Corporation workmen following its pollution; in 1953, the reflagging of paths, repair of the boiler (a constant subject of concern), and repair to the moulding over one of the bay windows; in 1958, repairs to a damaged wall in the bathroom; and in 1960, the renewal of gutters and fall pipes around the cycle shed. Security was also a concern: on the night of 31 December 1952, burglars broke into two rooms, stealing some student residents' belongings and damaging the fabric and wardrobes. 'In view of the number of burglaries and thefts in Derby Hall recently and the

Opposite top: Mr Reg Davies (seated, in the centre) and students resident at Greenbank House
(? 1953–56).
(Reproduced courtesy of the University of Liverpool Library, D.526/1)
Opposite bottom: Derby Hall students resident at Greenbank House, c. 1962.
(Photograph courtesy of Ian Aitken)

building operations in progress nearby,' in 1958 the doors of students' rooms were fitted with Yale locks. Perhaps coincidentally, nearby a new men's hall of residence, to be named 'Rathbone Hall,' was nearing completion. In 1958, it was additionally reported that 'rats were giving trouble in Greenbank.'

Greenbank House as a social centre – Greenbank House Club

In the knowledge that the new annex of Derby Hall, which would provide additional accommodation for students, including those who would transfer from Greenbank, would probably be ready for occupation by January 1962, the future use of Greenbank was discussed.[34] The Development Committee had proposed that it be used as a social centre for students living in the halls of residence and in lodgings nearby. On the Greenbank site, besides Rathbone Hall, two further halls, Gladstone and Roscoe halls, were erected in 1962–65, all set in a superb landscape of mature forest trees and gently sloping lawns executed to the design of Arnold Weddle, the University's landscape consultant. The development of the new halls was planned so that the buildings were placed towards the periphery of the site, leaving a large open space in the centre; in creating a single parkland landscape, the ha-ha, marking the edge of the old Victorian garden, was one of the landscape features preserved in the new design.[35]

The comments submitted by staff members were unanimous in support of such a social centre being established. Professor Robert Steel felt strongly that in the Greenbank area 'something of the communal life that is proper to the University during those hours when there is little or no life in the precinct itself' should be established. Facilities should be made available to all members of the University, including members of staff 'who are anxious to have a meeting point with the students away from departments.' Writing in March 1961 from Rathbone Hall, where he was now warden, Donald Coult deplored that there was 'nowhere in this University where students and older members of the University can sit down quietly and informally in the evening and take a meal together'; it would help a great deal if a small dining room could be booked for a simple meal: this could be used by moral tutors and their students living in the area and would also be valuable for twenty-first birthday parties 'and similar celebrations, of which in the nature of things we experience a plethora.' With a significant increase in the University population, a fair proportion of it in the Greenbank area, Professor Steel advocated much more integration of those living in lodgings and in halls of residence, with an ultimate aim of every student being attached to a hall, including those living at home. Anne Caunt, a lecturer in bacteriology, wrote that 'the few students who I know who live in lodgings in the area say their greatest need is for somewhere to meet their friends for an evening coffee occasionally.' As resident tutor at Greenbank, Reg Davies felt that staff-student relations would benefit from a common meeting ground, use of which was 'as of right' on both sides and that its potentialities as a 'social centre' were very considerable. For Dr Stanley Kennett, the major emphasis on the use of the house should be 'on activities which bring members of the teaching staff and students together.'

Present residents of Greenbank expressed the view that it should not lose its character as a house, the home of a rich, liberal, and benevolent family, its original features being restored as far as possible; but if it was to be felt to be a house, it must be lived in, Reg Davies arguing that residents would provide continuity and 'that sense of homeliness that is so important in achieving student confidence'; besides, such residents would also be able to 'supervise student activities which might, otherwise, rapidly deteriorate into those of an inferior sort of Union.'

A member of the University Council, Mr G. P. Holt, looked over Greenbank, leading him to argue strongly that it should be preserved and properly maintained in something approaching its original form, expressing his concern at the 'somewhat shabby and unpainted appearance of some of the exterior'; it would be a tragedy if the University, 'which is intended to be the nurse of culture, should demolish or neglect a building of this sort.'

Among the facilities which it was suggested should be provided at the 'social centre' were baths ('digs are often deficient in this and students put it as a very high priority'), laundering facilities ('particularly in these days of drip-dry fabrics'), coffee bar, licensed bar, and buffet bar, lounges (one with television), papers room, a library, a music room (acoustically sealed), games rooms (perhaps the attics and rooms over the bathrooms), rooms which could be made available for meetings of student groups or for staff members wishing to entertain groups of students, and accommodation for a resident caretaker and his wife to run the catering. The Halls of Residence Committee also had the benefit of the knowledge of the recreational facilities at several Oxford colleges which Mrs Lewis (Miss Jill Morton) and her husband conveyed.

The Halls Joint Committee accepted unanimously the view that Greenbank could be used as a social centre, believing that the time was ripe for a more experimental approach to staff-student relationships, and that it could be of special value to students who lived fairly near but had no association with a hall; 'the Greenbank Centre may well prove to be a testing ground and an apathetic reception by staff or students would inevitably affect future policy.'

An ad hoc committee appointed by the University Council and chaired by the vice-chancellor, Sir James Mountford, was assigned the task of considering the future of Greenbank in the light of the recommendations that had already been made. Recognising that the University had a responsibility for Greenbank's preservation and appropriate use, it was noted that the architect for the two new halls (Roscoe and Gladstone) had not incorporated it in his scheme. The Building (General Purposes) Sub-Committee, assisted by Dr J. Quentin Hughes (senior lecturer in the School of Architecture) as architect, had prepared a scheme for the conversion, for use as a social centre for members of staff and students. The choice of Dr Quentin Hughes was particularly appropriate; in 1964, the year he converted Greenbank House, he published *Seaport: Architecture and Townscape in Liverpool*, 'the first book to show the importance of British nineteenth century cities and the need to conserve their architectural wealth,' as he was to note in his later publication, *Liverpool, City of Architecture* (The Bluecoat Press, Liverpool, 1999) which features Greenbank House and many other buildings; in 1999 he was appointed OBE for services to architecture and conservation in northwest England. As a first step, it was agreed that a common room, part of the residential accommodation for a steward, and a snack bar and licensed bar, together with toilets and cloakrooms might be provided on the ground floor. Dr Quentin Hughes stressed his conviction that, in addition to the essential work of making good the exterior of the house and the electrical wiring, five of the six remaining rooms on the ground floor should be redecorated 'to ensure an air of purpose and activity.' Bertram Nelson, vice-president of Council, welcomed the proposals for a social centre, as a means of preserving a charming, historic house and providing an admirable experiment in bringing people together, as the vice-chancellor had advocated in his speech at the annual meeting of the Court. In his final address to the Court in November 1962, before his retirement, Sir James Mountford had spoken of one of the problems of the future that he foresaw, that with a greatly expanded University (to be expected when the Robbins Committee on Higher Education reported), the University would find it increasingly difficult to 'preserve our sense of unity'; 'if we are not going to be spiritually, intellectually and academically ruined by mere size,' it was very important 'that each one of us should consciously take every possible step to foster within the University a living sense of homogeneity, of unity, and of belonging one to the other.'[36]

In June 1963, Senate and Council agreed rules for Greenbank House Club. The management of the Club was to be entrusted to a Management

Committee comprising a chairman, two representatives each of the Council, the Senate, and the full-time academic staff (other than professors), together with five persons elected annually by the ordinary members of the Club.[37] All members of the University were eligible to become ordinary members, together with such other persons as the Committee elected. Provision was made for temporary membership and for ordinary members to introduce guests (though ordinarily not more than eight times in any one year). The annual subscription was initially fixed at ten shillings (fifty pence). The Club was to be open daily between 11.00 a.m. and 11.00 p.m. and the permitted hours for the supply of intoxicants were to be from 12.00 noon to 3.00 p.m. and 5.00 p.m. to 10.30 p.m. on weekdays and from 12.00 noon to 2.00 p.m. and 7.00 p.m. to 10.00 p.m. on Sundays, Christmas Day, and Good Friday.

At its first meeting, in June 1964, the Management Committee, chaired by Dr Nicholas Rast (senior lecturer, later reader, in geology), agreed that the Club's emphasis should be social rather than cultural, providing a meeting place for staff and students on a common footing, also providing recreational facilities for the large student population living in the Mossley Hill area, particularly for students in lodgings. The creation of an atmosphere which would attract both staff and students and their spouses to use the Club regularly was seen as a vital part of its functions; it was noted that the Robbins Report on Higher Education had recommended that 'universities should provide facilities for social contact between staff and students.' The University had agreed to be responsible for the fabric and for its interior and exterior redecoration and for an additional financial responsibility up to £1,000 annually.

After several months of sustained effort by the Management Committee and Dr Quentin Hughes, the Club opened on 1 December 1964, licensed, staffed, furnished, lighted, and heated. An advertisement for experienced bar staff was placed in the local press, offering good wages and working conditions, a forty-two-hour week, with opening in the evenings and Saturday and Sunday lunchtimes.[38] Major A. E. Smith, MBE, and his wife, who had been appointed to the joint post of resident steward and rendered good service in the early, difficult days, resigned within a few months, to be replaced in March 1965 by Gordon Milne (previously head barman at the Clifton Hotel, Southport) and his wife, Lillian. Because of the physical limitations of the size of the premises, the initial invitation to join the Club was restricted to members of the Council, the academic, senior administrative, and library staffs, post-graduate students, undergraduates in their third or more senior years (faculties of Arts, Science, Engineering, and Law), fourth or more senior years (faculties of Medicine and Veterinary Science), and to their spouses. Of a potential 3,500 to 4,000 members, 1,050 (including 280 members of staff and their spouses) had by the end of the year applied and been admitted

Top: Main entrance, Greenbank House Club, 1964.
(Reproduced courtesy of the University of Liverpool Library, P.8049)
Above: Looking toward Rathbone Hall, 1966.
(Reproduced courtesy of the University of Liverpool Library, P.8049)

Top: The south (Victorian) and west (Gothic) wings, 1969.
(Reproduced courtesy of the University of Liverpool Library, P.8049)
Above: The south elevations of the Victorian and Gothic wings, 1966.
(Reproduced courtesy of the University of Liverpool Library, P.8049)

to membership. Regrettably, the Committee had also to record damage by vandals – windows in the house broken and lead stripped from the roof of an outhouse.

Such was the success of the Club that by January 1966 the Management Committee had to introduce restrictions to ameliorate the overcrowding that frequently occurred as more members wished to use Greenbank during the evenings. Henceforth, the whole premises were not generally to be available for private functions during term and the ballroom was not to be available for private functions on Friday nights during term; at least one room was always to be available for ordinary members. Already, an impressive range of social functions, parties, dances, and meetings had been held over the previous months – twenty-first birthday parties of students (including for Paula Clyne, Lady President of the Guild of Undergraduates, 1964–65, herself an elected member of the Management Committee); a private dance (with band) for Alan Hudson Davies (a long-standing member of the University Council) and his wife; a wedding reception; a coffee morning of the University Women's Guild; a Graduation Ball for the Medical Students' Society; a Summer Ball

Small lounge, Greenbank House Club, 1964.
(Reproduced courtesy of the University of Liverpool Library, P.8049)

Opposite top: Small bar, 1964.
(Reproduced courtesy of the University of Liverpool Library, P.8049)
Opposite bottom and above: Large bar, 1964.
(Reproduced courtesy of the University of Liverpool Library, P.8049)

and a Christmas Ball, experience showing that 150 was the optimum number of tickets to be sold so that members might dance, drink, and eat in comfort. Arrangements had been made to enable those attending vacation conferences at the halls of residence who wished to use Greenbank's facilities to become temporary members of the Club. Greenbank was also fulfilling its intended role of providing a meeting place for staff and students on a common footing.

In his final year at the University and living at home, Dr Bill Shannon (BA Hons Geography, 1965) recollects that on a Sunday evening he and his future wife (who had spent her first two years at University Hall and was then in digs off Edge Lane) used occasionally to go to Greenbank, to meet a friend, living in Rathbone Hall, and his girlfriend, and that sometimes they would see and have a drink with Bill Rollinson, who had been their tutor in their first year in Geography.[39] As Dr Shannon acknowledges, it was Bill Rollinson who first got him interested in place-names and landscape history, leading to subsequent doctoral research and a series of publications relating to cartographic history and landscape history, with particular reference to the north-west of England.

Originating in the post-First World War era, what became the University of Liverpool Women's Club for many years arranged tea parties for its members, the summer tea forming a special occasion in the post-Second World War period. In 1955, according to *The University of Liverpool Recorder*, full membership of the Ladies Tea Club (the title being changed to Women's Club in 1964), was open to 'wives of members of Council, of academic staff and senior admin-istrative staff and to women academic staff.'[40] Usually held in one of the University's halls of residence, from 1972 until 1985 Greenbank House became the attractive setting for what was by then known as the 'Cream Tea.' Between 1979 and 1984, the event was made free to all members, including those who had retired. As Dr Anne Clough records, 'Part of the summer tea's attraction was no doubt the fare of strawberries and cream, which husbands were invited to share.' By the time of the famous occasion, perhaps in 1977, when no strawberries were available and bananas were successfully substituted, the Club's committee had for some years been adding home-cooked items to the basic tea; it was objections to this policy that were to lead to a split with Greenbank in 1986, the Vice-Chancellor's Lodge henceforth being established as the venue for the Cream Tea day.

Away from the University precinct, Greenbank provided a particularly attractive venue for meetings involving visitors to the University. Professor Christopher Allmand, who joined the staff of the Department of Medieval History in 1967, particularly recollects Greenbank as the place where Liverpool's medievalists used to hold seminars, on Saturdays, with their like-minded colleagues from the north-western universities (Keele to Lancaster) once or twice a year; very pleasant occasions, socially as well as academically, two or three papers were delivered, contributions from 'advanced' research students also being encouraged.[41] Mrs Priscilla Bawcutt recalls that the University's Centre for Medieval Studies also held some meetings at Greenbank; one meeting, sadly, was a near fiasco.[42] A distinguished medieval historian from Nottingham had been invited to lecture on an aspect of Anglo-Saxon England, but the audience was pathetically and uncharacteristically small – only four. They were told that many more would have been present if they had not been demonstrating in London with the slogan 'Rectify the Anomaly,' an Association of University Teachers lobby of Parliament on 15 November 1977. Greenbank also

Opposite top: Common room, 1964.
(Reproduced courtesy of the University of Liverpool Library, P.8049)
Opposite bottom: Ballroom, 1964.
(Reproduced courtesy of the University of Liverpool Library, P.8049)

provided the venue for a colloquium on the Trojan War which was organised by Professor John K. Davies of the Department of Ancient History and Classical Archaeology in 1981.[43]

To some degree, Greenbank might also be claimed as the birthplace of the University's Institute of Popular Music (established in 1988), the vice-chancellor, Professor Graeme Davies, convening a workshop there in April 1987 to consider the establishment of such an institute, those attending including Richard (later Sir Richard) Foster, Director of National Museums and Galleries on Merseyside, and Mike McCartney (known professionally as Mike McGear), the performing artist and rock photographer younger brother of Sir Paul McCartney.[44]

Greenbank also proved an attractive venue to which visitors to the University might be taken for a meal, as in the instance of Professor Alberto Navarro Gonzalez of the University of Salamanca, visiting the Department of Hispanic Studies in session 1973–74, who, together with his wife, was entertained to dinner by Professor Geoffrey Ribbans, accompanied by staff members of his department.[45] Besides twenty-first birthday parties, Greenbank was the preferred venue for a large number of wedding receptions of former students. Elizabeth Earl (BA General Studies, 1966) held both her twenty-first birthday party and, on her marriage in 1970 to David Batten (BEng Hons Electrical Engineering, 1966), her wedding reception there; perhaps uniquely, she can record that her mother, daughter of Mark Phillips Rathbone, remembered going to parties at Greenbank as a child and that she had found Eleanor Rathbone rather fearsome![46]

A large number of Liverpool graduates, relatives, and friends of Dr Jeff Green (BSc, 1969; MB ChB Hons, 1973; MD, 1979) and Dr Susan Hotson (BSc, 1970; BSc Hons Zoology, 1971; MB ChB Hons, 1976), attended their wedding reception at Greenbank in July 1976: the bridegroom's identical twin held a Liverpool BSc degree, an usher had also graduated in medicine, and, speaking at the reception in place of the bride's late father (Dr Richard Hotson, a former president of the Guild of Undergraduates, who had served as a member of the Greenbank House Management Committee since its formation) was Judge Frank Paterson, her godfather, who had studied law at Liverpool.[47] Before moving to a student house in Kensington for their final three years in the Medical School, Dr Daniel Ching (MB ChB, 1982) and Dr Avril Boyd (MB ChB, 1982; Diploma in Radiology – Radiodiagnosis, 1986) (whose wedding reception was to be held at Greenbank House in July 1983) lived for two years in Rathbone Hall, a mixed hall of residence, Daniel recollecting that he went to Greenbank for drinks some evenings with his future best man (a student in the School of Architecture), attracted by its lovely setting, a short walk from the hall; he adds that 'we met other people there but it was a special time for us because we were growing in our Christian faith, and were meeting our future wives at that time. We shared similar music, such as

Workshop to consider establishing an Institute of Popular Music, 1987. Front row: Professor (later Sir) Graeme Davies, vice-chancellor (second from left); second row from front: Mike McCartney (Mike McGear) (second from left), Professor Michael Talbot (James and Constance Alsop Professor of Music) (third from left) and Mr David Horn (appointed first director of IPM) (far right); back row: Mr (later Sir) Richard Foster, Director of National Museums and Galleries on Merseyside (far right).
(Photograph by Gordon Whiting taken at the request of the University)

Genesis. I was also playing basketball for the University.'[48] Their year (those who graduated in Medicine in 1982) was unusual inasmuch as between 10 and 15 per cent of the year married each other or students above or below their year.

From an early date, it was recognised that the Club's financial position was likely to be a difficult one, appreciating that, in common with all University catering enterprises, it suffered from the thirty- to forty-week limitations of the University year. With a view to reducing financial losses wherever possible, the normal rate of subscription was increased to £1 from session 1965–66. The deficit for the period ending 31 July 1965 had been reduced to £350. The Club had been pleased to receive £300 apiece from the trustees of the Eleanor Rathbone Charitable Trust and from the trustees of the E. L. Rathbone Charitable Trust for general expenses.

In its early days, the main attraction of the Club consisted of the bar facilities. The Buttery Bar, opened in November 1965, offered a full buffet service, waiter-served, with a main course at 6/6d or three courses at 8/6d being available to members from 6 p.m. each day, except Sunday when service started at 7 p.m. and Monday when the Buttery Bar was closed; last orders were taken at 10 p.m. Professor Fredric Taylor (BSc Hons Physics, 1966), who lived at Rathbone Hall from 1963 until 1966, has fond recollections of Greenbank, frequently studying until half an hour before closing time and then rushing over there for a convivial nightcap.[49]

The success of the Club led to proposals for its additional use of the first floor of Greenbank, Messrs J. B. Johnson being awarded a contract for extensive work in 1968 and to additional staff being recruited. A kitchen and dining rooms were provided on the first floor. In 1970, the Civic Trust's Commendations included those for Greenbank House and park, as also for the University's Alsop Centre and The Green.[50] In 1971, besides Gordon Milne and his wife, the staff comprised a head waiter, head barman, senior barman, barman, cook, chef, washer-up, kitchen assistant, waitresses, handymen, and cleaners. Following the increase in accommodation, eligibility for membership of the Club was

Wedding group of Dr Jeff Green and Dr Susan Hotson, July 1976.
(Photograph courtesy of Dr Susan Green)

extended in 1969–70 to second-year, and then also to first-year undergraduates and finally to all students who did not live in halls. Recorded profit increased from £404 in 1967–68 to £1,498 in 1968–69. In seeking an experienced chef to take charge of the kitchen in March 1974, it was stated that the Club had a small quality restaurant and a larger supper room; the chef was expected to work six days a week, from Monday to Saturday, 4.30–11 p.m.[51] For evening work, part-time bar staff and part-time waitresses were recruited, being paid 45p per hour plus threshold pay.[52]

Besides hosting exhibitions – a notable one in November 1967 being paintings and drawings by Mrs Vivien White (daughter of Augustus John), who had painted extensively in France, Italy, Germany, Spain, and Russia – Greenbank was fortunate to be able to acquire works of art to display on its walls, assisted by the University's Fine Arts Sub-Committee. In 1968 a tapestry by Geraldine Brookes was bought and displayed on the new main staircase, to be joined in 1972 by *Nude* by Ewan Uglow. At the AGM of the Club later that year, the committee reported that, though it was seeking suitable pictures to display, the search had to be conducted with considerable care to ensure any pictures were in keeping with the Club. In the context of paintings by Sam Walsh and Elizabeth Frink which had been obtained for display in 1969, the Fine Arts Sub-Committee (whose Secretary, John Brockbank, attended the Club's Management Committee to provide financial advice) was informed of the suitability of the Club premises for the display of eighteenth- and nineteenth-century works of art. It was through the generosity of the Rathbone family that in 1971 the University was able to acquire a watercolour of a robin which John James Audubon had painted while staying at Greenbank; following conservation at the British Museum, it was displayed over the fireplace in the first-floor lounge.

In the light of the forecast deficit of at least £4,000 – a deficit which was attributed to a lack of use of the restaurant – restaurant catering at Greenbank was terminated in March 1976. Function catering was resumed in session 1976–77, being provided by outside caterers, Barlow's Catering Co. Formal dinners could be provided for a minimum of twelve people (to a maximum of sixty-six) and buffets for a minimum of twelve and a maximum of one hundred. Publicity in the University and the halls advertising the Club's facilities unfortunately did not generate the expected number of membership applications, the membership in session 1978–79 standing at 1,653. The loss of £2,382 incurred in the year ended 31 July 1980 was followed by a surplus of £997 generated in the following five months; a newly installed pool table had proved very popular, 'providing a satisfactory profit for the Club.' The acquisition of a pool table was followed by the hire of a Space Invader machine which, it was agreed, would not impinge on the atmosphere of the rest of the Club as a separate Games Room had been set up. Disturbance of another nature was complained of by

Reg Davies, the warden of Roscoe and Gladstone halls: noise at the Club and students playing on the lawn facing the halls, concern also being expressed at the decision to admit first-year students to the Club. The Club's AGM in 1981 was informed that a deficit of £2,382 had been changed to a surplus of £2,753, this change in fortune being attributed to an increase in the hire of rooms, the installation of the pool table and the video machine, the reduction of measures from one-fifth to one-sixth of a gill, and a reduction of the electricity bill following a transfer to the chief engineer's budget of part of the security lighting. (Following an attempted burglary in 1978, five external floodlights had been installed.) A no-smoking area of the bar had also been introduced and proved most popular.

For those living within the vicinity of Greenbank, it continued to provide an attractive venue for a drink, a meal, or a party with friends. Though Tina Billinge (who graduated BSc in 1970) does not recall ever drinking there as an undergraduate, once she had settled with her first husband in a house a short and pleasant walk away, in Pitville Avenue, they were regular visitors:

> We met friends there, took friends and relatives there, ate in the restaurant once or twice on special occasions, and went to wine tastings organized by the lovely Mr Milne, the head steward. Mr Milne had a fantastic cellar of wines and spirits, of which we once had a tour .... We had two particular friends whom we introduced to Greenbank and also to each other. Many a sunny summer Sunday lunchtime we would meet with our children, and the Sunday papers, and have pushchair races across the grass, much to the children's delight ... Another special couple in my life were once on the verge of emigrating to Canada so I organized a farewell party for our group of friends at Greenbank. We hired it to ourselves and Greenbank House provided the catering. Our friends decided not to emigrate after all but the party was so good that we had it – at Greenbank, of course – a few more times with increasing numbers of toddlers on each occasion ... Another group of friends I enjoyed Greenbank with were 'Mums on the Ale.' Not an elegant name for us but coined by me in remembrance of my professional days before motherhood when one of my colleagues regularly referred to our social drinking as 'going on the ale.' We were a group of mothers of babies and toddlers whose only regular hope of an evening off was to leave fathers with babies and go out for a drink. And to Greenbank it was.[53]

For Dr Juliette Riddall (BVSc, 1990), a first-year veterinary science student at Roscoe and Gladstone halls in session 1985–86, besides recollections of going to Greenbank House for drinks and socialising, she had ' the vivid memories of the welcome sun' that, as an overseas student from Australia, she was missing so much: in the springtime, before the lead-up to examinations, she relaxed on the lawn in the sun outside Greenbank House after a long winter.[54]

In 1982, Gordon Milne retired as the Club's steward. In reviewing the future role of the steward, the Committee envisaged a greater emphasis on the Club as a conference centre, the steward being able to access other University facilities in liaison with the halls manager. Over forty applications were received for the post, Mr Neil D. Carter, assistant manager of a restaurant in County Durham, and his wife being appointed. To improve the appearance of staff, the steward was authorised to purchase jackets (for the men) and tabards (for the female staff). Though a supper room service had been introduced, selling foods such as chicken and chips, and was increasing in popularity, and Mr Carter had commenced the provision of an evening meals service on Thursdays, Fridays, and Saturdays in term time, by the time of the Club's AGM it was reported that the surplus of £2,753 in 1980–81 had been followed by a deficit of £2,372 in 1981–82. Costs had increased and bar sales had remained the same, reflecting a trend seen generally in the licensed trade at this time. Club membership numbers had also fallen, from 1,443 in 1980–81 to 1,282 in 1981–82, caused mainly by a reduction in membership by academic staff members. A £200 loss was attributed to the Club remaining open in the summer, at the request of the University's Conference Officer. For many years prior to the appointment in 1980 of Mr Peter Kenwright, formerly assistant halls manager, as the University's first, full-time conference officer, the University had hosted conferences and Saga holidays at its halls of residence during vacations, the income generated helping towards keeping student residential fees to a reasonable level. Under Peter Kenwright's leadership, the conference business grew very considerably, he being very active in the establishment of a Merseyside Conference Bureau.[55]

The following two years witnessed falling bar sales, attributed to students arriving later in the evening at the Club and spending less than previously. The Supper Bar, which had re-opened in October 1982, closed in late January 1983 owing to 'a lack of response,' though the increasing catering trade showed a net profit, 100 dinner plates, cups, and saucers, fish and side plates being purchased; the net surplus for catering over the period 1 August 1983–31 July 1984 reached £5,300. Over the same period the Club incurred an overall deficit of £4,881, the principal cause of concern being the bar operation. By now the Club's library was being used for functions and reflecting this change in use the purchase of newspapers was discontinued and a decision reached not to spend funds on the purchase of books, the University librarian not now being able to provide suitable volumes. Meanwhile, student membership had declined to 890.

One of the last meetings to be held at Greenbank House before the closure of the Club was the inaugural meeting of the Friends of the University, held on

22 September 1984. Recognising that the harsh cuts in the funding of higher education by the government in the early 1980s were probably the harbingers of a reduced level of support for universities in the future, Reg Davies, who had recently retired as reader in English literature, had formed a working party to draw up proposals for the establishment of what became the Friends, serving as its first chairman. Appropriately, as architect of the alterations of 1963–64, Dr Quentin Hughes gave a talk at this inaugural meeting about the history of the building. In the same year, three years after the 'Toxteth riots' of July 1981, as part of a dynamic programme led by the Merseyside Development Corporation to revitalise the south docks area of Liverpool, an International Garden Festival was held, to wide acclaim, reclaiming a 125-acre area of urban dereliction by the River Mersey; the University's many contributions to the Garden Festival included a 'New Lands for Old' Garden and a stand in the Festival Hall which served as a window on the whole of the University, promoting it to prospective students and their parents, to commerce and industry, and to the general public.[56]

At what turned out to be the last meeting of the Management Committee, on 24 June 1985, it was reported that Mr Carter had resigned with effect from the end of the month. The Committee recognised that it had become increasingly difficult for Greenbank House to maintain its financial viability as an exclusive members' club. Steps had been taken to maintain its solvency, but it was recognised that radical changes were required to provide a facility which would be more appropriate to the present circumstances and requirements of staff and students and would permit the University to make more profitable use of its facilities. Identifying a desire to develop the Greenbank site as a conference/seminar centre, the committee recommended to Senate and Council that the Management Committee should be dissolved; that the remaining works of art on display in the Club should now come under the control of the curator of Art Collections (Audubon's painting of a robin already being held in Art Collections on grounds of security); and that the stocks of fine wine held by the Club be transferred to the control of the University's Wine Committee. An end to an era at Greenbank was also sadly marked by the news of the recent death of Gordon Milne, who had so ably served as manager of the Club from 1965 until his retirement in 1982. Gordon and Lillian Milne were regarded with great affection by all who knew them. One of the last outside functions to be hosted by Greenbank House was the reception which Wing Commander Kenneth Stoddart, Lord Lieutenant of Merseyside, gave in July 1985 for the commissioning of seven new Deputy Lieutenants of Merseyside.[57]

6 Under new management – Greenbank House and its future

From June 1985, the management of Greenbank House was placed under the overall control of Alan Thorpe, the halls manager, and his deputy, Ian Thomson. From August 1986 the management of all licensing activities on the Greenbank site was centred on Greenbank House, with the individual halls' bars being operated as satellite stations, providing the opportunity to make Greenbank House a 'premium' location. At the time, 44 per cent of the income was attributable to student business. Future market targets for Greenbank House were identified as corporate business, function business, and an older, year-round population; the importance of redirecting students to University bars, rather than their custom being lost to private publicans, was recognised. In 1985–86, cash income (from bars and other sources) and function income (from the sale of food, drinks, and accommodation) amounted to 64 per cent and 34 per cent of income respectively, with company training business, weddings and dinners accounting for 47 per cent of function business.

Greenbank House offered two large meeting/function rooms, each seating up to ninety persons, with several smaller rooms able to accommodate up to forty persons; three fully equipped bars; and a first-floor kitchen. In a business plan for Greenbank drawn up by Dr Ray Buss, senior assistant registrar (later director of administrative services), and Alan Thorpe and colleagues in the Finance Office in October 1987, the major market target groups which Greenbank House aimed to develop were identified as training and business meetings, wedding business, and University short courses and development programmes; the potential was recognised of introducing bar meals utilising the cook/chill facility on the Greenbank site and promoting the general use of Greenbank House by non-University customers to whom the link with the University and the attractiveness of the house and its grounds might appeal. While recognising that in Greenbank House the University had an asset of tremendous potential, the report noted that it was currently underdeveloped, requiring significant funds for its refurbishment. In July 1987, the University Council had been informed that the Residences Group was examining ways in which income from outside sources, including vacation activity, could be increased and that a business plan for Greenbank House would be submitted in the near future 'in support of a proposal that a major refurbishment be undertaken.'[1] Expenditure of £367,800 was estimated to be required, on bars, conference suite, ball room, ground-floor toilets, cook/chill finishing kitchen, reception and office facilities, first-floor function suite, and general redecoration; also specialised audiovisual equipment and catering and bar equipment, and furniture.

Since taking over responsibility for Greenbank House, the Halls Management Group staff, and in particular Ian Thomson, the deputy halls manager, managed to increase turnover by 60 per cent, and although the results for 1986–87 showed a modest operating deficit, it was noted that additional sums had been spent on the fabric of the building.[2] The operating deficit on the Club's income and expenditure had been gradually reduced, from £17,000 in 1984–85, to £8,500 in 1985–86, and £1,100 in 1986–87. But the stark warning was given that it would not prove possible to maintain the present level of business in Greenbank House unless there was capital investment, 'urgently required to reverse the rapid deterioration of internal décor and fittings' that was now taking place and which was having a detrimental effect on customer perception of the services provided. Such was the further deterioration by May 1988 that the halls manager, in recommending the closure of the bar facilities, observed that students regarded Greenbank as 'that grotty place.' In response to the October 1987 proposals, on behalf of the Residences Group, Professor Bernard Wood saw little alternative between two 'extreme' courses of action: (1) to restore Greenbank as a historically important Liverpool merchants' house which in its fine surroundings would be an attractive venue for meetings, functions, etc., and (2) to cease expenditure on it and to run it as an increasingly 'seamy' bar which attracted students away from the halls' bars and thus threatened their financial viability. From a personal point of view, to let such a historic building deteriorate into 'seaminess,' even if the fabric was maintained, went against the grain of the vice-chancellor, Professor Graeme Davies; commending the enterprising document as exemplary in its thoroughness, he was obliged to note that the University would need to bear in mind the current competition for resources.

Even at the time of the submission of the business plan in October 1987, such was deterioration of the building that the halls management staff had begun to run down outside bookings and just concentrate more on the in-house business, with the proviso that 'clients' accepted the facilities as seen. In the absence of any indication that refurbishment was imminent, in the following January a decision was taken to cease all future bookings, the Club therefore becoming little more than a student bar. Nevertheless, the local press continued to advertise a Rotaract Club, a social club for those aged 18–28 years, as meeting at Greenbank House.[3] In the knowledge that funds for refurbishment would not be available in the near future, in May

1988 Alan Thorpe strongly recommended that the bar facilities be closed until funds to upgrade the Club internally could be approved; Greenbank House had become 'a financial burden to ourselves as well as to the University and is sapping management strength that would, for the time being, be better applied elsewhere.' The old adage that 'if you keep something looking decent students will respect it, if not they will abuse it,' seemed to have been realised; the main bar and toilet area had suffered especially and were in a particularly appalling state. The morale of those staff who had not left the University's employ or transferred to other posts was by now at an all-time low. The two other student bars on the Greenbank site had also suffered in competition with Greenbank. In June 1988, Council was told that a bid for £368,000 had been submitted in respect of Greenbank House, but the proposed development was deferred. In the meantime, the Residences Group took the decision to close Greenbank House at the end of session 1987–88.

In 1989 the University's Planning and Resources Committee allocated £50,000 towards the cost of improving and developing Greenbank House, with a view to bringing it back into use for 'Short Course activity, in-house training, and some external functions.' Though Dr Buss in May 1989 recommended the refurbishment of the main bar and the toilet areas (it being noted that the rooms for the proposed short course and other functions were nearly all situated on the first floor, reached only by way of the main bar area), he noted that the allocated sum would have to be supplemented, perhaps by between £25,000 and £50,000, from other sources, the Residences' budget and perhaps also from the Friends of the University and local business. In February 1990, Council was informed that the sum of £50,000 allocated towards the cost of refurbishment had not yet been committed; a separate working group had been established by the vice-chancellor 'to consider what the long-term development plans for this property should be.'[4] A limited amount of building maintenance work was carried out, during which, in early 1990, some papers of the Rathbone family were found in the rafters. They included two photographs, one of which was identified by Dr B. L. Rathbone as that of his grandmother, the second wife of William Rathbone the sixth, who died in 1918. Also found was a letter in which a family member writes movingly of the death of her young son, in the context of a reflection on a hymn which draws a connection between death and the falling of a leaf.[5]

To help assess the possible demand for Greenbank House as a residential centre for conferences and short courses, Margaret Pegg, of the University's Short Courses Office, prepared a report in March 1990. The report drew attention to the fact that the number of short courses that could be marketed was restricted by the lack of both teaching rooms and residential facilities and noted that there was a major shortage of conference facilities in the North West. 'A well managed conference centre, which has the atmosphere of a country house' would be 'a much better learning environment than a hotel.' Adopting a 'devil's advocate' role in testing Mrs Pegg's hypothesis that research 'strongly suggests that the Greenbank House development would be successful,' Dr Buss concluded that, though he remained enthusiastic about the idea of developing Greenbank House, there was not yet sufficient evidence to convince him of the viability of running it as a conference centre on the basis of repaying some of its capital cost. Though an ideal building and its parkland setting very attractive, he had doubts about how such a conference centre would be perceived by potential clients because of its proximity to Greenbank Lane and to Toxteth. Even if a more optimistic view was taken of the income estimates, there would still be the need to generate £1m through the University's Development Campaign and to run the Centre through its 'start-up' period of at least three years. With the large number of conference centres already in existence, for instance at Keele University, or being planned, as at UMIST, coupled with the then current recession in the economy, he felt that the chances of achieving success were even lower.

The suggestion that Greenbank House might serve as a conference centre resurfaced in April 1991 when the University's senior management team received a memorandum from Dr Buss on an option of entering into a partnership with a hotel company which would build a sixty-bedroom hotel as an extension to Greenbank House, which would be refurbished as a conference centre. Dr Buss and Adrian Simmons, Assistant Director of Estates, had met representatives from Crown House Hotels (which owned the Royal Clifton Hotel in Southport and had developed the Lancashire Lodge just off the M58), and sketch plans for a possible development were attached.

In limbo
In 1989, a Conference Office was established at the University, the team setting up home in the former servants' quarters at Greenbank House. There they remained until dry rot forced their departure in 2000, leaving no one else to occupy the house. It was during the Office's occupation that a level of spirit/ghost activity was reported; the team reported running footsteps on the first floor, flushing toilets, filing cabinet drawers opening and closing of their own accord, lights being switched on when they had been switched off, and stones being thrown at them when they parked their cars in front of the house. Joyce Hunt, who had worked at the house when it was a staff-student club, spoke of a white lady being seen on the veranda at regular intervals by staff and students despite the absence of flooring there. On 23 September 1993, the *Liverpool Echo* highlighted the mysterious reported sightings and activities in an article headed 'White Lady Riddle in Ghost Hunt, Gothic goings-on at mansion.' A medium was recruited to visit Greenbank, evidently suggesting, presumably after some research had been undertaken in the Rathbone family

archives, that the spirits remaining in the house were those of Theophilus Rathbone (the son of William Rathbone the fourth and his wife Hannah, who, born in 1798, had died, allegedly of smallpox, as a young child), Jane Vaucher (the Rathbone children's governess in the mid-nineteenth century), and a coachman who had committed suicide.[6]

When, on a lovely warm, sunny day on 29 June 2001, Mr William Rathbone the tenth unveiled an English Heritage ceramic Blue Plaque on Greenbank House, commemorating both William Rathbone the sixth and his daughter, Eleanor, 'politicians and social reformers,' there was a certain degree of embarrassment on the part of the University that Greenbank House, closed, was not in a fit state for its interior to be visited and admired, not that those present were aware of its deterioration.[7] In October 1992, the University Archives had mounted an exhibition, 'An Investment in Education, The Rathbones and the University of Liverpool,' at the reception which Rathbone Brothers held at St George's Hall, Liverpool, as part of its 250th anniversary celebrations.

In the light of the demand by students for self-catered, en suite accommodation, in 2006 the University explored the potential to convert 269 rooms on the Greenbank site from catered places to self-catered, en suite accommodation. The 'hybrid' residences strategy that the University wished to deliver also envisaged 'the disposal of some assets, the capital receipts from which could be re-invested in residences,' and the provision of new self-catered accommodation at or near the University campus.[8] The Planning and Resources Committee had considered the future of Greenbank House and had concluded that it could play no part in delivering the residences strategy; accordingly, its sale was recommended, it being noted that 'it was understood that this would be acceptable to the Rathbone family.' In giving approval for the sale, it was agreed that this should 'if possible [be] with conditions relating to its use and development, and that consideration be given to consulting the Rathbone family about the use of proceeds from its sale.'[9] During the summer of 2007, there was an investment of £4.5m at the Greenbank site involving the addition of en suite facilities to 200 rooms, with associated kitchen facilities, and the extension and renovation of Roscoe and Gladstone halls' dining hall and server which 'would improve marketability of the halls and also the student experience.' A study undertaken in 2007 had concluded that quality university student accommodation was essential to ensure Liverpool maintained its competitiveness against other Russell Group universities.[10]

Following the publication in 1949 of Professor W. G. Holford's *Proposals for the Development of a Site for the University of Liverpool*, the University's Development Committee published a series of quinquennial reports chronicling the development of the University's estate. Then in the mid-1990s the University produced the first in a series of Estate Strategies; revised and updated in 2000, the Strategy was incorporated in the University's Corporate Plan 2004–07. Under a £200m capital programme completed in 2008/09, improvements were made to a number of buildings across the University precinct, including the extensive refurbishment of two major listed buildings designed by Alfred Waterhouse, the old Royal Infirmary building (£12m), occupied by the Faculty of Medicine in late 2009, and the iconic red-brick Victoria Building (£8.5m), providing accommodation for the University's new Victoria Gallery and Museum and accommodation for Widening Participation activities, the Victoria Gallery and Museum being formally opened by HRH The Princess Royal on 28 May 2008.

Not by coincidence, the restored Victoria Building opened in 2008, the year Liverpool celebrated its status as European Capital of Culture, with a large programme of events as also an exploitation of its heritage. The recent revival in the fortunes of the city and its architectural inheritance had been celebrated in the restoration of St George's Hall, the designation by UNESCO in 2004 of the large waterfront and commercial centre of the city as a World Heritage Site,[11] and the revival of the city's Georgian and early Victorian streets and squares, including those in the vicinity of the University. Promoting a better understanding and appreciation of the city's architectural heritage and its historic parks and gardens, in 2008 English Heritage published several Liverpool titles in its Informed Conservation series.[12] The city's modern-day resurgence also emerged in such new buildings as the waterfront Arena, the Liverpool One commercial development, and the opening in 2011 of the Museum of Liverpool. Liverpool, which had in the past prospered from Britain's imperial markets and global reach, was now, some decades after the end of empire, enjoying a resurgence in its fortunes.

Provision for the compilation of lists of buildings of special architectural or historic interest had been first set out in the Town and Country Planning Act of 1947, which gave powers to local authorities to preserve such buildings. The University had a total of forty-seven Grade II-listed non-residential properties, the bulk in the University precinct, including the houses in Abercromby Square and Oxford Street. While providing accommodation for key activities, the age and listed status of such buildings rendered them expensive to maintain and modify, listed status in most cases protecting the entire building, interior and exterior. Conscious that the external environment and appearance of its buildings provides a first impression for staff, students, and visitors to the campus, the University developed a maintenance investment plan which would see the eradication of a maintenance backlog over ten years from 2011.

Following consultation with the various stakeholder groups and partners, including the City Council and NHS Trusts, an Estates Strategy for 2011–16 was prepared in collaboration with the University's Strategic Management Team and Estates Advisory Board. The aim was to provide a strategy whereby the University could continue 'to develop its physical assets in a way that enriches the student experience and provides the stimulating environment required to achieve teaching, learning and research excellence, through which the University can become a world-class institution.' The preferred option was to reduce, rationalise, and enhance its estate. A significant growth in student numbers was forecast, targeted to rise by c. 2,000 by 2014/15. At the time, 944 of the University's 3,354 student residential study beds were located at the Greenbank site (Derby and Rathbone halls, and Roscoe and Gladstone halls). Consultation of students had identified a preference for self-catered residential facilities and the Residence Strategy aimed at developing new facilities on the main campus and at Greenbank. Most of the University's current residential accommodation was found to be showing signs of age, a condition survey in 2010 concluding that there was a high level of risk, with a number of key infrastructure elements in some buildings at risk of complete failure within the next two years. The poor quality and condition of the accommodation was having an adverse effect on recruitment of students; besides, it was noted that students, as customers, expected a high standard of accommodation including en suite facilities and that the University had the lowest number of en suite rooms in the higher education sector, at 9 per cent, whereas on average 60 per cent of student rooms in Russell Group universities were en suite.[13]

Recognition of Greenbank House as an integral part of the redevelopment of the Greenbank campus

Though the Estates Strategy 2011–16 makes just passing reference to Greenbank House as a listed building, an appendix concerning Greenbank recommended that consideration be given to 'ways of bringing the heritage assets of Grade II* listed Greenbank House and the parkland setting into wider use. This could include renovation of the house as a conferencing and wedding type venue, restaurant etc., as covenants allow.' The University was willing to explore the encouragement of more public access to the greenspace, which would be seen as part of Liverpool's rich store of parkland environments which included the adjacent Sefton and Greenbank Parks.

In the summer of 2011 the University announced plans to invest £600 million in its academic and residential estate across the Liverpool City Region, including a £250m redevelopment of its student accommodation, alongside new teaching, research, and sustainable energy infrastructure. To provide more self-catered student accommodation on the University campus, in 2011 the University employed Ocon Construction Limited of Manchester to build Vine Court, on Chatham Street, on the south side of the campus, providing en suite accommodation for 749 students, including retail space and a restaurant on the ground floor. On the successful completion of this project in 2012, Ocon won a design and build contract for Crown Place, adjoining Brownlow Hill, providing 1,259 en suite rooms, together with retail space on the ground floor. Part way through the construction of Crown Place, in March 2013 Ocon unfortunately entered administration on account of its insolvency, presenting the University with a difficult decision, of whether to close down the site, lay off all the workers, and re-tender the works to another contractor.

If such a decision had been taken, a year would probably have been lost such that the residences would not have been available for occupation by the September 2014 intake of students. Fortunately, the University already had its own registered company as a developer, the University of Liverpool Construction Company (ULCCO), and the decision was now quickly taken to create its own contractor, ULCCO-SP (Special Projects), and thereby ring-fence and employ all those Ocon employees who were working on Crown Place to complete the project; remarkably, the site management lost just a couple of weeks dealing with the upheaval of a changing employer and Crown Place was completed on time and to budget. The creation of such a Special Projects contractor to undertake capital projects was – and continues to be – unique in the higher education sector.

Even before the practical completion of Crown Place on 12 September 2014, in November 2013 the University Council took the decision to continue ULCCO-SP to ensure its completion and thereafter to refurbish the student residences at Melville Grove and deliver planned student residences at Greenbank.[14] On a day-to-day basis, the University's department of Facilities Management managed ULCCO's work, ULCCO-SP being effectively a project design and management team, the majority of the actual construction work being subcontracted. Though recognising that the activity of ULCCO-SP was not the University's core business, continuing its work had the distinct advantage of safeguarding the completion of Crown Place by retaining key ULCCO staff, the team's knowledge of the University and its expectations significantly contributing to an enhanced ability to effectively manage and deliver major projects and their associated risks; besides, such a proposal was estimated to achieve financial savings on future projects compared to the costs associated with working with an external contractor. The momentum for the delivery of the University's overall capital plan in a cost-effective way was to be maintained while providing high-quality work and supporting the retention of high-quality staff.

The planned developments at Greenbank comprised not only the creation of a student village, incorporating new self-catering student residences, Rathbone Hall and Roscoe and Gladstone halls, on the sites of their predecessor halls which were considered to be out of date and failing to attract the highest calibre of students to the University and were accordingly to be demolished, and also the restoration of Greenbank House. The £106m redevelopment of Greenbank was to form the final major element of the £250m redevelopment of the University's student accommodation and as such was to make it the most significant investment by the University in any one project.

The production of a heritage appraisal for Greenbank

In advance of planning permission being sought, in 2011 discussions with Liverpool City Council, also involving a representative of English Heritage, highlighted the need for a 'statement of significance' heritage report for the whole Greenbank site, to understand the heritage value of the site being within the Mossley Hill Conservation Area and that Greenbank House was a Grade II* listed building. Heritage statements are required for any planning application or listed building consent which affects the significance of a heritage asset; besides providing a supporting document for an application, they generally also provide a useful resource of baseline information which can inform an appropriate scheme of development, repair, or conservation. That Greenbank House was Grade II* listed meant that it was in the top 6 per cent of buildings of special architectural or historic interest in the country, ranking it alongside the Palm House in Sefton Park, the Philharmonic Hall, and the Picton Reading Room in Liverpool, requiring a significant amount of attention to detail by all involved, with a higher degree of scrutiny by the local planning authority and other bodies, including Historic England, becoming statutory consultees. Four heritage consultants/heritage architects were accordingly invited to quote for the production of such a report, KMHeritage, a consultancy for the historic built environment, headed by Kevin Murphy, who trained and worked as an architect and had served as an Inspector of Historic Buildings in the London Region of English Heritage, being chosen; historical research and assistance in the production of the report was provided by Lee Hutchings.

KMHeritage's report, submitted in May 2012, provided a detailed history of Greenbank House as the main heritage feature of the site, followed by an assessment of its heritage significance: providing evidence of the pre-Rathbone eighteenth-century nature of the site and documenting the Rathbones as a family and as a record of how they lived, the early nineteenth-century Gothic part of the house and the more humble earlier parts close to Greenbank Lane contrasting with the red sandstone extension of the 1860s. In its study of the anatomy of the building, it concludes that if the earliest part of the house 'has very little by way of surviving internal features,' its architectural interest resides in its 'evidently early external appearance and

Plan illustrative of the successive phases in the evolution of Greenbank House. (KMHeritage, redrawn by David O'Leary, ULCCO-Special Projects)

external features such as the round stair turret.' As Richmal Wigglesworth has observed, this oldest part of the house has a solid brick construction which can be read visually by the headers (the end faces of bricks) which are present in the brickwork, the 'Penny Struck' pointing in lime also dating this brick wing.[15] Assessed as of high significance architecturally are the early nineteenth-century Gothic section (both internally and externally) and the western extension of the late 1860s (externally), constructed of face-bedded red sandstone. The face-bedded stonework of this Victorian wing was to present a particular problem, the sandstone having been bedded with its natural sedimentary layers vertical, meaning the face could be easily and delicately tooled; however, the freeze-thaw process forces the front 'sheet' of stone off the blocks very easily, resulting in a loss of surface. To have remedied this detail would have required removing and replacing the entire external sandstone skin of the wing; instead, the surface of loose stone was to be defrassed, though this wing will continue to deteriorate. Assessed by the report as of low significance were the yard buildings to the west of the early–mid-nineteenth-century stable block, while the later twentieth-century interventions, including the internal alterations carried out by the University, were adjudged 'uniformly of low or no significance,' detracting from the house's special interest as a listed building and its contribution to the conservation area. The proposed scheme would remove 'all inappropriate later changes such as the external 20th century stairs' and 'see the recovery and rejuvenation of an important heritage asset and provide it with a long-term sustainable future.'[16]

The *Planning for the Historic Environment Practice Guide* published by English Heritage, in setting out the requirements of the Planning (Listed Buildings and Conservation Areas) Act 1990, notes that, in reaching decisions, local planning authorities must 'have special regard to the desirability of preserving a listed building or its setting or any features of special architectural or historic interest which it possesses.' In respect of listed buildings, which account for approximately 2 per cent of England's built heritage, it is generally appreciated that each local planning authority varies in its approach to what is and is not acceptable in terms of extensions or renovations.

The purpose of the report being to agree with the City Council and English Heritage which assets were of most value, Knight Frank LLP, who had been employed to provide planning advice to the University for the Greenbank campus, were able in August 2012 to report that agreement had been reached with both bodies that Greenbank House should be retained but that the Council would accept extensions to the property and minor internal and external alterations to facilitate a proposed use. Derby Hall and its annex were considered of 'listable status' and were to be retained, but the Council and English Heritage would not object to the demolition of the remaining buildings, Rathbone Hall and Warden's Lodge and Roscoe and Gladstone halls, providing their replacement preserved and enhanced the character of the conservation area.

The appointment of architects

In 2013, through the principal medium of the *Official Journal of the European Union*, the University invited expressions of interest from architectural practices in a scheme to develop Greenbank as a student village with all the associated amenities to meet the changing needs of future students.[17]

From those companies which expressed an interest, a shortlist was drawn up, these companies being provided with tender documents including a brief, *Guidance Document for Greenbank* (August 2013). Bringing together guidance on the history and purpose behind the residences strategy and its objective for the Greenbank site, it sought to identify the aspirations of the University 'to deliver a newly developed Greenbank as a form of student village with a single centralized reception/welcome point.' A link was to be provided between the design brief and key University processes and minimum requirements; the design brief was expected to be based on the adoption of all of the best aspects from the previous new developments, of Vine Court and of Crown Place, both of which had been designed to embed sustainability and robustness in their design. There was a requirement for tenderers to demonstrate how they had developed the brief to provide the required accommodation 'in the most effective and efficient use of space,' demonstrating compliance with the heritage and conservation criteria for the site. A key requirement was the ability to demonstrate an awareness of cost implications, 'so that at all times the proposals are cost effective and remain within the available budget ... This is **not** an opportunity to impress the University with a scheme that cannot be built within the stated budgets. We are seeking the best possible design for the available budget.' The target programme for tender purposes envisaged the design process and the planning process (from an initial meeting to a final planning approval) extending in tandem from early December 2013 until late August 2014, followed by a construction period of new build and refurbishment from January 2015 until early August 2017, ready for occupation at the start of the 2017–18 academic year.

Following the delivery of their tender documents, including design proposals, in late October 2013 the shortlisted architectural practices attended a tender evaluation meeting with their presentations. Assessed and scored on the fee, the experience of their team, their understanding and interpretation of the brief, the design and phasing of the project, risks, and acceptance of terms and conditions, Sheppard Robson came out top and were awarded the project. Founded in 1958 by Sir Richard H. Sheppard (1910–82), Sheppard Robson is the fourth largest architectural practice in the UK. From the seminal buildings for Churchill College, Cambridge (founded in 1960), over the succeeding decades the practice had built up a substantial portfolio of projects for a large number of universities, tailored to their individual needs and respectful of their heritage. Demonstrating its empathetic approach, at Liverpool it had already been responsible for the University's Active Learning Laboratory for the engineering department (completed in 2009) and the Liverpool School of Tropical Medicine's Centre for Tropical and Infectious Diseases (completed in 2007). For Liverpool City Council's Liverpool Schools Investment Programme, it had designed Notre Dame Catholic College, Archbishop Beck Catholic Sports College, and Archbishop Blanch School, to be completed over the years 2013–15. Its residential accommodation for universities in the north-west of England included that for the universities of Leeds (Storm Jameson Court, completed in 2009) and Salford (completed in 2015). No fewer than eight of Sheppard Robson's architects were to work on Greenbank House.[18]

Discussions with the City Council and English Heritage

A further pre-application meeting with the City Council in April 2014 was attended by representatives of Sheppard Robson, Knight Frank, English Heritage, the University, and the City Council (including its conservation officer). Of Greenbank House, the minutes record that, though work was underway to make the building safe, much of it was still largely unsafe, collapsed, and dangerous, Graham Ives (English Heritage) warning that the general condition of the building needed to be addressed immediately to prevent English Heritage publicly from registering it as 'at risk'; he was happy that Greenbank House was now to move away from being a catering facility and more towards a study space, Rupert Goddard (Sheppard Robson) advising that the house would become a study area, almost like a sanctuary for students. The University was conscious of its legal responsibilities under the Listed Buildings and Conservation Areas Act 1990, of keeping the building in a good state of repair, and the far-reaching damage that would be attached to its reputation should the building be included in the national Heritage at Risk Register which English Heritage (later Historic England) maintained and published; the press releases issued by the University regarding the promised investment in the Greenbank site had specifically highlighted a planned significant investment into Greenbank House. It was fortunate that Greenbank House was not featured in the exhibition 'Triumph, Disaster and Decay,' the SAVE Britain's Heritage survey of Liverpool's Heritage, or the report which accompanied it in 2009; of the officially 137 listed buildings at risk in Liverpool, the report featured some of the most pressing cases.

In July 2014, after an internal structural survey had been completed by the structural engineer, the Booth King Partnership, Brian McGorry, ULCCO-SP's site manager, together with three scaffolders, met at Greenbank House armed with propping drawings, 43 sheets of plywood and 240 Acro props. The main areas to be propped were ground-floor rooms G/18–19–21, the adjoining corridor G/001, and accessible basement areas, which would then allow works to commence on the refurbishment. Upon works starting it was realised that other areas would require propping due to the uncovering of concrete floors laid on first-floor timber floors and the decay of other timber floors which would require another sixty Acro props. Besides the support of the floors, various other types of propping were employed to support walls in danger of collapse and also bay windows.

In an internal report in July 2015, the Director of Capital Projects and Estates Strategy acknowledged that Greenbank House had been poorly maintained by the University since its last use, the degradation growing 'due to vandalism and theft resulting in ongoing water penetration through the roof structures leading to severe rot and mould growth ... In the past a member of staff had fallen through a soaked floor, plaster is falling from ceilings and walls and the majority of the building is becoming unsafe and relying on propping works.'

It was acknowledged that it would prove difficult for plans for Greenbank House to be included within a wider site planning application, given the need for more certainty concerning the structural issues of the building. Accordingly, a condition survey of the building was conducted by Richmal Wigglesworth, an associate of Sheppard Robson, over three days in October 2014.

A condition survey of Greenbank House

During the years of neglect of the building, roof coverings and flashings had been lost and rainwater pipes and gutters had become blocked and ineffective. This had inevitably led to water ingress throughout the building, particularly above the central corridor of the Gothic wing where rainwater had collected in a poorly drained 'hidden' and confined 'valley' of the roofscape and eventually percolated into the building. As Mark Moppett, managing director of Booth King Partnership Ltd, the structural engineers for the project, has additionally noted, when untreated timber elements become repeatedly exposed to water in poorly ventilated space their moisture content can rise and they become prone to fungal attack, typically wet and dry rot.[19] 'Wet rot causes the breakdown of timber elements at locations where they are wettest (moisture contents typically in excess of 50%). Dry rot however can generally germinate and grow on timbers with a lower moisture content (upwards of 20%) which means its effects can be far more widespread. Significantly it will also grow and travel behind plasterwork on concealed brickwork where it attacks and disrupts mortar and spreads to other timbers in contact with affected masonry. Timber affected by rot loses all structural integrity and can be crushed to a powder with very little effort.' The original rainwater pipes from the roof had a very typical swan neck lead detail to get the water from the parapet gutter into the down pipe.[20] This detail was inherently poor as it blocks with leaves exceptionally easily. In order to mitigate this, hoppers with weirs were to be installed so that should the downpipe become blocked, water would shoot out clear of the building; this would both alert users to the blockage and keep the building fabric dry.

In Richmal Wigglesworth's report of 113 pages, illustrated by photographs and location plans, each room was described, its condition noted, its significance and risk assessed, and recommendations made. The report concluded that Greenbank House was 'in a generally poor condition with some areas very poor. Further water ingress will only accelerate the decline in structural stability and damage to significant building elevations. A full temporary roof is recommended to allow the structure to dry out, and remain dry until the repair works have been carried out.'

In the ground-floor library (Room G/026, now the Shaftesbury Room), whose significance was rated high, it recorded 'Dry rot penetration to all timber in this area. Head of the bay is collapsing and celium is visible. (It is assessed the roof of the bay was lead and has been stolen – unable to visually inspect.) Water penetration has caused the floor area in the bay to collapse and is currently boarded with plywood.' Fortunately, the original in situ mahogany bookcase with its cupboards and drawers below was found in a good condition, 'unaffected by rot. A rare survival,' the white marble fireplace also being in a good condition. When later the areas of ceiling of this room affected by rot were taken down, it was found that the rot extended to the joists which were then cut and spliced, using new timber and splicing plates.[21] On rot starting to appear in other areas, it proved necessary for the whole of the ceiling and a number of joists to be removed and replaced like for like. All the plaster on the walls had to be removed due to rot and a section of the bookcase dismantled and stored while some rotted timbers behind were removed. The whole bay area had to be propped while structural works were done, and the new lintel built into position. The windows to the south elevation were fortunately found not to be affected by rot and were able to be repaired and restored, as were the window shutters.

Besides the in situ bookcase and the white marble fireplace, also found in good condition was the stone staircase with its cast iron balusters and hardwood handrail. Areas, including in the eighteenth-century wing, had been propped by the University due to structural instability; window security boarding and boxed beams also restricted access and inspection. A number of ceilings in the first-floor rooms had collapsed. In the basement area significant dry rot was observed, though numerous brick piers supported the ground floor to the west of the Gothic area of the house, the only area of interest in the basement being the wine cellar which retained its stone bins. It was clear that specialist skills would be required to undertake repairs and that areas of particular significance might need detailed drawings and method statements detailing their repair.

Mahogany bookcase which was found 'unaffected by rot; a rare survival,' 2019.
(Photograph courtesy of Richmal Wigglesworth)

Wider consultations

Already between 21 January 2013 and 3 March 2014 a series of briefings had
been held with senior officers and elected members of Liverpool City Council
to discuss the University's investment plans for the Greenbank campus.
There then followed meetings with and consultation of staff and students
of the University, neighbours, and local community and residents groups,
and the distribution of over 2,600 newsletters to residences and business
addresses within the area inviting them to attend a public exhibition on
13 November 2014. Such pre-application consultation was required by the
Localism Act 2011 and the Statement of Community Engagement, which in
January 2015 recorded such consultation could state that the vast majority of
feedback had been overwhelmingly supportive of the proposals; the feedback
on such issues as renewable energy technologies and local transport and
parking provided the project with important data informing the emerging
masterplan.

Feedback forms at the public exhibition were completed with such expressions of pleasure as that the University was staying on the site 'as it provides a
bit of character/interest to the area rather than another housing development,'
that it would 'enhance the area and retain the student population in the area

supporting local businesses,' and that it was 'a great scheme and much needed to bring the university back into the 21st century.' The refurbishment of Greenbank House was raised by both local councillors and residents who were assured that the University had worked closely with English Heritage and the City Council's planning and conservation officers to develop a design brief covering design, heritage, and conservation.

Further surveys

Though English Heritage had anticipated the inclusion of Greenbank House within the wider master plan for Greenbank Student Village and raised serious concerns about its omission, Knight Frank were able to outline the programme for converting the building, confirming further survey work, and assuring them that the University aimed to submit a detailed listed building consent application in August 2015 with the aim of starting on site in October 2015 and completing the conversion in September 2017. Whereas the accommodation design for the student residences was well advanced, Greenbank House required many surveys and inspections before any design work could take place, such that the detail required for a planning application could be supplied. To have waited until a planning application covering Greenbank House could have been submitted would have seriously delayed the first student intake into the new halls. Satisfied that the building would be brought forward as an integral part of the campus, English Heritage did not maintain an objection to the planning application for a master plan that they had supported through the pre-application process.[22] In turn, the City Planning department's case officer recommended approval of the plan to erect replacement halls of residence as representing 'an enhancement of the area and an attraction to the student community to the benefit of the local economy.'[23]

The Condition Survey strongly recommended surveys and appraisals by specialist subcontractors, including a detailed survey and analysis of the early nineteenth-century two-storey cast-iron veranda to the south elevation. Restoration projects require a good deal of patience and a keen eye for detail. Following a site survey of the veranda's condition in June 2015, The Ironwork Studio, an architectural metalwork design and consultancy company, observed that it was 'an elegant piece of work made using finely detailed quality castings and constructed using a very high standard of crafts-manship.' Though obviously much neglected, taking into consideration its age it was found that there was 'little missing and few repairs, meaning the vast majority is original work.' The previous repairs that had been carried out were found not to be in keeping with the original design intent; for instance, the balustrade within one bay was all new, made from mild steel/wrought iron, welded to the veranda. Due to the failures of the drainage and the condition of the paint, active corrosion was found all over; the broken paint surface with cracks and blisters, trapping water, was accelerating the corrosion. The veranda was not stable or structurally sound enough for use. Concluding that the ironwork required a major overhaul, a full restoration to conservation standards, involving full dismantling, was recommended, all the restoration work to be carried out in the workshop, rather than an attempt to carry out the work in situ; thereby, the veranda could be returned to full working order, corrosion stabilised, broken components repaired using sympathetic techniques which minimised any visual intrusion, and the ironwork returned to as-new condition.

Commencing in June 2015, regular meetings were held at Greenbank of representatives of ULCCO-SP, Sheppard Robson (the architects), Booth King Partnership (structural engineers), Currie & Brown UK Ltd (health and safety consultants and principal designers under the health and safety-related Construction (Design and Management) Regulation 2015), and WYG (White Young Green, mechanical and electrical consultants) to deal with the structural, servicing, and alteration requirements, initially as the results of the various surveys and investigations became available, as parts of the building were opened up, and as alternative proposals and specifications were considered. When structural inspections were initially carried out in 2014–15, generally all the ornate plasterwork and finishes were in place. Damp patches were evident in some locations on walls and ceilings and in these areas the floor and roof structures were suspected of suffering from rot and so such areas were propped as a precaution.

Already in February 2015, a cherry picker photographic survey had been undertaken of the exterior, in particular the various roof structures. Besides the survey of the veranda by The Ironwork Studio, other surveys were undertaken by specialist firms, in particular by Ornate Interiors of Leeds (a plaster and render survey), Ventrolla (window survey), and Quadriga Contracts Ltd of Northwich (survey, pricing, and specification work for the historic fabric repairs). When permission was finally obtained, it became clear that wet rot, but more significantly dry rot, was widespread. The majority of timber floor and roof elements were severely damaged and had to be replaced. Similarly, timber lintels over door and window openings and mortar between bricks to many walls had also been affected. Cracking was evident and large areas of brickwork were loose. This meant that many walls had to be taken down and rebuilt. Rotten timber lintels were replaced in this process.[24] The City's conservation officer was involved at an early stage, giving approval for the opening of ceiling access hatches for inspection, visiting the site to agree details of replacement plastering and ceilings, etc. As investigative work progressed, so the plans and drawings issued by Sheppard Robson and by Booth King and WYG, showing repair and replacement works required, were revised and specifications for tenders to undertake the agreed works drafted. Accordingly, the budget had periodically to be revised.

Following the approval given on 21 April 2015 to the campus-wide planning application,[25] in December 2015, planning permission and listed building consent were granted by the City Council in respect of Greenbank House 'to make internal changes and external alterations and restore listed building for use as a meeting, training and performance space and for ancillary facilities for the student village [and] to carry out external works and landscaping.'[26] Accompanying the plans and various reports submitted to the Planning Authority in support of the grant of this permission and consent was a Design and Access Statement prepared by Sheppard Robson, Knight Frank, and Landscape Projects in July and revised in November 2015. Greenbank House was 'to be the key focal point of the Greenbank campus,' the campus regeneration ensuring that 'this century's graduates can enjoy Greenbank House and appreciate the history of the University which they attend.' Though the walled garden, pond, and outhouses of Greenbank House had been demolished in 1972 to make way for the erection of Roscoe and Gladstone halls, the surviving key spaces of the garden, the lawn, and the fishpond were to be restored to form a distinctive foreground, separated from the more distant woodland and garden by clumps of evergreen trees and the ha-ha wall (to the south of the house); the formal terraces close to the house, providing seating spaces and access to the main entrance, were to transition to the more flowing landscape to the south and west, with the sweeping driveway to the house being reinstated. As the brief for the wider site plan had evolved, so feasibility options had been carried out and revisions made so that the house might accommodate differing social and study functions; with the proposed shop and café relocated to the main student hub in Derby Hall, so the brief for the house required a combination of group study rooms, bookable meeting spaces, and music rooms.

By January 2016, ULCCO-SP could report that a roof strip had commenced and that interior demolition and soft strip works were to start on 30 January 2017; in the meantime, a large part of ceiling had fallen down, Booth King looking at providing a temporary works scheme to make the area safe to work in, though this would prove difficult as there was nothing obvious from which to support the structure. Negotiations with the conservation officer proved necessary to determine how the decorative plasterwork and timber window works were to be conserved. It was recognised that the majority of the existing decorative plasterwork cornices could not be removed and then re-installed; in respect of new cornices to be spliced in next to existing sections, moulds were to be taken for these new elements with the existing paint layers left on, so ensuring that they retained the same appearance when spliced in. The complicated nature of the works required for the timber window works led to a subcontractor declining to submit a quotation. As the subcontractors began to be appointed, the University's ability to obtain the prior agreement of the conservation officer concerning samples of materials, details, and sample repair works was facilitated. Over the period of the works, there was a succession of four different conservation officers, each having a slightly different view and approach, their heavy workloads in a city undergoing a period of rapid change affecting conservation areas and many listed buildings – Liverpool having one of the highest number of listed buildings in the UK outside London – limiting the time they could devote to a particular building. It was unfortunate that Liverpool understandably encountered problems recruiting and retaining conservation officers; at one stage, in the absence of an officer in post, decisions were delayed, slowing site progress.[27] That Cerys Edwards (later Mrs Cerys Robinson), a Master of Planning graduate of the University of Liverpool and a Building Conservation MSc graduate of the University of Central Lancashire, appointed as Urban Design and Conservation Officer in November 2017, was to remain in post while the works were completed was very much welcomed. The care taken over the restoration and new lease of life granted to Greenbank House was to mirror a successful period of physical urban renewal and regeneration and the exploitation of its cultural attractions and heritage which Liverpool had undertaken, presenting a very different picture to the world from that of the 1980s.

Planning permissions

Following the submission of amended plans, on 31 August 2016, as local planning authority the City Council granted planning permission for the erection of the new halls of residence and the refurbishment of Derby Hall (providing 1,361 bedrooms in total, with ancillary support accommodation), the erection of a sports hall and sports pavilion, and the layout of sports pitches/facilities.[28] In the case officer's report to the Planning Committee, it was noted that the Council had approved the University's planning and listed building application for Greenbank House and that it was considered that the plans for the new halls etc. would have no detrimental impact on the condition of Greenbank House or the conservation area. Of particular note, as stated by English Heritage, was the retention and internal modernisation of Derby Hall; that the new residential blocks would provide effective replacements for those existing; and that the architectural approach of presenting a series of understated elevations to the public highways, while presenting more flamboyant inner courtyards which respect the conservation area, provided the scheme with distinctiveness. In February 2015, even before the redevelopment at Greenbank began, the University Council was pleased to learn that there had been a significant improvement in the quality of student accommodation since 2011, with a rise in the percentage of the ensuite stock from nine to fifty-three, bringing the University into line with its fellow members of the Russell Group.[29]

In February 2015, the University Council was informed that overall the expected cost of delivering the residential estate strategy, which had been agreed in 2011, was c. £216m; when estimated receipts from property sold off were taken into account, the net cost was estimated at £170m, which would be raised through commercial loans. The refurbishment of the Greenbank element of the estate was estimated at £90m. Subsequent changes in cost driven by the finalisation of design, responses to planning restrictions, and the deterioration of the site, among other factors, were to lead to an increase in expenditure.[30] In January 2018, the University was reported as investing £116.5m in the Greenbank estate with significant funds being spent on refurbishing and remodelling Greenbank House 'to return it to its former glory in terms of conservation and aesthetics but in compliance, where appropriate, with current building standards, modern building user requirements and expectations and increase [of] the life of the building.' The financial model employed to digest the various estimates forecast that the strategy would pay for itself over a period of about forty years.[31]

In granting planning permission in July 2016 for repairs to the pond, external alterations to Greenbank House (including new windows, doors, roof lights, and fire escape), and alterations to the boundary wall and installation of new gates, the City Council, as was usual, attached a number of conditions. Six of the conditions were stated to be 'in the interests of design and conservation,' including the requirement that a sample of any new stone, brick, slate, or stucco render (which should match the original materials in composition, size, colour, and texture) to be used for repairs or reinstatement had to be approved by the planning authority before work commenced; that all masonry work and repointing should be carried out using an appropriate hydraulic lime mortar mix without colour or other additives; that all new windows and external doors were to have a material finish in a colour to be approved by the authority; and that all new gutters, rainwater goods, and soil pipes were to be cast iron and painted in a colour to be agreed prior to implementation.[32] In respect of the condition relating to repointing with lime mortar, it is perhaps not generally appreciated how much time and effort is required, using old-fashioned hand tools, carefully to rake and chisel out old cement mortar which acts as a barrier, trapping moisture within walls.

To inform discussions with the Council, Sheppard Robson produced proposals for the paint colours to be employed on the exterior.[33] Noting that the existing colour of the early nineteenth-century wing was pink/peach, previously blue, it was recommended that a neutral/muted version of the original 'bath stone' colour be adopted, it being felt that the original 'bath stone' colour was 'too strong and rich for current taste.' Analysis of the many layers of paint on the veranda had revealed that over the years three primary colour schemes, of dark green, black, and white respectively, had been adopted; as the original 'holly green' colour was also felt to be 'too strong a colour statement for contemporary use,' it was recommended that it be 'de-saturated to generate a warm grey with similar tonal properties.' To match the original, there was no hesitation in recommending black for the drainage, pipes, gutters, etc.

The redevelopment of the residential campus proceeds

Though Sheppard Robson had been commissioned to lead the refurbishment of Greenbank House and the replacement and expansion of the student residential accommodation and the refurbishment of Derby Hall's 'Old Court,' given the extensive investigations and surveys of Greenbank House which had to be made to determine how to bring the building back into long-term use, it proved necessary to split it out of the main planning application. Accordingly, the replacement and expansion of the residential accommodation and the refurbishment of Derby Hall proceeded on a separate timeline to that for Greenbank House's restoration.

The brief to the Sheppard Robson team for the wider site was to replace outdated 1960s student accommodation with a full en suite residential development that would provide prospective students with a high-quality alternative to city-centre living, building on the unique qualities of the site. This included the following spatial requirements: 1,367 en suite bedrooms (increasing on-site provision by 40 per cent); a gym, outdoor courts, and an indoor multi-use space; a variety of social spaces; pastoral support spaces; a surgery, music practice rooms, games facilities, and study spaces; and an energy centre. The development was to be phased and to be BREEAM (Building Research Establishment Environmental Assessment) Excellent. (BREEAM is the world's longest-established method of assessing, rating, and certifying the sustainability of buildings.)

Phase One of the new Greenbank Student Village was successfully completed in September 2017, with the provision of new Derby and Rathbone halls on the sites of their predecessors, providing 509 en suite bedrooms, with the completion of the refurbishment of Derby Hall's Old Court, to provide a further 167 en suite bedrooms to the same standard as that of the new halls, a year later. The welcoming, attractive, and high-quality environment was reflected in full occupation from the halls' opening; students were provided with en suite bedrooms, a reception hub, gym facilities, an energy centre with low-carbon technology, and new external multi-use games areas (MUGA). In turn, the new Roscoe and Gladstone halls were erected on the site of their predecessors, providing 709 en suite bedrooms, opening in August 2019, completing the University's student residence investment programme.

Rupert Goddard, a Partner in Sheppard Robson, has provided the following account of the architects' design response to the brief:

> The complex package of redevelopment replaced six 1960s buildings with three new student accommodation blocks offering full en-suite accommodation and a range of social spaces. Derby Hall, Rathbone Hall and Roscoe and Gladstone Halls all take advantage of their unique setting and open up key sight lines and linkages across the site.

> The new accommodation blocks have been created around three distinct landscaped courtyards and range in height from five to eight storeys, making use of natural sight levels. The materials, scale and massing of the design have been developed to reflect both the character of the conservation area and the distinctive mature landscape of the Greenbank site.

A view of the new Derby Hall courtyard, 2020.
(Photograph courtesy of Adrian Lambert Photography)

The overall effect is of a series of distinct blocks with a shared architectural language that balances modernity with contextual references, allowing improved sightlines into the park landscape and reinforcing the setting of Greenbank House.

The materiality of the new blocks responds to the context by using a sympathetic brick as the primary material. This is contrasted with a PVDF-coated metal shingle that changes from yellow-gold to green accordingly to the angle of the sun, which is used on the park-facing side of the scheme. Window reveals and frames are picked out to refer to aspects of the conservation area, to be both respectful and distinctive.

Within Derby Old Court, the challenge was to undertake significant internal reorganization of the plan. This included taking rooms that were thermally and spatially inefficient and replacing them with a more social arrangement to give this important building a new lease of life.

The elevation composition of the outward-facing 'formal' elevations follows controlled guidelines, using feature windows to reduce vertical proportions to respond to the language of the conservation area. The park-facing 'informal' facades feature a contrasting composition using window arrangements that stagger across the façade, used in combination with a metal shingle cladding system.

The outer, formal elevations which face onto the surrounding neighbourhood and conservation area are finished in brick, the predominant material of existing buildings such as Derby Old Court. In contrast, the inner park-facing façades to Rathbone and Derby Hall are finished with shimmering metal shingles, introducing a range of tone, textures, richness and character to the inner courtyards and park setting.

A key focus during the concept development was the selection of two opposing materials that worked together in a contrasting yet complementary manner. A PVDF aluminium standing seam system was selected, as used on our nearby Notre Dame Catholic College project for the Liverpool Schools programme.

PVDF is a resin based coating which is applied to the aluminium during the coil manufacture process. Pigments are then added to the resin which imparts colour, depth and brightness. The resulting finish has pearlescent quality and a highly reflective finish which varies under natural light from green to gold.

As at Notre Dame, the material was selected to soften the perceived mass of the building and add variety and interest to the façades. At Greenbank we chose to apply the material as a tiled shingle rather than a sheet standing seam, in order to enhance the tonal variation of the PVDF finish and to be sympathetic to the unique character of the conservation area.

In order to determine the ideal shingle size, 3D testing was undertaken to ensure that the format worked with the fenestration and was well balanced across the face. We worked collaboratively with Range Roofing, who were also involved at Notre Dame, and focused heavily on the key interfaces such as the mansard junction, the relationship with the brickwork to the shingle and the window projection reveal.

The resulting finish is testimony to a positive working relationship between architect, main contractor and sub-contractor, enhancing the character of the Mossley Hill conservation area.

The recruitment of specialist subcontractors

It takes a huge amount of skill and technical expertise to restore historic buildings. The University was most fortunate that it was able to draw on specialist subcontractors, remarkably almost all based in the north-west of England, principally Merseyside and Cheshire, to undertake the more specialist work in restoring Greenbank House to the highest standards required. Of the forty or so separate subcontractors who worked on the building, the following might be identified as among those doing the main elements of the restoration works: Quadriga Contracts Limited, of Northwich (main masonry, stone, roof carpentry, flooring, and window restoration works); W. Swindles & Son (Roofing), of St Helens (all slate roofing and lead work); Calibre Metalwork Ltd, of Stockport (restoration of the iron veranda); Peter Cox Limited, of Liverpool (all timber treatment and damp proofing work); Ornate Interiors Limited, of Stanningley, West Yorkshire (all traditional lath and lime plaster work, including decorative replica plaster mouldings); R. J. C. Joinery Ltd, of Knowsley Industrial Park (all internal joinery, including replica doors); R. J. Clarke, of Fleetwood (internal painting decoration works); Kimpton Ltd, of Birkenhead (all mechanical, electrical and plumbing works); Axiom Group, of Ampthill, Bedfordshire (floor coverings); and Broadstock Office Furniture Limited, of Macclesfield (internal furniture). The restored house is an outstanding testament to the revival of traditional English craft skills in more recent decades. In the quality of the work, the conservation of Greenbank House demonstrates that conservation is both an art and a science, drawing on a diverse range of skills.

Above and opposite top: Work in progress on the eighteenth-century, Gothic, and Victorian wings, April 2019.
(Photographs courtesy of ULCCO-Special Projects)

Above: Applying the first coat of lime plaster
to the prepared lath wall, September 2019.
(ULCCO-Special Projects)
Right: New Gothick panelling and window
frame, April 2019.
(ULCCO-Special Projects)

The structural engineering challenges

The challenges presented to the structural engineer, Booth King Partnership Limited, and how they were addressed is outlined by Mark Moppett, the company's managing director:

> The role of the structural engineer was to repair the listed structure using like-for-like materials to accord with the principles of building conservation and to facilitate the architectural modifications. This is difficult in any listed and heritage-sensitive building but Greenbank House presented additional complications.

> The many modifications and extensions that had been carried out over time made the construction of the building extremely variable and unpredictable. The quality of the construction and details in many locations was of a poor standard.

> The building had almost been extensively destroyed by rot. Barely a joist, rafter, lintel or wall escaped.

> The widespread structural breakdown was due to fungal attack, combined with the many poorly constructed historical modifications rendered the building extremely dangerous and unsafe in many areas. These effects demanded extensive stabilization, followed by intensive repair works and making good before the new modifications could be implemented.

> Repair and Conversion Works
> Before repair works could begin all floor, wall and roof structures which were known or suspected to be damaged by rot and therefore potentially at risk of collapse were propped to maintain their stability and to make the building safe. In addition, a covered scaffold structure with an integral temporary roof was erected around and over the entire building to protect it from the weather and to provide access to the facade walls and roof at each level.

> The repairs and conservation works to the structure were carried out by a Historic Building Repair and Restoration specialist, Quadriga Contracts Limited of Northwich, working as sub-contractors to the University of Liverpool Construction Company. All repair works were designed and detailed by the Structural Engineer, Booth King, sub-contractor to ULCCO SP.

Roofs
Area by area the roof coverings were stripped off and each element of the roof structure was assessed and then retained, repaired or replaced with new structural timbers that had been pretreated with pressure impregnated preservatives. All wall surfaces and original timber elements that could be salvaged were treated with antifungal sprays.

(Writing about the roof, Brian McGorry, the Site Manager, has recorded that 'after the roof survey was completed, it was realized that all the slates would have to be removed to enable a proper intrusive survey of the timbers to be taken which exposed a number of problems, mainly rotted timbers. The main area of concern was the 18th century area where all ridge timbers and spars had to be replaced due to severe rot whilst the main trusses were able to be saved and restored where required. The central core of the roof running through the Gothic area to the 18th century area was also badly rotted due to this being the main gutter from which the lead protection had been removed. Once all the timbers to all roofs had been repaired, all the original slates were put back on. There were also the three chimney stacks built through the roof which also required dismantling and rebuilding.')

Walls
As areas of plasterwork and other wall finishes were removed, it became clear that dry rot was effectively universal throughout the building and so the wholesale removal of finishes was necessary.

Many walls were variously loose, cracked, distorted, or damaged by dry rot and each one was taken down and rebuilt or stitched together where conditions permitted. Where masonry could be retained it was treated with antifungal compounds following any partial demolition.

Most chimney stacks were dilapidated, heavily inclined and consequently unsafe. They were each taken down and rebuilt.

All timber lintels were replaced due to degradation.

Façade walls were repointed to building conservation standards, using appropriate lime mortars which are more sympathetic to brickwork. Lime mortars breathe and permit more movement than modern cementitious mortars. As part of the repointing, the mortar joints were 'struck' to match and replicate the appropriate historic pointing style.

Floors
Floors at ground and first floor levels were mostly beyond repair and were extensively replaced.

Examples of Repair Work
The range and extent of the repair works was considerable and the following photographs provide a sample of the issues that the building posed.

The impressive temporary roof soars over the building and the roof coverings have been stripped back to reveal the timber carcass.

The sagging of the roof ridge beams can be seen. The sagging has occurred because the ridge beams were not of an adequate size to resist the weight applied by the roof. Over time the deflection of the timber increases or 'creeps' under sustained loading. This mechanism leads to the supporting walls being pushed outwards as the roof drops and spreads.

The picture shows the rotten end of a timber roof 'truss' (a triangular frame) over the early 18th century wing. The effect of the rot was to render the truss unsafe and prone to collapse.

Here the same truss end has been repaired using new treated timber and steel plates. It is also noticeable that the structure of the roof in this area has been completely removed pending wholesale replacement.

One of the dividing walls in the 18th century wing where water ingress caused large vertical cracks to develop and dry rot degraded the mortar, loosening the bricks. The wall was taken down to sound brickwork, the cracks were stitched together, and the wall was treated with an antifungal spray.

This is an example of temporary beams or needles that were inserted to prop a brickwork wall to allow repairs to be carried out on the dilapidated structure below.

This photograph shows the complete degradation (due to dry rot) of the timber elements which once supported the curved brick and stone parapet wall above a bay window on the west side of the Gothic wing. The large weight of masonry above the bay window was close to collapse. It is significant that the original roof structure has been removed due to severe rot.

Pieces of the iron veranda in the workshop awaiting repair. This element was completely renovated by expert craftsmen, Calibre Metalwork Ltd of Stockport.

The south façade of the Gothic wing following the removal of the iron veranda for conservation, April 2019. (ULCCO-Special Projects)

Documenting the work carried out in individual rooms over the course of the three-to-four-year period of the renovation works, Brian McGorry, the site manager, observed what was revealed when more intrusive inspections were undertaken following the various surveys. The work undertaken in individual rooms witnesses that in the restoration of the house the University was endorsing what some might regard as lost trades, encouraging a very high standard of craftsmanship that is unusual nowadays; a large team of craftsmen working together towards one goal. The intangible heritage of historical skills was being cared for. Of Room G/001 (adjoining what is now the main entrance), he notes that when all the plaster was removed, a very rusted and inadequate steel beam which supported the floor above was exposed. When the rotted floor was removed, an old culvert under the building was exposed which had partly collapsed and required clearing out. The ceiling to the basement is constructed in brick arches and part was exposed when the floor was removed; a dumb waiter shaft introduced, possibly in the 1970s, had damaged the floor and had to be repaired. The room was floored with old York stone flags which had to be removed due to damp issues; upon lifting the flags, a kitchen midden was discovered which suggests that this part of the building was a later addition to the original.

Part of the suspended timber floor above the original cellar removed due to dry and wet rot and being prepared for replacement, September 2019.
(ULCCO-Special Projects)

On the first floor, in what Brian McGorry noted was possibly the most structurally unstable part of the building, the main beam of Room 1/002 carrying the brickwork that was supporting part of the roof was found to be constructed of a 15mm steel beam with a timber lintel bolted either side that had rotted due to the ingress of water over a number of years; following propping, the lintels were replaced and a new steel beam built in position, the brickwork being taken down and new brickwork built. The room's original floor, comprising timber joists supported by two large timber beams with floorboards on the joists, had at some later time been overlaid by a concrete floor; considerable concern about the weight of the concrete on the timber floor and the discovery of rot within the two supporting beams led to the floor being fully propped from below while the concrete was broken out and the timber floor and beams replaced.

Whereas in other rooms it proved possible to retain existing walls, addressing structural cracks in the brickwork, in some cases rebuilding walls with the same bricks (as in G/008–9, 029 and 032) or, as in the case of Room 1/002, new brickwork following the replacement of a defective steel beam, major cracks to all the walls and trees growing through external walls necessitated a new build between the house and the old stables (G/005–007 and 031), the old building being taken down brick by brick and rebuilt in the same brick, these rooms thus becoming a new build.

Though in the course of the work no records were found secreted, the removal of plaster from walls in some areas revealed features which had long been lost – in Room G/027, the removal of the plaster from the wall to the east elevation revealed a section adjoining the south elevation which had been rebuilt along with a section of the south elevation wall, suggesting either subsidence or possible bomb damage during the Second World War; in Room G/028 (the 'Macadam Room'), an arch over a bricked-up door opening was found; in Room G/016, once the ceiling was taken down, a large supporting riveted steel beam was exposed which looked as if it could have been part of a ship's construction; in Room G/012, a chimney breast was found built around an existing chimney breast; and in Room G/006, five recessed arched openings that had been bricked up were found behind the plaster, a decision being made to open them up to bring the room back to its original design.

Lath and plaster removal to allow rotted timber to be removed was in turn replaced with new lath and plaster. Where windows and other original features had to be replaced due to extensive rot, they, too, were replaced like for like; in the porch to the east entrance (Room G/024) and on the first-floor balcony, in Room 1/024, moulds were taken of the ceilings before their removal to allow the timber work behind to be replaced, exact copies being fixed in place.

A new foundation excavation for a section of the outbuildings that had to be taken down and rebuilt; rebuilding on the site of the stable block, looking towards the rear of the eighteenth-century wing.
(ULCCO-Special Projects)

The choice of room names

The refurbishment of Greenbank House was intended 'to showcase the importance and history of the Rathbone/University relationship.'[34] Operating as a modern-day conference centre within a heritage environment, it was intended to provide an additional facility from which to conduct University business; to provide facilities in which student groups and societies could meet, enhancing the student experience and helping to build a student community; and to make rooms available to external organisations to hold meetings and events. The individual seminar/society rooms provided for both small and large groups, the Knowsley and Somerville Rooms for six persons, the Carnatic and Lightbody Rooms for eight, the Shaftesbury Room for ten, the Macadam Room for eleven, the Bridgewater, Granby, and Kensington Rooms for twelve, the Holt Room for eighteen, and the Brodie Room for thirty persons. Two of the additional three social rooms on the ground floor could accommodate up to ten, the third twenty-five persons.

The choice of room names was made by Mike Kelley, director of the University's Residential and Commercial Services, who had previously contacted a member of the Rathbone family, the Guild of Students, and others. They commemorate members of the Rathbone family and benefactors: the first William Rathbone to settle in Liverpool (William Rathbone the second) was born at **Gawsworth** near Macclesfield in 1696; in 1768, his son, William Rathbone the third, was the first of a succession of family members to occupy a house and warehouses, the base of the Rathbone business, adjoining the Duke of **Bridgewater**'s dock; the **Lightbody** Room commemorates Hannah Lightbody who married Samuel Greg (of Quarry Bank Mill) and whose eldest daughter, Elizabeth, married William Rathbone the fifth in 1812; Eleanor Rathbone spent a year at **Kensington** High School, 1889–90, later studying at **Somerville** College, Oxford, 1893–96, forming a close relationship with Elizabeth **Macadam**, with whom she was to share a home, serving as an independent member of Liverpool City Council, representing the **Granby** Ward, 1909–35, standing, unsuccessfully, for the East **Toxteth** division at the General Election in 1922 before she won election, as an Independent, as an MP for the Combined English Universities in 1929. Numbered among the principal benefactors of the University, besides members of the Rathbone family, are successive earls of Derby, whose family home is at **Knowsley** Hall; and George **Holt** and his daughter Emma, who left the family home, Sudley, and its contents to Liverpool Corporation. The Shaftesbury Room recollects that in nearby Sefton Park there is a cast of the famous Shaftesbury Memorial in Piccadilly Circus, London, commemorating the seventh Earl of **Shaftesbury** (1801–85), evangelical Christian, factory reformer and philanthropist, who piloted successive factory acts through Parliament, regulated conditions in the coal mines, and provided lodging houses for the poor. The **Carnatic** Room recalls that the University's former Carnatic Halls of Residence at Elmswood Road and North Mossley Hill Road (which closed in June 2019) were erected on the site of Carnatic Hall, named after the French East Indiaman 'Carnatic,' captured in 1778 by a privateer, the 'Mentor,' owned by Peter Baker, the profits from some of the prize money allowing him to erect the first Carnatic Hall. Though John Alexander **Brodie** (1858–1934) has achieved lasting fame for his patent (1890) for goal nets for football and other games, as Liverpool's City Engineer, 1898–1926, he was responsible for improving the provision of acceptable working-class housing, for improving the city's road systems, and for work on the construction of the Mersey Tunnel, completed in 1934; he was an Honorary Associate Professor of Municipal Engineering and an Honorary Lecturer in Civic Design at the University of Liverpool.

7   Greenbank House reopens

After five years of painstaking repair and restoration, Greenbank House was handed back to the University in January 2020. For the first time in 200 years, the house had been thoroughly restored, remedying the defects in its original construction, successive extensions, and subsequent alterations, installing modern technology, and providing a new lease of life to a tired building; the house now appeared in full glory, representing an outstanding example of restoration work. Advances in technology in recent years had allowed a seamless join between old and new, integrating thermally efficient heating, ventilation, lighting, audiovisual, and communication systems into the fabric of the building.

After a delay, the City Council signed off the house from a planning and listed building perspective, issuing certificates to this effect on 5 March 2020. On 4 March 2020, the first Covid-19 case in Liverpool had been confirmed and a week later, on 11 March, the World Health Organisation declared a global pandemic in respect of the spread worldwide of the coronavirus disease. From 16 March, all face-to-face classes, including lectures, laboratory-based classes, seminars, and tutorials at the University were cancelled for the remainder of the 2019/20 academic year. On 23 March the prime minister announced an immediate closure of all but essential services such as health, pharmacies, and food stores and the banning of gatherings of more than two people in public, with travel to and from work to be only undertaken when absolutely necessary. The University had already been reducing the number of its services over the previous few weeks in order to protect staff and students, the vast majority of staff now working from home, the Harold Cohen and Sydney Jones Libraries finally closing to users from after 20 and 23 March respectively, with the announcement on 24 March that outside

Opposite top: The completed building looking towards the south and west elevations of the Victorian and Gothic wings respectively.
(Reproduced courtesy of Adrian Lambert Photography)
Opposite bottom: The restored Victorian sandstone wing with prospect on the corner on the right and the rebuilt, remodelled and extended single-storey section (social spaces, plant room, etc.) to the left.
(Photograph courtesy of Mark Moppett)

the halls of residence all other buildings would now close. Following the easing of lockdown restrictions in June–August, a second lockdown was announced on 31 October, lasting until 2 December, with a third national lockdown entered on 6 January 2021. As lockdown restrictions were eased in April 2021, Professor Dame Janet Beer, the vice-chancellor, expressed her pride in the many ways the University's students, staff, and alumni had responded to the pandemic, from final-year medical students and nurses who supported frontline staff throughout the pandemic, to the University's researchers who worked tirelessly in laboratories trying to understand the developing disease, also the alumni who contributed more than £450,000 in response to the University's appeal to fund vital research, support students in financial hardship, and provide personal protective equipment for frontline workers.[1] 'Fiat Lux' proclaims the University's coat of arms, and with light now emerging at the end of the Covid-19 tunnel it will surely not be long before Greenbank House is able to play its part in fulfilling the University's motto, 'Haec Otia Studia Fovent.'

Public recognition of the quality of the restoration of Greenbank House was afforded in November 2020 when Sheppard Robson and the University were 'Highly Commended' in the 'Fit-out or Refurbishment of the Year' category of the 2020 Liverpool City Region Property Awards (the winner of this category being the Royal Liver Building, restored to its former glory) and in August 2021 a 'Very Good' BREEAM Certificate was awarded for the refurbishment of Greenbank House, this being the highest category that can be achieved for a refurbishment project.

Opposite top: The restored east elevation of the Gothic wing.
(Photograph courtesy of Mark Moppett)
Opposite bottom: The restored east elevation of the Gothic wing with the early eighteenth-century brick façade to the right.
(Photograph courtesy of Mark Moppett)

The restored entrance hall and staircase to the Gothic wing. (Photograph courtesy of Mark Moppett)

The restored entrance hall and staircase to the Gothic wing. (Photograph courtesy of Mark Moppett)

Top: The Shaftesbury Room, the south-eastern room of the Gothic wing, set out as a meeting space with the fully replaced, craftsman-made windows at the far end of the room.
(Photograph courtesy of Mark Moppett)
Above: The restored veranda.
(Reproduced courtesy of Adrian Lambert Photography)

The Gawsworth Room. (Reproduced courtesy of Adrian Lambert Photography)

The Shaftesbury Room, with the restored bookcase. (Reproduced courtesy of Adrian Lambert Photography)

Corridor. (Reproduced courtesy of Adrian Lambert Photography)

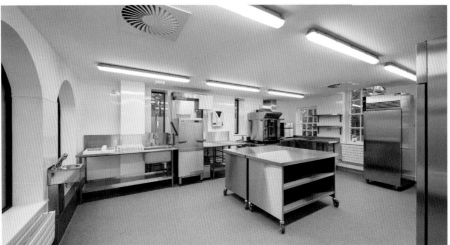

Top: The entrance corridor (on the right), viewed from Greenbank Lane.
(Reproduced courtesy of Adrian Lambert Photography)
Above: Kitchen.
(Reproduced courtesy of McCoy Wynne Photography, Liverpool)

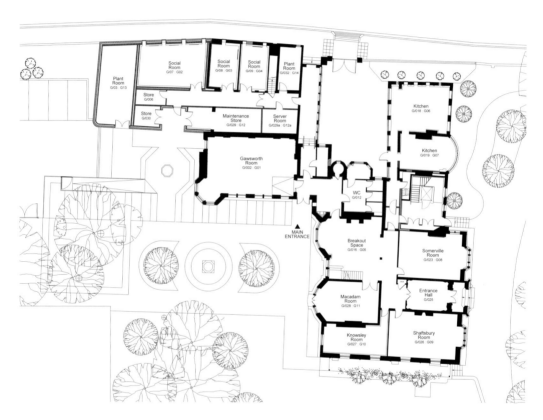

Ground-floor plan, Greenbank House.
(Daniel Anderson, ULCCO-Special Projects)

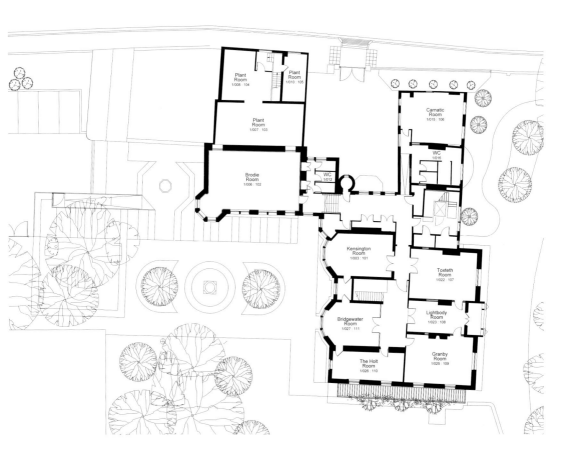

First-floor plan, Greenbank House.
(Daniel Anderson, ULCCO-Special Projects)

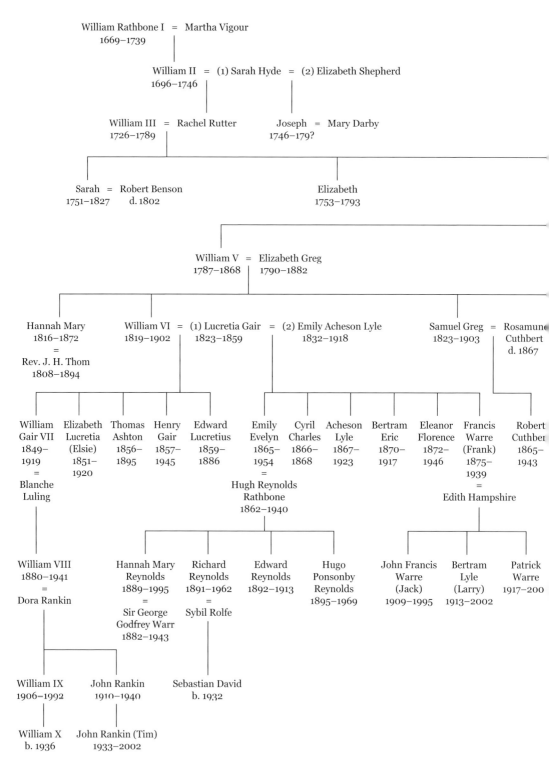

William Rathbone I = Martha Vigour
1669–1739

William II = (1) Sarah Hyde = (2) Elizabeth Shepherd
1696–1746

William III = Rachel Rutter   Joseph = Mary Darby
1726–1789   1746–179?

Sarah = Robert Benson   Elizabeth
1751–1827   d. 1802   1753–1793

William V = Elizabeth Greg
1787–1868   1790–1882

Hannah Mary   William VI = (1) Lucretia Gair = (2) Emily Acheson Lyle   Samuel Greg = Rosamund
1816–1872   1819–1902   1823–1859   1832–1918   1823–1903   Cuthbert
=   d. 1867
Rev. J. H. Thom
1808–1894

William   Elizabeth Thomas   Henry   Edward   Emily   Cyril   Acheson Bertram Eleanor   Francis   Robert
Gair VII   Lucretia   Ashton   Gair   Lucretius   Evelyn   Charles Lyle   Eric   Florence Warre   Cuthbert
1849–   (Elsie)   1856–   1857–   1859–   1865–   1866–   1867–   1870–   1872–   (Frank)   1865–
1919   1851–   1895   1945   1886   1954   1868   1923   1917   1946   1875–   1943
=   1920   =   1939
Blanche   Hugh Reynolds   =
Luling   Rathbone   Edith Hampshire
                                                      1862–1940

William VIII   Hannah Mary   Richard   Edward   Hugo   John Francis Bertram   Patrick
1880–1941   Reynolds   Reynolds   Reynolds   Ponsonby   Warre   Lyle   Warre
=   1889–1995   1891–1962 1892–1913 Reynolds   (Jack)   (Larry)   1917–200
Dora Rankin   =   =   1895–1969   1909–1995   1913–2002
                      Sir George   Sybil Rolfe
                      Godfrey Warr
                      1882–1943

William IX   John Rankin   Sebastian David
1906–1992   1910–1940   b. 1932

William X   John Rankin (Tim)
b. 1936   1933–2002

188

RATHBONE
FAMILY TREE

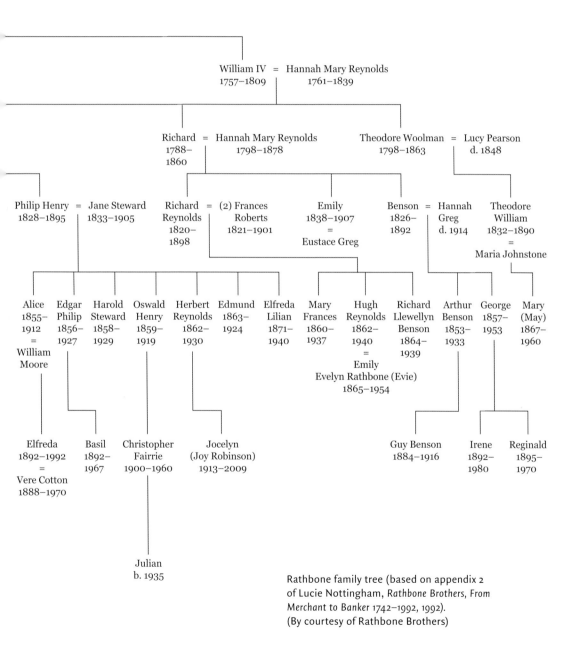

Rathbone family tree (based on appendix 2
of Lucie Nottingham, *Rathbone Brothers, From
Merchant to Banker 1742–1992*, 1992).
(By courtesy of Rathbone Brothers)

Notes

Acknowledgements

1   Adrian Allan, *Greenbank: A Brief History* (Liverpool: University of Liverpool, 1987).

2   In his insightful book, *The Future of Capitalism, Facing the New Anxieties* (Allen Lane, 2018), the distinguished Oxford economist, Professor Sir Paul Collier observes that in a healthy society those who become successful have been reared into acceptance of the web of reciprocal obligations, triggering support for those whose lives have turned out to be less fortunate (p. 213).

3   As the *Liverpool Mercury*, 14 December 1892, recorded, the Principal of University College, Liverpool, read the letters of apology that had been received, noting that 'Mr William Rathbone, M.P., who was perhaps the most resolute and most sympathetic supporter of the College – (applause) – was also unable to be with them, being now on the Continent.'

Chapter 1

1   Lancashire Archives, DDM/50/201.

2   See, in particular, Richard Lawton, 'From the pool of Liverpool to the conurbation of Merseyside' in William T. S. Gould and Alan G. Hodgkiss, eds., *The Resources of Merseyside* (Liverpool: Liverpool University Press, 1982). Another instance of a Liverpool merchant acquiring a small estate in Toxteth Park is that of Moses Benson (1738–1806), who settled in Liverpool where he carried on business as an African trader. Besides a large town house in Duke Street, he acquired a leasehold estate of about 32 acres from Lord Sefton which on his death was advertised in *The Liverpool Courier and Commercial Advertiser* from 27 April 1808 onwards as including a mansion, the garden having hot-houses, grapehouse, and a pinery. Confusingly described as 'Greenbank House and Estate,' some of the property fronting Smeaton [Smithdown] Lane, it is believed the property was not far distant from the Rathbones' Greenbank.

3   William Enfield, *An Essay Towards the History of Leverpool Drawn Up from Papers Left by the late Mr George Perry, and from Other Materials Since Collected* (London: Joseph Johnson, 1774), p. 114.

4   William Wallace Currie, ed., *Memoir of the Life, Writings and Correspondence of James Currie M.D. F.R.S. of Liverpool*, vol. 1 (London, 1831), p. 360.

5   William Rathbone, *A Sketch of family history during four generations, compiled from old letters and papers, and rough notes written by William Rathbone (6) for the use of his children* (typescript, 1894), p. 119.

6   *Victoria History of the Counties of England: Lancashire*, vol. 3 (1907), pp. 40–5. See, too, Joseph Boult, 'The former and recent topography of Toxteth Park' in

Proceedings of the Liverpool Architectural and Archaeological Society, 20th Session, 2nd Meeting, 16 October 1867, 1867, pp. 18–34, and Robert Griffiths, *The History of the Royal and Ancient Park of Toxteth* (Liverpool, 1923).

7   John Belchem, ed., *Liverpool 800: Culture, Character and History* (Liverpool: Liverpool University Press, 2006), p. 158.

8   *Williamson's Liverpool Advertiser*, 15 September 1788.

9   For the estate of the earls of Sefton and its system of tenure, see Andrew Gritt, '"For want of reparations": Tenants and the built environment on the estates of south-west Lancashire, 1750–1850' in *Transactions of the Historic Society of Lancashire and Cheshire*, vol. 150, 2003, especially pp. 34, 40–3, and 47–9.

10 Lancashire Archives, DDM/50/201.

11 Special Collections & Archives, Liverpool University Library, RP XX.1.1; note that the estate is named St Onslow otherwise Green Bank.

12 'Chapter 8, The Lerpinieres,' at users.adam.com.au/easby/Chapter%2208%20-%20The%20Lerpinieres.html, accessed on 31 May 2019.

13 *Leeds Intelligencer*, 21 July 1761; *Gore's Liverpool Advertiser*, 23 April 1795; Wikipedia's entry for 'Liverpool porcelain'; and entry for 'William Reid & Co. (1756–61)' on The British Museum's website. The site of the factory, on the south side of Brownlow Hill, was excavated in 1997 and 1999, by-products of the research being Maurice R. Hillis and Roderick J. Jellicoe, *The Liverpool Porcelain of William Reid: A Catalogue of Porcelain and Excavated Shards* (London: Roderick Jellicoe, 2000) and Maurice Hillis, *Liverpool Porcelain, 1756–1804* (Great Britain, 2011).

14 Francis E. Hyde, *Liverpool and the Mersey: An Economic History of a Port 1700–1970* (Newton Abbot: David & Charles, 1971), pp. 19–20.

15 Lancashire Archives, DDM/10/6.

16 See, in particular, Joseph Sharples, *Liverpool* (Pevsner Architectural Guides, New Haven, CT and London: Yale University Press, 2004). For Abercromby Square, see Adrian R. Allan, *The Building of Abercromby Square* (Liverpool: University of Liverpool, 1986).

17 Rathbone Papers, RP III.1.147.

18 *Williamson's Liverpool Advertiser*, 15 September 1788.

19 RP III.1.138 (letter of 29 October 1786).

20 RP III.1.154.

21 Lancashire Archives, DDM/14/11.

Chapter 2

1   Daniel Defoe, *A Tour through England & Wales*: vol. 2 of Everyman's Library edition, with an Introduction by G. D. H. Cole (London, 1928), pp. 255–6.

2   Lancashire Archives, WCW/Supra/C536A/7.

3   John Belchem, ed., *Liverpool 800: Culture, Character and History* (Liverpool: Liverpool University Press, 2006), p. 169.

4   *A Tribute to the Memory of Mr William Rathbone of Liverpool who died at his house, at Greenbank, 11th February, 1809, 'by a friend'* (Liverpool, 1809).

5   Letter of 30 November 1804, Liverpool Record Office, 920 ROS 5796.

6   Lucie Nottingham, *Rathbone Brothers, From Merchant to Banker 1742–1992* (London: Rathbone Brothers, 1992), pp. 11–12 and 17. For Liverpool and the slave trade, see, in particular, Roger Anstey and P. E. H. Hair, eds., *Liverpool, the African Slave Trade, and Abolition*

(Historic Society of Lancashire and Cheshire, 1976) and Anthony Tibbles, *Liverpool and the Slave Trade* (Liverpool: Liverpool University Press, 2018).

7   Letter of 22 April 1807, Liverpool Record Office, 920 ROS 3060.

8   William Rathbone, *A Sketch of family history*, p. 100.

9   William Wallace Currie, ed., *Memoir of the Life, Writings and Correspondence of James Currie, M.D. F.R.S. of Liverpool*, vol. 1 (London: Longman, Rees, Orme, Brown, and Green, 1831), p. 147.

10 Thomas Kelly, *For Advancement of Learning: The University of Liverpool 1881–1981* (Liverpool: Liverpool University Press, 1981), p. 20; Arline Wilson, 'The cultural identity of Liverpool, 1790–1850: The early learned societies,' *Transactions of the Historic Society of Lancashire and Cheshire*, vol. 147, 1998, pp. 55–80; for the origins of the Botanic Garden, see Eric Greenwood, Steve Lyus, and Ray Lampert, 'Liverpool Botanic Garden: Early curators and gardeners,' *Transactions of the Historic Society of Lancashire and Cheshire*, vol. 167, 2018, pp. 111–30.

11 Robert Southey, *Letters from England*, quoted in Nicholas Murray, *So Spirited a Town: Visions and Versions of Liverpool* (Liverpool: Liverpool University Press, 2007), p. 74.

12 Martin Murphy, *Blanco White: Self-banished Spaniard* (New Haven, CT: Yale University Press, 1989), p. 171.

13 15th edition, n.d. [c. 1852], p. 27.

14 The whole of John Dalton's letter is reproduced in Emily A. Rathbone, ed., *Records of the Rathbone Family for private circulation only* (Edinburgh: R & R Clark, 1913), pp. 111–15.

15 RP III.1.158. Though there is very limited information on the garden at Greenbank House, a lively 'potted' history of gardening in Britain is provided by Jenny Uglow, *A Little History of British Gardening* (London: Chatto & Windus, 2004).

16 RP III.1.160.

17 RP III.1.171.

18 RP III.1.175.

19 RP III.1.178.

20 RP III.1.202.

21 RP III.1.210.

22 RP III.1.251.

23 These extracts are taken from Mrs Eustace Greg, ed., *Reynolds-Rathbone Diaries and Letters 1753–1839* (London: Constable, 1905), which includes entries from Hannah Rathbone's diaries, 1761–62 and 1784–1809, and from her original diary for 1790, RP III.3.1; SCA also holds her diary for 1795, RP III.3.2.

24 Dr John Rutter (1762–1838), born in Liverpool, brought up a Quaker; graduated MD at Edinburgh University in 1786; appointed a Physician to the Liverpool Dispensary in 1792; recognised as a clinician of ability and as a skilful diagnostician; president of the Liverpool Medical Library (precursor of Liverpool Medical Institution), 1826–27 and 1834–38, he long advocated the continued and improved education of the doctor; founder of the Liverpool Medical Institution (whose building was erected 1835–37). One of the founders of the Liverpool Athenaeum (1797). A keen plant collector, he also helped to found Liverpool Botanic Garden in 1802. See John Shepherd, *A History of the Liverpool Medical Institution* (Liverpool: Liverpool Medical Institution, 1979).

25 Revd Theophilus Houlbrooke (1745–1824), a former Anglican clergyman who became a Unitarian in c. 1785. He was elected a Fellow of the Royal Society of Edinburgh in 1792 for his contributions on botany. Both Houlbrooke and William Rathbone were subscribers to the Liverpool Botanic Garden from its opening; besides serving on the Botanic Garden's committee, he was president of the Liverpool Athenaeum, 1808–11.

26 It was in opposition to the government's Orders in Council promulgated in 1806 – in response to Napoleon's decree which declared the British Isles to be in a state of blockade – which prohibited neutral ships from trading with any French ports and declared all French ports and those of her allies to be in state of blockade, so adversely affecting British overseas trade, particularly that with North America, that William Rathbone led the opposition, giving evidence before a committee of the House of Lords.

27 RP XXII.1 p.73.

28 William Rathbone, A Sketch of family history, p. 9.

29 Lancashire Archives, WCW/Supra/C656A/5.

30 Liverpool Record Office, Plan Chest 1 Drawer 3 Map Case 16A.

31 Billinge's Liverpool Advertiser and Marine Intelligencer, 21 July 1800.

32 On page 301. It might be noted that Park Lodge, at the corner of Sefton Park Road, which is understood to incorporate masonry from one of the lodges of the former royal hunting ground of Toxteth Park, was to become the home of Dr Larry Rathbone in the latter half of the twentieth century.

33 For a photocopy of this letter, see RP XIX.3.7.

34 The revised Buildings of England guide Lancashire: Liverpool and the South-West (New Haven, CT and London: Yale University Press, 2006), p. 442, suggests that the veranda could be by the Coalbrookdale Company or perhaps by the local foundry of Joseph Rathbone and William Fawcett.

35 Quentin Hughes, Liverpool: City of Architecture (Liverpool: The Bluecoat Press, 1999), pp. 38–40, and Joseph Sharples, Liverpool (Pevsner Architectural Guides, New Haven, CT and London: Yale University Press, 2004), pp. 264–65 and 293–94.

36 2019 saw the completion of a major conservation project by English Heritage to protect the future of the bridge.

37 In her book, Relatively Rathbone (Richmond: Trotman, 1992), p. 14, Joy Robinson provides this transcript of Revd Houlbrooke's letter, the original of which is not among the University's Rathbone Papers.

38 KMHeritage, University of Liverpool – Greenbank Campus, History and Heritage Significance (April 2012), p. 47.

39 Emily A. Rathbone, ed., Records of the Rathbone Family, p. 364.

40 Ibid., pp. 322–23, quoting from chapter 2 of Henry Chorley's Memoirs, 1873.

41 Lucie Nottingham, Rathbone Brothers, pp. 30–31.

42 The Times Digital Archive, 26 May 1849, drawing on a report in the Liverpool Mercury.

43 William Rathbone, A Sketch of family history, pp. 102–5.

44 RP XXII.1, p. 126.

45 The whole of the letter is reproduced in Daniel Patterson, ed., *John James Audubon's Journal of 1826: The Voyage to The Birds of America* (Lincoln, NE, and London: University of Nebraska Press, 2011), p. 398.

46 The following extracts are reproduced from Daniel Patterson, ed., *John James Audubon's Journal of 1826*, by kind permission of the University of Nebraska Press, © 2011 by the Board of Regents of the University of Nebraska.

47 John Chancellor, *Audubon, A Biography* (London: Weidenfeld and Nicholson, 1978), p. 117.

48 Daniel Patterson, ed., *John James Audubon's Journal of 1826*, p. 155.

49 In 1826, the site of what is now No. 24 Abercromby Square, close to the junction with Bedford Street North, is recorded as being leased by Liverpool Corporation to Theodore Rathbone, a cotton broker, a younger brother of William Rathbone the fifth, and as a house in 1828; presumably the house had been very recently erected.

50 Dr Thomas S. Traill (1782–1862), graduated MD at Edinburgh University in 1802; he was subsequently in general practice in Liverpool until 1832 when he returned to Edinburgh as Regius Professor of Medical Jurisprudence. A Whig and a member of the 'Roscoe group,' he was a founder member and first secretary of the Liverpool Literary and Philosophical Society and a prime mover in the establishment of the Liverpool Royal Institution, where he lectured on chemistry.

51 Lady Isabella Margaret Douglas (1760–1830) was the eldest daughter of Dunbar Douglas, fourth Earl of Selkirk (d. 1799); though her brother, Thomas Douglas, fifth Earl of Selkirk (d. 1820), did not serve as a governor [general] of Canada, he is noteworthy as a Scottish philanthropist who sponsored immigrant settlements in Canada. As noted on p. 27, Lord Selkirk visited Greenbank in 1801.

52 In his journal entry for 29 September 1826, Audubon records that the previous evening at Greenbank, Hannah Rathbone had invited him to place the 'good likeness' of himself in a 'beautiful frame of Rose wood.'

53 Daniel Patterson, ed., *John James Audubon's Journal of 1826*, pp. 171–72.

54 Maria R. Audubon, *Audubon and his Journals*, vol. 1 (London: John C. Nimmo, 1898), p. 269.

55 Ibid., p. 274.

Chapter 3

1 The text of this letter of 10 June 1808 is transcribed in William Rathbone, *A Sketch of family history*, pp. 44–5.

2 Eleanor F. Rathbone, *William Rathbone: A Memoir* (London: Macmillan, 1905), p. 39.

3 Nowadays No. 24 Abercromby Square forms part of the School of Architecture and Building Engineering.

4 RP XXII.1, p. 75.

5 'How cheap washing may be provided for the poor: letter from the late William Rathbone, Esq., a letter of 26 January 1848, republished in the local press,' n.d., RP XXII.1a; and William Rathbone, *A Sketch of family history*, pp. 84 and 108–19. See, too, Susan Pedersen's entry on Catherine (Kitty) Wilkinson (1786–1860) in the *Oxford Dictionary of National Biography*. Buried in St James' cemetery,

6 A description of this silverware, accompanied by photographs of the candelabrum-epergne and the basket, is to be found in The University of Liverpool Recorder, No.78, October 1978, pp. 4–6. For a contemporary description of the plate, see RP XXII.1, p. 102.

7 Steven Brindle, 'Upstaging the world: St George's Hall, Liverpool', Country Life, 3 July 2019, pp. 50–55.

8 See the obituaries which the local press published on her death, aged 92, in 1882: RP XXII.1 and 1a.

9 See, too, the text of the letter of 15 November 1836 which William Rathbone wrote entreating his 'brother Reformers in the Council' not to abandon the Irish system, 'one of the most effectual means by which the moral and religious education of the people is to be accomplished', RP XXII.1, pp. 91–3.

10 William Rathbone, A Sketch of family history, pp. 56–7.

11 Dugald Stewart (1753–1828) held the Chair of Moral Philosophy at Edinburgh University, 1785–1810 and 1820, his students including Lord Brougham and Lord John Russell; Sir John Archibald Murray, Lord Murray (1778?–1859), Whig politician, Lord Advocate, 1834–39, and later a Judge of the Court of Session, Edinburgh; Francis Jeffrey, Lord Jeffrey (1773–1850), editor of The Edinburgh Review for about twenty-six years until 1829, and later a Judge of the Court of Session; Henry Brougham, Lord

Brougham and Vaux (1778–1868), Whig politician, Lord Chancellor, 1830–34. All were key figures of the Scottish Enlightenment of the eighteenth and early nineteenth centuries. (Dugald Stewart's publications include an Account of the Life and Writings of Adam Smith [1795], Adam Smith's own most influential publications comprising The Theory of Moral Sentiments [1759] and An Inquiry into the Nature and Causes of the Wealth of Nations [1776].)

12 William Rathbone, A Sketch of family history, p. 96.

13 Ibid., p. 100. Lord John Russell, first Earl Russell (1792–1878), Whig politician, prime minister 1846–52 and 1865–66, foreign secretary, 1859–65; Mr Edward J. Stanley (1826–1907), Conservative MP for Somerset West 1882–85 and for Bridgwater 1885–1906, married the daughter of Henry Labouchere, Baron Taunton; Daniel O'Connell (1775–1847), Irish nationalist leader; Henry Labouchere, Baron Taunton (1798–1869), Whig politician, MP for Taunton 1830–59, held ministerial office including as president of the Board of Trade, 1839–41 and 1847–52.

14 William Rathbone, A Sketch of family history, p. 99.

15 The life of Robert Owen written by himself with his preface and an introduction by John Butt (London, 1971), p. vii.

16 William Rathbone, A Sketch of family history, p. 101.

17 For a study of the life and work of Blanco White, see Martin Murphy, Blanco White: Self-banished Spaniard (New Haven, CT: Yale University Press, 1989); see, too, his entry for Blanco White in the Oxford Dictionary of National Biography

in which he judges Blanco White's 'most enduring legacy has proved to be his life, read as a paradigm of the struggle to reconcile faith with doubt and reason with imagination.'

18 Martin Murphy, *Blanco White: Self-banished Spaniard*, p. 172.

19 Special Collections and Archives, University of Liverpool Library, BW 1/124.

20 Lancashire Archives, DRL 1/80.

21 RP XXII.1, p. 177.

22 Richard Rathbone (1788–1860) was in partnership with his elder brother, William Rathbone the fifth, as merchants, from 1809 until his retirement in 1835. Richard Rathbone was the grandfather of Hugh R. Rathbone, whose children in 1944 were to gift Greenbank to the University.

23 RP XX.1.4.

24 Will accessed online per the government's Probate Search Service.

25 *The Porcupine*, 6 May 1865, p. 11; copy: RP XXII.1, p. 79. A black and white photograph of the portrait, by James H. Millington, is reproduced in the Walker Art Gallery's catalogue, *Merseyside Painters, People & Places: Catalogue of Oil Paintings – Plates* (Liverpool: Merseyside County Council, 1978), p. 118.

Chapter 4

1 Lancashire Archives, DDX 162/78/09.

2 R. A. Cordingley, 'Three houses,' *Blue Pigeon, The Magazine of Derby Hall*, 1949, pp. 11–14.

3 Lancashire Archives, DDX 162/10/04 and DDX 162/89/50.

4 Sheila Marriner, *Rathbones of Liverpool 1845–73* (Liverpool: Liverpool University Press, 1961).

5 B. Guinness Orchard, *Liverpool's Legion of Honour* (Birkenhead: B. Guinness Orchard, 1893), p. 581.

6 William Rathbone, *A Sketch of family history*, p. 132. See, too, Frank Prochaska, *Royal Bounty: The Making of a Welfare Monarchy* (New Haven, CT and London: Yale University Press, 1995), p. 3. Somewhat later, in his short treatise, '*Unto This Last*' (1862), John Ruskin emphasised the importance of human relations in a capitalist system: 'That country is the richest which nourishes the greatest number of noble and happy human beings; that man is richest who, having perfected the functions of his own life to the utmost, has also the widest helpful influence, both personal, and by means of his possessions, over the lives of others.'

7 Aristotle, *The Politics*, translated with an Introduction by T. A. Sinclair (Harmondsworth: Penguin Books, 1962), pp. 25 and 28. Even before entering Oxford to read Greats (which included the study of Plato and Aristotle), William Rathbone's daughter Eleanor was attempting to read Aristotle (Susan Pedersen, *Eleanor Rathbone and the Politics of Conscience* (New Haven, CT and London: Yale University Press, 2004), p. 51).

8 John Bowle, *Western Political Thought from the Origins to Rousseau* (London: Methuen, 1961), p. 64.

9 RP IX.4.187 (letter to Elizabeth Lucretia ('Elsie') Rathbone (1851–1920), n.d. [? c. 1866]).

10 Eleanor F. Rathbone, *William Rathbone: A Memoir*, p. 428.

11 RP IX.6.411 (letter of 4 February 1900).

12 Eleanor F. Rathbone, *William Rathbone: A Memoir*, p. 156. The bas-relief memorial to Lucretia Rathbone was relocated from the Ashton Street Nurses' Home to the new Nurses' Home, what is now known as Cedar House, in 1931. In 2006 Cedar House was inaugurated as the home of the University's School of Medical Education and the Centre for Excellence for Teaching and Learning in Developing Professionalism in Medical Students.

13 William Rathbone, *A Sketch of family history*, p. 140.

14 See Meg Parkes and Sally Sheard, *Nursing in Liverpool since 1862* (Lancaster: Scotforth Books, 2012), which reproduces engravings of the Nurses' Training School and Home for Nurses and of its floor plans from Florence Nightingale's *Organisation of Nursing in a Large Town* (1865).

15 R. G. Huntsman, Mary Bruin, and Deborah Holttum, ''Twixt candle and lamp: The contribution of Elizabeth Fry and the Institution of Nursing Sisters to Nursing Reform,' *Medical History*, vol. 46, 2002, p. 377.

16 B. Guinness Orchard, *Liverpool's Legion of Honour*, p. 582.

17 Thomas Kelly, *For Advancement of Learning*, p. 39.

18 Edward Morris and Timothy Stevens, *History of the Walker Art Gallery, Liverpool 1873–2000* (Bristol: Sansom & Co., 2013), especially pp. 10–14.

19 Special Collections and Archives, P.5508/154 (letter of 20 May 1878).

20 William Rathbone, *A Sketch of family history*, p. 160; Thomas Kelly, *For Advancement of Learning*, pp. 47–8.

21 Thomas Kelly, *For Advancement of Learning*, p. 48.

22 Eleanor F. Rathbone, *William Rathbone: A Memoir*, p. 356.

23 RP IX.6.185.

24 RP IX.6.402.

25 RP IX.6.180, 181.

26 RP IX.6.183.

27 RP IX.6.392 (letter of 13 November 1892).

28 William Rathbone was latterly accustomed to making short visits in the spring or autumn to his little villa at the small seaside town of Alassio on the Italian Riviera, between Nice and Genoa. In the verses celebrating his eightieth birthday in 1899, tribute was paid to

Alassio, blessed retreat
Where our warrior lies when by pressure he's beat;
When his 'eight-hour's day' to a 'tenner' has grown,
And no day of repose for a year has been known.
Then to Italy's Mediterranean coast,
Where anemones bloom and good fishermen boast,
With his argument offspring, and sweet-tempered wife,
Who has been his support through her generous life.
(Liverpool Record Office, 920 MD 355).

29 RP IX.6.184.

30 RP IX.6.187.

31 RP IX.6.406.

32 Special Collections and Archives, D.166.

33 Liverpool Record Office, 920 MD 355.

34 Ibid.

35 Victoria Gallery and Museum, CE 390.

36 Adrian Allan, *Greenbank: A Brief History* (Liverpool: University of Liverpool, 1987), pp. 9–10.

37 1901 census schedule accessed per Ancestry.

38 Eleanor F. Rathbone, *William Rathbone: A Memoir*, p. 483.

39 Will accessed online per the government's Probate Search Service.

40 RP IX.6.203.

41 Susan Pedersen, *Eleanor Rathbone and the Politics of Conscience*, pp. 9 and 377.

42 Special Collections and Archives, S.2967–69.

43 Susan Pedersen, *Eleanor Rathbone and the Politics of Conscience*, p. 61.

44 Susan Pedersen, 'Eleanor Florence Rathbone (1872–1946)' in *Oxford Dictionary of National Biography*, vol. 46, 2004, pp. 94–5.

45 *Liverpool Daily Post*, 20 March 1945.

46 John Belchem, ed., *Liverpool 800*, p. 47; Margaret Simey, *Charitable Effort in Liverpool in the Nineteenth Century* (Liverpool: Liverpool University Press, 1951); Margaret B. Simey, *Eleanor Rathbone 1872–1946, A Centenary Tribute* (Liverpool: University of Liverpool, 1974); *Merseyside's Philanthropic Past: Inspiring a New Generation of Philanthropy: Philanthropy Report 2010* (Community Foundation for Merseyside, 2010).

47 1911 census schedule accessed per Ancestry.

48 Margaret Simey, *Eleanor Rathbone 1872–1946*, pp. 1 and 12.

49 Susan Pedersen, *Eleanor Rathbone and the Politics of Conscience*, p. 266.

50 Oration of Professor W. Lyon Blease, Public Orator, Special Collections and Archives, S.82.

51 This account draws on Adrian R. Allan, *A History of the Convocation of the University of Liverpool* (Liverpool: University of Liverpool, 2012), pp. 65–7.

52 One might deduce that Mrs Evelyn Rathbone was making particular reference to Eleanor's work on behalf of refugees both before, during, and after the war, the subject of Susan Cohen, *Rescue the Perishing: Eleanor Rathbone and the Refugees* (London and Portland, OR: Vallentine Mitchell, 2010).

53 Susan Pedersen's entry for Eleanor Rathbone in *Oxford Dictionary of National Biography*, vol. 46, 2004, p. 101.

54 RP XIV.6.4.

55 A list of the Eleanor Rathbone Memorial Lectures which were delivered from 1948 until 2003, the majority published by Liverpool University Press, may be found in Susan Pedersen, *Eleanor Rathbone and the Democratic Faith* (Liverpool: University of Liverpool, 2004); Professor Pedersen's lecture, delivered in 2003, appears to be the last in the series of Memorial Lectures to have been delivered and published.

56 Special Collections and Archives, D.284/1/22/4.

57 RP XX.I.11.

58 RP XX.1.10.

59 KMHeritage, *University of Liverpool – Greenbank Campus, History and Heritage Significance* (April 2012), pp. 56–7.

60 RP XV.A2.47. Joseph Sharples has kindly drawn my attention to a nineteenth-century photograph of Greenbank House viewed from across the stretch of water with a man standing in a rowing boat, which is held by the Library of the Athenaeum Club, Liverpool, reference Miscellaneous Box, Folder 31, Item no. 21.

61 RP XV.A2.48.

62 *Liverpool Echo*, 19 September 1925.

63 RP XX.1.13.

64 Obituary in the *Liverpool Daily Post*, 20 January 1940.

65 David Lascelles, *The Story of Rathbones since 1742* (London: James & James, 2008), pp. 101, 103.

66 Special Collections and Archives, S.82 part one.

67 Special Collections and Archives, S.81.

68 RP XV.A4.47,48.

69 RP XV.A3.114.

70 RP XV.A3.161.

71 P. J. Waller, *Democracy and Sectarianism: A Political and Social History of Liverpool 1868–1939* (Liverpool: Liverpool University Press, 1981), pp. 275, 279; pp. 274–80 are devoted to 'The decline of the Liberal plutocracy'.

72 RP XXII.97a.

73 RP XV.A3.161.

74 This paragraph draws on the exhibition which Special Collections and Archives mounted, October 2018– January 2019, as a product of a project to trace and record the books donated to the University by the Rathbones. RP XV.A6.30 comprises a list (May 1945) of the books presented by the family to the University.

75 RP XX.1.8.

76 RP XV.A2.78.

77 RP XV.A3.162; *The Times*, 22 January 1940.

78 RP XV.A.1.3; letter of 25 January 1940. For further information about the roles of Col. Cotton (1888–1970) as a partner in Rathbone Brothers, as a member of Liverpool City Council, and as a lay officer of the University, see Lucie Nottingham, *Rathbone Brothers*, Edward Morris and Timothy Stevens, *The Walker Art Gallery Liverpool*, and Thomas Kelly, *For Advancement of Learning*.

79 RP XX.1.34.

80 RP XX.1.29; letter of 7 March 1929.

81 RP XX.1.33.

82 RP XX.1.30 (letter of the University Registrar, 9 July 1929).

83 RP XV.A3.118.

84 RP XV.A2.13 (letter of 14 September 1936).

85 A description of Derby Hall, with plans, was published by *The Builder*, 21 May 1948, pp. 610–16.

86 Sir Frank Kermode (1919–2010) graduated in English in July 1940. His publications include *Not Entitled: A Memoir* (London: Harper Collins, 1996), and *The Uses of Error* (London: Collins, 1990), which includes an essay, 'My Foundation.'

Chapter 5

1 RP XX.1.18.

2 RP XX.1.21.

3 John Belchem, ed., *Liverpool 800: Culture, Character and History* (Liverpool: Liverpool University Press, 2006), p. 38.

4 RP XV.A1.125.

5 John Goodall's two-part illustrated article on Chequers Court in *Country Life*, 6 May 2020, pp. 62–7, and 13 May 2020, pp. 68–73.

6 RP XV.A4.2.

7 RP XX.1.15.

8 John Belchem, ed., *Liverpool 800*, p. 42.

9 The National Archives, RG 101/4354E/016/11.

10 *Manchester Evening News*, 20 August 1940; at the time, five maids were kept.

11 RP XX.1.94. Though we do not have the recollections of those who served in the household, such publications as *Born to Serve – Domestic Service in Liverpool 1850–1950*, n.d. [c. 1986] (the product of a Second Chance to Learn project) provide some contextualised insights.

12 RP XV.A3.161.

13 Special Collections and Archives, S.82 (Oration of the Public Orator, Professor Lyon Blease).

14 *Liverpool Daily Post*, 28 July 1954.

15 RP XV.A7.1

16 The text of most of Mrs Emily Rathbone's letter is published in Joy Robinson, *Relatively Rathbone* (Richmond: Trotman, 1992), pp. 74–5.

17 RP XX.1.16 and RP XV.A3.188.

18 RP XV.A2.175.

19 RP XV.A2.17.

20 RP XV.A1.369.

21 RP XX.1.17.

22 RP XV.A1.485.

23 Special Collections and Archives, D.284/1/22/4.

24 Special Collections and Archives, D.284/1/22/5.

25 Special Collections and Archives, P.7622/2.

26 Special Collections and Archives, S.236 (minutes of the Development Committee).

27 *Report of the Development Committee to the Council and Senate of the University on Building Progress 1949–1954* (Liverpool, 1955), pp. 21–2.

28 Special Collections and Archives, S.244.

29 KMHeritage, *University of Liverpool – Greenbank Campus*, pp. 25–8.

30 Email from Ron Green forwarded by Caroline Mitchell, 25 January 2019.

31 Professor R. A. Cordingley (1896–1962), Professor of Architecture at the University of Manchester, 1933–62; his publications include a notable seventeenth revised edition of Sir Banister Fletcher's major work, *A History of Architecture on the Comparative Method* (1961).

32 Adrian Allan, 'Derby Hall – the early years', *The University of Liverpool Recorder*, No. 118, April 1999, p. 13.

33 Email from Ian Aitken forwarded by Caroline Mitchell, 25 January 2019.

34 Special Collections and Archives, P.738/1.

35 *The University of Liverpool Recorder*, No. 90, a Special Landscape Edition, June 1985, pp. 20–1.

36 Sir James Mountford's address is reproduced in *The University of Liverpool Recorder*, No. 31, January 1963, pp. 5–6.

37 Special Collections and Archives, S.2930 and S.4240 (Minutes of the Management Committee of Greenbank House, 1964–85).

38 *Liverpool Echo*, 30 December 1964.

39 Email from Dr Bill Shannon, 5 July 2018. Dr William Rollinson (1937–2000), a noted historical geographer, spent nearly all his career on the staff of the University, first in the Geography department, 1962–69, and then in what became latterly known as the Department of Continuing Education, 1969–90.

40 Anne Clough, *'Ladies wore Hats': A History of the University of Liverpool Women's Club* (Liverpool: University of Liverpool Women's Club, 2000), p. 22.

41 Email from Professor Christopher Allmand, 30 August 2018.

42 Email from Mrs Priscilla Bawcutt, 31 August 2018.

43 Lin Foxhall and John K. Davies, *The Trojan War: Its Historicity and Context: Papers of the First Greenbank Colloquium, Liverpool 1981* (Bristol Classical Press, 1984).

44 The country's first specialist academic centre for the subject, the Institute

was established with support from the vice-chancellor's development fund. The principal aims of the Institute, under its director, David Horn, were to undertake teaching, research, and publication in the area of popular music; to undertake collaborative work with, and commissioned work for, outside bodies; and to have an advisory and co-ordinating role in popular music culture and the popular music industry (*University of Liverpool Annual Report 1988*, p. 9). In 2015, the year in which the 175th anniversary of establishment of The Liverpool Philharmonic Society was celebrated, UNESCO conferred City of Culture status on Liverpool, as a city in which creativity is recognised as a vital part of urban development.

45 Emails from Professor Geoffrey Ribbans, 23 October 2018, and from Professor Ann Mackenzie, 27 October 2018.

46 Email from Mrs Elizabeth Earl forwarded by Caroline Mitchell, 25 January 2019.

47 Email from Dr Susan Green forwarded by Caroline Mitchell, 25 January 2019.

48 Email from Dr Daniel Ching forwarded by the Alumni Relations Team, 12 March 2019.

49 Email from Professor Fred Taylor forwarded by the Alumni Relations Team, 25 January 2019.

50 *The University of Liverpool Report to the Court 1969–70*, p. xv.

51 *Liverpool Echo*, 19 March 1974.

52 *Liverpool Echo*, 27 April 1974.

53 Email from Tina Billinge forwarded by Caroline Mitchell, 25 January 2019.

54 Email from Dr Juliette Riddall forwarded by Caroline Mitchell, 25 January 2019.

55 Email from Peter Kenwright, 4 June 2019.

56 Adrian R. Allan, 'An inner-city partnership: The University of Liverpool at the Liverpool International Garden Festival,' *The University of Liverpool Recorder*, No. 96, October 1984, pp. 23–36.

57 A group photograph of the Lord Lieutenant and the Deputy Lieutenants was published in the *Liverpool Echo*, 8 July 1985.

Chapter 6

1 University Council, 2 July 1987, minute 228.6.

2 'Greenbank 1987–91,' a folder of papers received from the Vice-Chancellor's Office, Special Collections and Archives, VCS/8054.

3 Advertisements in the *Liverpool Echo*, 10 October 1987–23 September 1989. Rotaract clubs aimed to foster the exchange of ideas with leaders in the community and to develop leadership and professional skills.

4 University Council, 15 February 1990, minute 149 (g).

5 Adrian Allan, 'Passports to another world,' *Precinct*, 6 July 1990, p. 7.

6 This paragraph is based on the information provided by Nicola Gilmore, Conference Co-ordinator, in an email, 7 February 2019. See, too, the reports in the *Liverpool Echo*, 23 September 1993 and 27 September 1995.

7 In response to the University's nominations, further English Heritage Blue Plaques were unveiled in 2001 in honour of Sir Ronald Ross on the laboratories in the University quadrangle in which

he worked; Captain Noel Chavasse, VC and Bar, on his former home, the former bishop's palace, at no. 19 Abercromby Square; and Sir Charles Reilly, on his former home in Chatham Street. There are entries for all three in the *Oxford Dictionary of National Biography*. Another Blue Plaque in honour of Eleanor Rathbone, 'Pioneer of Family Allowances,' was unveiled by the Greater London Council on her Tufton Court, Tufton Street, Westminster, home.

8   University Council, 28 June 2006, minute 172.

9   University Council, 28 June 2006, minute 172 (g) (iii).

10 Guidance Document for Greenbank, Facilities Management, August 2013, p. 1.

11 UNESCO's designation of the World Heritage Site covered Pier Head, the Albert Dock, and Stanley Dock Conservation Areas, as also the Castle Street/Dale Street/Old Hall Street Commercial Area, the William Brown Street Cultural Quarter, and Lower Duke Street. See *Maritime Mercantile City, Liverpool: Nomination of Liverpool – Maritime Mercantile City for Inscription on the World Heritage List* (Liverpool: Liverpool University Press, 2005). In July 2021, the World Heritage Committee of UNESCO 'decided to delete the property "Liverpool – Maritime Mercantile City" (UK) from the World Heritage List, due to the irreversible loss of attributes conveying the outstanding universal value of the property'.

12 Liverpool titles in English Heritage's Informed Conservation series include Colum Giles, *Building a Better Society: Liverpool's Historic Institutional Buildings*

(2008); Joseph Sharples and John Stonard, *Built on Commerce: Liverpool's Central Business District* (2008); Katy Layton-Jones and Robert Lee, *Places of Health and Amusement: Liverpool's Historic Parks and Gardens* (2008); and Sarah Brown and Peter de Figueiredo, *Religion and Place: Liverpool's Historic Places of Worship* (2008). Reference should also be made to earlier publications concerning Liverpool's architectural heritage, including Liverpool Heritage Bureau, *Buildings of Liverpool* (Liverpool City Planning Department, 1978); *Liverpool Heritage Walk: Illustrated Companion Guide* (Liverpool City Planning Department, 1990); Maggi Morris and John Ashton, *The Pool of Life: A Public Health Walk in Liverpool* (Liverpool: Maggi Morris, 1997); Quentin Hughes, *Liverpool: City of Architecture* (Liverpool: The Bluecoat Press, 1999), a beautifully illustrated description and appreciation of a selection of key buildings, including Greenbank House; and Richard Pollard and Nikolaus Pevsner, *Lancashire: Liverpool and the South West* (The Buildings of England series, Yale University Press, 2006), the account of Liverpool being the text of Joseph Sharples, *Liverpool* (Pevsner Architectural Guides, Yale University Press, 2004) suitably adapted. *Maritime Mercantile City* (Liverpool: Liverpool University Press, 2005) provides an illustrated description of the property within the World Heritage Site and a history of the development of the site's individual areas.

13 Facilities Management: Guidance Document for Greenbank, August 2013, p. 5.

14 University Council, 19 November 2013, minute 5.2.

15 Email from Richmal Wigglesworth to Gary Meinert, 15 October 2019.

16 University of Liverpool – Greenbank House: Heritage Appraisal, vol. 1, July 2015, p. 3.

17 The competition for the £58m redevelopment of the University's Greenbank site was announced in *The Architects' Journal*, vol. 237, no. 24, 27 June 2013, responses to be received by 8 July.

18 View the website of Sheppard Robson, https://www.sheppardrobson.com. The architects, members of staff of Sheppard Robson, who worked on Greenbank House were Rupert Goddard, Mary-Ann Crompton, Jonathan Davies, Johnathan Djabourouti, Luke Green, Robbie Haworth, Eirini Tsianaka, and Richmal Wigglesworth.

19 Mark Moppett, 'Greenbank House: The Structural Engineering Repair and Remodelling', February 2020.

20 Email from Richmal Wigglesworth to Gary Meinert, 15 October 2019.

21 Descriptions of the work carried out in individual rooms were kindly provided by Brian McGorry, site manager.

22 Letter from Graeme Ives, Principal Inspector of Historic Buildings and Areas, North West Office of English Heritage, Manchester, to Nicola Gallagher, Liverpool City Council Planning department, 18 March 2015.

23 Case Officer Report on Planning Application 15F/0288, 2 February 2015.

24 Mark Moppett, 'Greenbank House: The Structural Engineering Repair and Remodelling.'

25 Liverpool City Council Planning department, planning permission, 15F/0288.

26 Liverpool City Council Planning department, planning permission, 15F/1991 and 15L/1896.

27 Concern about the fall in the number of conservation officers in England since 2010 was expressed in an article, 'Conservation officers are the heroes of our heritage,' in *Country Life*, 29 November 2017.

28 Planning application 15F/0288.

29 University Council, 10 February 2015, minute 4.4.

30 University Council, 6 July 2016, minute 4.1.

31 Email from Gary Meinert, 7 March 2019.

32 Grant of planning permission, 16F/1371, 29 July 2016.

33 Sheppard Robson, *Greenbank House: External Finishes Proposals*, August 2017, revised January 2018.

34 Report on Greenbank House, January 2018.

Chapter 7

1 2021 edition of the University's Alumni Magazine which provides an account of the University's response to the pandemic.

Bibliography

I Primary Sources

Lancashire Archives

DDM/10/6, Lease Register, 1745 onwards.

DDM/14/11, entry for 'St Anslow' in survey of Toxteth Park, 1754.

DDM/14/70, R. Lang's map of Toxteth Park, 1754.

DDM/50/201, Lease of Greenbank, 1 May 1788.

WCW/Supra/C536A/7, will of William Rathbone the third, 1789.

WCW/Supra/C656A/5, will of William Rathbone the fourth, 1805.

DRL 1/80, Tithe Map of Toxteth Park, 1847.

DDX 162/78/09 (plans of western extension of Greenbank House, 1868), 162/93/78 (plan of Greenbank estate, c. 1892), 162/10/04 and 162/89/50 (plans of fish pond, 1868).

Liverpool Record Office

Plan Chest 1 Drawer 3 Map Case 16A, sketches of lots of land for sale, July 1800.

920 ROS 3060 and 5796, letters of William Roscoe and William Rathbone, 1804 and 1807.

920 MD 355, verses in celebration of William Rathbone's eightieth birthday, 1899.

Special Collections and Archives, University of Liverpool Library

RP III.1, IX, XIV, XV.A1-4, XIX, XX.1, XXII, Rathbone family papers.

BW 1/124, letter from J. Blanco White, September 1836.

P.5508/154, letter from William Rathbone to the Mayor of Liverpool, 1878.

S.2967–69, Day Student Address Books, 1891–93.

SF/CS439.R.R23. William Rathbone, *A Sketch of family history during four generations, compiled from old letters and papers, and rough notes written by William Rathbone (6) for the use of his children* (1894).

D.166, Testimonial of Engineering staff and students, 1899.

S.81, Gifts Book, 1903–62.

S.82, Honorary Degree Orations, 1925 and 1931.

P.7622/2, Papers of Professor J. Mclean Thompson, 1938–39, 1945–47.

S.244-46, Halls of Residence Committee minutes, 1940–62.

D.284/1/22/4,5, Deeds, 1944–45.

S.236, Development Committee minutes, 1946–57.

P.738/1, Papers on the future of Greenbank House, 1961–63.

S.2930 and S.4240, Greenbank House Management Committee minutes, 1964–85.
VCS/8054, Papers of Vice-Chancellor, 1987–91.

II Secondary Sources

A Tribute to the Memory of Mr William Rathbone of Liverpool who died at his house, at Greenbank, 11th February, 1809, 'by a friend' (Liverpool, 1809).

Allan, Adrian R., 'An inner-city partnership: The University of Liverpool at the Liverpool International Garden Festival,' The University of Liverpool Recorder, 96 (1984).

Allan, Adrian R., The Building of Abercromby Square (Liverpool, 1986).

Allan, Adrian, Greenbank: A Brief History (Liverpool: University of Liverpool, 1987).

Allan, Adrian, 'Derby Hall – the early years,' The University of Liverpool Recorder, 118 (1999).

Allan, Adrian R., A History of the Convocation of the University of Liverpool (Liverpool: University of Liverpool, 2012).

Anstey, Roger and Hair, P. E. H., eds., Liverpool, the African Slave Trade, and Abolition (Liverpool: Historic Society of Lancashire and Cheshire, 1976).

Audubon, Maria R., Audubon and his Journals (London: John C. Nimmo, 1898).

Belchem, John, ed., Liverpool 800: Culture, Character and History (Liverpool: Liverpool University Press, 2006).

Billinge's Liverpool Advertiser and Marine Intelligencer.

Born to Serve – Domestic Service in Liverpool 1850–1950 (Liverpool, c. 1986).

Boult, Joseph, 'The former and recent topography of Toxteth Park' in Proceedings of the Liverpool Architectural and Archaeological Society (1867).

Bowle, John, Western Political Thought from the Origins to Rousseau (London: Methuen, 1961).

Brindle, Steven, 'Upstaging the world: St George's Hall, Liverpool,' Country Life, 3 July 2019.

Brown, Sarah and de Figueiredo, Peter, Religion and Place: Liverpool's Historic Places of Worship (Swindon: English Heritage, 2008).

The Builder.

Butt, John, The life of Robert Owen written by himself with his preface (London, 1971).

Chancellor, John, Audubon, A Biography (London: Weidenfeld and Nicholson, 1978).

Clough, Anne, 'Ladies Wore Hats': A History of the University of Liverpool Women's Club (Liverpool: University of Liverpool Women's Club, 2000).

Cohen, Susan, Rescue the Perishing: Eleanor Rathbone and the Refugees (London and Portland, OR: Vallentine Mitchell, 2010).

Cordingley, R. A., 'Three houses,' Blue Pigeon, The Magazine of Derby Hall (Liverpool, 1949).

Currie, William Wallace, ed., Memoir of the Life, Writings and Correspondence of James Currie M.D. F.R.S. of Liverpool (London: Longman, Rees, Orme, Brown, and Green, 1831).

Defoe, Daniel, *A Tour through England and Wales*, ed. Cole, G. D. H. (London, 1928).

Enfield, William, *An Essay Towards the History of Leverpool Drawn Up from Papers Left by the late Mr George Perry, and from Other Materials Since Collected* (London, 1774).

Foxhall, Lin and Davies, John K., *The Trojan War: Its Historicity and Context: Papers of the First Greenbank Colloquium, Liverpool 1981* (Bristol Classical Press, 1984).

Giles, Colum, *Building a Better Society: Liverpool's Historic Institutional Buildings* (Swindon: English Heritage, 2008).

Gore's Liverpool Advertiser.

Greenwood, Eric, Lyus, Steve, and Lampert, Ray, 'Liverpool Botanic Garden: Early curators and gardeners,' *Transactions of the Historic Society of Lancashire and Cheshire*, 167 (2018).

Greg, Mrs Eustace, ed., *Reynolds-Rathbone Diaries and Letters 1753–1839* (London: Constable, 1905).

Griffiths, Robert, *The History of the Royal and Ancient Park of Toxteth* (Liverpool, 1923).

Gritt, Andrew, '"For want of reparations": Tenants and the built environment on the estates of south-west Lancashire, 1750–1850,' *Transactions of the Historic Society of Lancashire and Cheshire*, 150 (2003).

Hillis, Maurice, *Liverpool Porcelain, 1756–1804* (2011).

Hillis, Maurice R. and Jellicoe, Roderick J., *The Liverpool Porcelain of William Reid: A Catalogue of Porcelain and Excavated Shards* (London: Roderick Jellicoe, 2000).

Hughes, Quentin, *Liverpool: City of Architecture* (Liverpool: The Bluecoat Press, 1999).

Huntsman, R. G., Bruin, Mary and Holttum, Deborah, ''Twixt candle and lamp: The contribution of Elizabeth Fry and the Institution of Nursing Sisters to Nursing Reform,' *Medical History*, 46 (2002).

Hyde, Francis E., *Liverpool and the Mersey: An Economic History of a Port 1700–1970* (Newton Abbot: David & Charles, 1971).

Kelly, Thomas, *For Advancement of Learning: The University of Liverpool 1881–1981* (Liverpool: Liverpool University Press, 1981).

Kermode, Frank, *The Uses of Error* (London: Collins, 1990).

Kermode, Frank, *Not Entitled: A Memoir* (London: Harper Collins, 1996).

KMHeritage, *University of Liverpool – Greenbank Campus, History and Heritage Significance* (2012).

Lascelles, David, *The Story of Rathbones since 1742* (London: James & James, 2008).

Lawton, Richard, 'From the pool of Liverpool to the conurbation of Merseyside' in Gould, William T. S. and Hodgkiss, Alan G., eds., *The Resources of Merseyside* (Liverpool: Liverpool University Press, 1982).

Layton-Jones, Katy and Lee, Robert, *Places of Health and Amusement: Liverpool's Historic Parks and Gardens* (Swindon: English Heritage, 2008).

Leeds Intelligencer.

Liverpool Daily Post.

Liverpool Echo.

Liverpool Heritage Bureau, *Buildings of Liverpool* (Liverpool: Liverpool City Planning Department, 1978).

Liverpool Heritage Walk: Illustrated Companion Guide (Liverpool: Liverpool City Planning Department, 1990).

Manchester Evening News.

Maritime Mercantile City Liverpool (Liverpool: Liverpool University Press, 2005).

Marriner, Sheila, *Rathbones of Liverpool 1845–73* (Liverpool: Liverpool University Press, 1961).

Merseyside Painters, People & Places: Catalogue of Oil Paintings (Liverpool: Merseyside County Council, 1978).

Merseyside's Philanthropic Past: Inspiring a New Generation of Philanthropy: Philanthropy Report 2010 (Liverpool: Community Foundation for Merseyside, 2010).

Morris, Edward and Stevens, Timothy, *History of the Walker Art Gallery, Liverpool 1873–2000* (Bristol: Sansom & Co., 2013).

Morris, Maggi and Ashton, John, *The Pool of Life, A Public Health Walk in Liverpool* (Liverpool: Maggi Morris, 1997).

Murphy, Martin, *Blanco White: Self-banished Spaniard* (New Haven, CT: Yale University Press, 1989).

Murray, Nicholas, *So Spirited a Town: Visions and Versions of Liverpool* (Liverpool: Liverpool University Press, 2007).

Nottingham, Lucie, *Rathbone Brothers, From Merchant to Banker 1742–1992* (London: Rathbone Brothers, 1992).

Orchard, B. Guinness, *Liverpool's Legion of Honour* (Birkenhead: B. Guinness Orchard, 1893).

Parkes, Meg and Sheard, Sally, *Nursing in Liverpool since 1862* (Lancaster: Scotforth Books, 2012).

Patterson, Daniel, ed., *John James Audubon's Journal of 1826: The Voyage to The Birds of America* (Lincoln, NE, and London: University of Nebraska Press, 2011).

Pedersen, Susan, *Eleanor Rathbone and the Democratic Faith* (Liverpool: University of Liverpool, 2004).

Pedersen, Susan, *Eleanor Rathbone and the Politics of Conscience* (New Haven, CT and London: Yale University Press, 2004).

Pollard, Richard and Pevsner, Nikolaus, *Lancashire: Liverpool and the South-West* (New Haven, CT: Yale University Press, 2006).

The Porcupine.

Prochaska, Frank, *Royal Bounty: The Making of a Welfare Monarchy* (New Haven, CT and London: Yale University Press, 1995).

Rathbone, Eleanor F., *William Rathbone: A Memoir* (London: Macmillan, 1905).

Rathbone, Emily A., ed., *Records of the Rathbone Family for private circulation only* (Edinburgh: R & R Clark, 1913).

Report of the Development Committee to the Council and Senate of the University on Building Progress 1949–1954 (Liverpool, 1955).

Robinson, Joy, *Relatively Rathbone* (Richmond: Trotman, 1992).

Ruskin, John, 'Unto This Last': Four Essays on the First Principles of Political Economy (London, 1862).

Sharples, Joseph, *Liverpool* (New Haven, CT and London: Yale University Press, 2004).

Sharples, Joseph and Stonard, John, *Built on Commerce: Liverpool's Central Business District* (Swindon: English Heritage, 2008).

Shepherd, John, *A History of the Liverpool Medical Institution* (Liverpool: Liverpool Medical Institution, 1979).

Simey, Margaret, *Charitable Effort in Liverpool in the Nineteenth Century* (Liverpool: Liverpool University Press, 1951).

Simey, Margaret, *Eleanor Rathbone 1872–1946, A Centenary Tribute* (Liverpool: University of Liverpool, 1974).

Sinclair, T. A., trans., Aristotle, *The Politics* (Harmondsworth: Penguin Books, 1962).

Smith, Adam, *The Theory of Moral Sentiments* (1759).

Smith, Adam, *An Inquiry into the Nature and Causes of the Wealth of Nations* (1776).

Tibbles, Anthony, *Liverpool and the Slave Trade* (Liverpool: Liverpool University Press, 2018).

The Times, 22 January 1940.

Uglow, Jenny, *A Little History of British Gardening* (London: Chatto & Windus, 2004).

Victoria History of the Counties of England: Lancashire, vol. 3 (1907).

Waller, P. J., *Democracy and Sectarianism: A Political and Social History of Liverpool 1868–1939* (Liverpool: Liverpool University Press, 1981).

Williamson's Liverpool Advertiser, 15 September 1788.

Wilson, Arline, 'The cultural identity of Liverpool, 1790–1850: The early learned societies,' *Transactions of the Historic Society of Lancashire and Cheshire*, 147 (1998).

Index